Disaster Risk Reduction

Methods, Approaches and Practices

Series Editor

Rajib Shaw, Keio University, Shonan Fujisawa Campus, Fujisawa, Japan

Disaster risk reduction is a process that leads to the safety of communities and nations. After the 2005 World Conference on Disaster Reduction, held in Kobe, Japan, the Hyogo Framework for Action (HFA) was adopted as a framework for risk reduction. The academic research and higher education in disaster risk reduction has made, and continues to make, a gradual shift from pure basic research to applied, implementation-oriented research. More emphasis is being given to multi-stakeholder collaboration and multi-disciplinary research. Emerging university networks in Asia, Europe, Africa, and the Americas have urged process-oriented research in the disaster risk reduction field. With this in mind, this new series will promote the output of action research on disaster risk reduction, which will be useful for a wide range of stakeholders including academicians, professionals, practitioners, and students and researchers in related fields. The series will focus on emerging needs in the risk reduction field, starting from climate change adaptation, urban ecosystem, coastal risk reduction, education for sustainable development, community-based practices, risk communication, and human security, among other areas. Through academic review, this series will encourage young researchers and practitioners to analyze field practices and link them to theory and policies with logic, data, and evidence. In this way, the series will emphasize evidence-based risk reduction methods, approaches, and practices.

More information about this series at http://www.springer.com/series/11575

Rajib Shaw · Suvendrini Kakuchi ·
Miki Yamaji

Editors

Media and Disaster Risk Reduction

Advances, Challenges and Potentials

 Springer

Editors
Prof. Rajib Shaw🆔
Graduate School of Media
and Governance
Keio University
Fujisawa, Japan

Suvendrini Kakuchi
University World News
Tokyo, Tokyo, Japan

Miki Yamaji
Graduate School of Media
and Governance
Keio University
Fujisawa, Japan

ISSN 2196-4106 ISSN 2196-4114 (electronic)
Disaster Risk Reduction
ISBN 978-981-16-0284-9 ISBN 978-981-16-0285-6 (eBook)
https://doi.org/10.1007/978-981-16-0285-6

This Springer imprint is published by the registered company Springer Nature Singapore Pte Ltd.
The registered company address is: 152 Beach Road, #21-01/04 Gateway East, Singapore 189721, Singapore

Preface

Media has always been playing a critical role in different phases of disaster risk reduction. The use of media is very much dependent on the governance and cultural context. There are traditional media as well new media. New media, including social media, is playing critical roles in disasters with live updates on the event. Citizens play a critical role in this. Of course, there are challenges in social media, including fake news, etc. Responsible journalism is one of critical issues of disaster risk reduction.

This book has 15 chapters, which deal with various aspects of disaster risk reduction and addresses different types of media. The first section discusses the concepts of and its current status in Asia. The second section deals with various types of media, and the third section deals with different cases of the use of different types of media in different contexts.

Covering significant aspects of media and disaster risk reduction, this book is intended for students, researchers, academia, policymakers, and development practitioners in the fields of disaster risk reduction as well as media sectors, especially in the Asia-Pacific region. It will help to better understand the proactive media role in different phases of disaster. We will be happy if the readers find this book useful and relevant.

Fujisawa, Japan   Rajib Shaw
Tokyo, Japan   Suvendrini Kakuchi
Fujisawa, Japan   Miki Yamaji

About This Book

This book analyzes recent advances, trends, challenges, and potentials of the role of media in disaster risk reduction. Collaboration, co-design, and co-delivery with other stakeholders in science technology, private sectors, and civil society are found to be effective in reaching people and communities.

The media is considered to be of utmost importance in all phases of disasters, before, during, and after, with different types of media having different proactive roles to play in disaster risk reduction. Before disasters, they play essential roles not only in bringing an early warning to people but also in enhancing their perception of the need to take action. At during- and post-disaster response recovery phases, community radio and social media are the key. These necessitate a resilient media infrastructure as the core of uninterrupted coverage.

Media literacy has become an important issue for several stakeholders, including governments. In addition, more focus is placed on media governance to look at the priorities of disaster risk reduction initiatives within the media. All of these are considered to lead to trust in the media, which further improves people's disaster response actions based on information from the media, before and during disasters.

Covering different aspects of media, this book is a valuable source for students, researchers, academics, policy-makers, and development practitioners.

Contents

Editors and Contributors

About the Editors

Rajib Shaw is a Professor in the Graduate School of Media and Governance at Keio University, Japan. He is also a senior fellow of the Institute of Global Environmental Strategies (IGES) Japan, and the chairperson of SEEDS Asia and CWS Japan, two Japanese NGOs. He is, additionally, the co-founder of the Delhi (India)-based social entrepreneurial start-up Resilience Innovation Knowledge Academy (RIKA). Earlier, he was the executive director of Integrated Research on Disaster Risk (IRDR) and was a professor at Kyoto University. His expertise includes disaster governance, community-based disaster risk management, climate change adaptation, urban risk management, and disaster and environmental education. Professor Shaw was the chair of the United Nations Science Technology Advisory Group (STAG) for disaster risk reduction and is the co-chair of the Asia Science Technology and Academic Advisory Group (ASTAAG). In addition, he is the CLA (Coordinating Lead Author) for the Asia chapter of IPCC's 6th Assessment Report. He is the Editor-in-Chief of the Elsevier journal *Progress in Disaster Science* and Series Editor of a Springer book series on disaster risk reduction. Professor Shaw has published more than 48 books and over 400 academic papers and book chapters.

Suvendrini Kakuchi is a Sri Lankan journalist and author based in Tokyo. She focuses on development journalism covering such issues as education, environment, disasters, gender, and conflict resolution. Her long reporting career of more than 30 years has spanned South Asia and the Asia-Pacific region, and her work comprises writing for traditional media and research-based publications and books. Among her disaster reporting assignments from the field is the Indian Ocean tsunami in 2004, the Great Hanshin earthquake in 1995, and the Great East Japan disaster in 2011. She has also produced disaster risk-reduction publications, documentary films, and journalist training, and has developed media manuals with guidelines for news editors making assignments on disasters.

Miki Yamaji is pursuing her graduate studies on media and governance at Keio University. She is also a senior producer at NHK Educational, conducting several programs on disaster education. In her earlier career, she had long experience as an editor for a publishing company and also as a journalist for a newspaper company in Japan.

Contributors

Suman Basnet World Association of Community Radio Broadcasters Asia Pacific (AMARC AP), Kathmandu, Nepal

Mario Antonius Birowo Universitas Atma Jaya Yogyakarta, Yogyakarta, Indonesia

Dhrupad Choudhury International Center for Integrated Mountain Development (ICIMOD), Kathmandu, Nepal

Adnan Fabyandi Graduate School of Media and Governance, Keio University, Fujisawa, Japan

Junichi Hibino FMYY Community Radio, Kobe, Japan

Hiromi Hirose Broadcasting Culture Research Institute, Japan Broadcasting Corporation (NHK), Tokyo, Japan;
Center for South, Asian Studies of Gifu Women's University, Gifu-shi, Gifu, Japan

Shodai Honzawa Faculty of Policy Management, Keio University, Fujisawa, Japan

Shunya Hosokawa Faculty of Policy Management, Keio University, Fujisawa, Japan

Sayaka Irie NHK Broadcasting Culture Research Institute, Japan Broadcasting Corporation (Nippon Housou Kyoukai), Tokyo, Japan

Russell Isaac Asia Pacific Broadcasting Association, Kuala Lumpur, Malaysia

Tianhai Jiang Institute of Mountain Hazards and Environment, Chinese Academy of Sciences, Chengdu, China

Suvendrini Kakuchi Tokyo Correspondent, University World News, Tokyo, Japan;
Inter Press Service and Tokyo Foreign Correspondents Club, Tokyo, Japan

Aye Nge Khin NHK WORLD Department, Japan Broadcasting Corporation, Tokyo, Japan

Midori Kusagaya NHK Educational Corporation, Tokyo, Japan

Aleksandrina V. Mavrodieva Graduate School of Media and Governance, Keio University, Fujisawa, Japan

Himanshu Shekhar Mishra New Delhi Television Limited (NDTV), New Delhi, India

Osamu Mizuno Institute for Global Environmental Strategies (IGES), Hayama, Japan

Sri Purwanti Graduate School of Media and Governance, Keio University, Fujisawa, Japan

Rajib Shaw Graduate School of Media and Governance, Keio University, Fujisawa, Japan

Binaya Raj Shivakoti Institute for Global Environmental Strategies (IGES), Hayama, Japan

Vibhas Sukhwani Graduate School of Media and Governance, Keio University, Fujisawa, Japan

Miki Yamaji Graduate School of Media and Governance, Keio University, Fujisawa, Japan

Part I
Overview

Chapter 1
Media and Disaster Risk Reduction

Rajib Shaw, Suvendrini Kakuchi, and Miki Yamaji

Abstract Media is an effective and essential stakeholder in disaster risk reduction and can enhance citizen perspectives through timely and science-based information dissemination. Media has a role in all phases of disaster management, from preparedness to during disaster, response and recovery. Different media have different target groups. Traditional media covers all age groups, while new media (like social media) is more popular among the younger generation. Role of media has been observed very strongly in addressing the global pandemic COVID-19. Citizen reporters are becoming popular to inform the ground realities during a disaster situation. This chapter draws some specific lessons on the role of media in disaster risk reduction. The chapter also provides an outline of the book.

Keywords Traditional media · New media · Global pandemic · Media governance · Science-based reporting

1.1 Introduction

Media can be classified into different ways. Broadly speaking, there are three types of media: print media (newspaper, magazine), broadcast media (television and radio) and online media (internet, social media, apps, blogs, Wikis, streaming video and music, podcast, etc.). Among these, traditional media includes print and broadcast media; while the new media includes mainly online media. Other characterization of media can be mass media (reaching a large number of people), and local or community media (like community radio, which has a restricted number of people).

Media has a direct link and outreach to people. That makes media very special when it comes to different aspects of a disaster. Before a disaster, media can play a critical role to inform and sensitize people on the importance of preparedness. There

R. Shaw (✉) · M. Yamaji
Graduate School of Media and Governance, Keio University, Fujisawa, Japan
e-mail: shaw@sfc.keio.ac.jp

S. Kakuchi
Inter Press Service and Tokyo Foreign Correspondents Club, Tokyo, Japan

© Springer Nature Singapore Pte Ltd. 2021
R. Shaw et al. (eds.), *Media and Disaster Risk Reduction*, Disaster Risk Reduction,
https://doi.org/10.1007/978-981-16-0285-6_1

can be educative programs on TV, edutainment (education with entertainment), talk shows, panel discussion, etc. on different aspects of preparedness and preventive measures. Media can also share important information on disaster risk before a disaster strikes and can inform people what to do. For certain types of disasters like typhoon or tsunami (which has a lead time), media can provide real-time early warning and can enhance safe evacuation. There are different researches on how effectively the urgency of "early" warning can be communicated so that people take it seriously and evacuate to safe place. During a disaster, citizen reporters can play a vital role in providing local information through social media and providing critical alerts. After a disaster, media plays an important role in sharing information on missing and casualty and damage and losses. Local media like community radio plays important roles in the local information, which becomes vital to the local residents (affected people), while mass media plays important role to disseminate the information nationally, regionally and globally and helps in disseminating requests for aid and assistance. Social media has taken key roles in many recent disasters in disseminating real-time information. Several match-making services (like specific need for assistance at local level, and its supply by aid agencies) have been effectively provided by social media. Both local media and mass media, along with social media play critical roles in postdisaster recovery. One of the key issues of social media is fake news, which often creates panic and provides hindrance in disaster relief, rescue to postdisaster rehabilitation operations. Different countries have undertaking specific measures to address fake news in legal and through other governance mechanisms creating a techno-legal regime.

With this context of media and disaster risk reduction, this chapter provides overviews and draws a few critical lessons.

1.2   Global Pandemic and Role of Media

The timing of the book coincides with the global pandemic COVID-19, which affected the globe in different ways. COVID-19, being an invisible disaster, "*infodemic*" becomes a critical issue in risk communication (Hua and Shaw 2020). Media has been in the forefront of the pandemic response, providing non-stop information, coverage on different aspects of the disease, infection spread, mitigation measures, etc. Different heads of states had virtual meetings with media groups with an appeal of cooperation and collaboration. A great example is Indian Prime Minister Narendra Modi had a meeting with the head of media groups as early as March 2020 and appealed to them to work with governments to spread the right information and generate more citizen literacy about COVID-19.

Positive aspects of the role of media in the pandemic are quite prominent. Irrespective of the country, media groups provided free sites and services on information related to COVID-19. There have been several media dialogues, especially on the expert advice on what are the best protection measures from COVID-19. Several media groups have started social media and traditional media campaign on the use of masks, sanitizers as well other protection gears. Role of the journalists covering different infection hit areas is commendable while risking their own lives. We also had reports of infection and death in the journalism fraternity. Role of media saving and coming to people was possibly never been so prominent. Media groups have also done fund-raising campaign in collaboration with different development agencies to help the most-needy people. Strict protocols were in place in continuing media operations, and many new measures were undertaken.

In the era of *"infodemic"*, fake news became a real challenge. In different countries, there were numerous fake news on the remedy of COVID-19, as well as the reasons for its spread, including many conspiracy theories. Some countries had strict measures for fake news (including penalty), and there were several portal sites developed to nullify or test the fake news. Of course, social media provided several positive sides as well. Many social media were positively used to reach out to different communities, especially to younger population during pandemic. TikTok or Instagram videos became very popular on what to do during the pandemic. Celebrities took their social media account to sensitize people and appeal to people for undertaking several control measures.

Traditional media also played useful roles. Community radios were able to spread the news to the rural and remote communities. Several local language programs suitable to the local cultural contexts were delivered through community radio to reach out to rural population. Many local governments used community radios not only for one-way information flow but also to receive information from the community, especially on their immediate needs and priorities, and to customize the assistance based on those priorities.

In summary, the role of media during pandemic was a mixed one, with definitely more positive impacts. Over time, media roles have changed, and citizen reporting became stronger. Of course, there was panic created by some fake news (which prompted panic buying in many cities across the globe), however, gradually citizen's awareness on fake news has also enhanced. Different age groups used different types of media to get "trusted" information. Thus, information provider sides also need to provide uniform sets of basic information to all types of media to reach different age groups.

1.3 Ten Key Lessons on Media and DRR

Following are some of the key observations and lessons while discussing the role of media in disaster risk reduction.

1. **Timely and precise information with a proper delivery mode can save lives**: **Timely** information is key to saving life. For any types of disasters, where early earning is feasible, time becomes critical. For some disasters like earthquake, where early warning has minimal lead time, pre-disaster information becomes critical. There have been different training to the announcers (in all different

types of media: TV, radio, community radio, etc.) on how to convey the urgency of an early warning. Japan is a classic example, where after the 2011 East Japan Earthquake and Tsunami, there has been specialized training and protocol of emergency announcement. This has been found to be effective for evacuation during other disasters like typhoons, where the scale and severity of the typhoon and urgency of evacuation need to be communicated properly.

2. **Media governance is an important aspect in enhancing its role in DRR**: Media is not always about the TRP. While for the private media houses, it is important to raise sponsorships by increasing their TRP, media houses also have social responsibilities. There, media governance plays an important role. Sensitizing higher authorities in media groups is an important task, and this can be done through multi-stakeholder consultative process. Science plays an important role here, and science-based journalism can play a neutral role in disseminating proper information timely. Media governance also includes safety concerns of journalists during a disaster reporting, especially from ground zero. There needs to be a strict safety protocol to be maintained during disaster reporting.

3. **Technology plays critical role to bring media to the most-needy people**: These days, media can access different types of technologies, including drones, IOT (Internet of Things), AI (Artificial Intelligence), etc. Sources of information have widely broadened over last past few years. Citizen science and crowd reporting have increasingly played important roles in disaster risk reduction. The key challenge is how to integrate these technologies to have effective use and benefit to the neediest and vulnerable people. The target vulnerable groups are different in different countries. For some countries, this is the aged population living in rural/coastal/mountain regions. Providing appropriate and timely early warning and encouraging them to evacuate is one of the key targets. For some countries, people living in slum/informal settlements are most exposed to different types of vulnerability. For some countries, urban non-engineered constructions are the key to vulnerability to some specific hazards like earthquakes. Media can bring the benefit of the integration of different technologies to these most vulnerable people.

4. **Role of media needs to be looked on the local governance and cultural context**: Media is very much linked to governance as well as cultural context in the local environment. This in a way defines the role of media. In several socialistic countries, media plays an important role as government spokesperson. In democratic countries, media is often biased or aligned to certain political parties. In some democratic countries, media plays a role with certain boundary conditions. These contexts often influence the role of media before, during and after a disaster, from government criticism to watchdog to neutral role as well as pro-government propaganda. This has also been reflected in the role of media during pandemic.

5. **Generating trust in media for DRR needs time and effort**: Trust in media is a very important issue for disaster risk reduction. The trust can be gained through science-based media coverage, highlighting the grass-root/people's

vulnerability issues, and timely early warning system. Popular media anchors can also be effective in gaining people's trusts.

6. **Social media role is becoming important**: Social media is gaining increasing importance due to its easy usage and deep penetration in different parts of society. This media can be linked properly with traditional media and can play an important role, provided the source of information and its authenticity is made clear. For example, during the COVID-19, WHO (World Health Organization) has used extensively Twitter, Facebook, Instagram and TikTok to spread safety information in different languages.

7. **Contents research as well as dissemination ways are equally important**: Disaster risk reduction is increasingly becoming important in higher education and research. Different inter-, multi- and trans-disciplinary researches are performed on different aspects of disasters in the universities and research institutions. Media content research is a key topic in many universities. It is important to put research emphasis on the delivery mechanism of information as well. This coupled with content research can make a breakthrough in generating new innovation in media research in DRR.

8. **Journalist training needs to be linked to real-life scenario**: There are different online and face to face training courses on DRR for journalists. Different regional bodies like ABU (Asia Pacific Broadcasting Association) took key efforts enhancing capacities of journalists from developing countries. An effective journalist training needs to be linked to real-life scenario, with specific and direct link to the field realities and disaster cases. A holistic training would require to focus on contents, delivery mechanism, basic protocols in disaster situations, disaster reporting, etc.

9. **Citizen journalism is becoming popular and can be effective**: This is increasingly becoming a popular trend, especially to cover wide area disaster situation. Many media groups have previous citizen volunteers with certain level of training for disaster reporting. Some media groups use more ad-hoc citizen reporters, collecting materials from the social media sites with certain levels of verification. An organized citizen reporter's group can help effectively and real-time information sharing during a disaster.

10. **Edutainment becomes a crucial learning tool**: Disaster is often considered as a negative subject. However, education for disaster risk reduction can be fun and can attract children and their parents if properly designed. Edutainment (education and entertainment) can be effectively used by media to make effective imprints on children at an early age. Different education channel or different programs with cartoon (manga in Japanese) can be effective in sharing the right message to the children. Both broadcasting as well as print media would be effective means for that.

1.4 Outline of the Book

This book consists of fifteen chapters in three parts. Part 1 provides two overview chapters. Part 2 explains three types of media and Part 3 provides actual cases of utilizing media in different aspects of disaster risk reduction.

Chapter 1 outlines the key issues of media and disaster risk reduction, and also provides an overview of different chapters o f he book.

Chapter 2 provides an outline of activities of Asia Pacific Broadcasting Union. During the second decade of the twenty-first century, members of the Asia Broadcast Union staff and associated consultants and trainers worked across the Asia–Pacific region on various training and consultation projects related to Climate Change and Disaster Risk Reduction programs. Some of their experiences are highlighted in this paper, which is aimed primarily at outlining the lessons that have or should have been learned. Despite the logistic and practical challenges facing Asian and Pacific broadcasters and media outlets, the analysis offers a way forward regarding strategy and approaches that can be adopted for the development and improvement of mass audience awareness, safety and well-being.

Chapter 3 focuses on community radio experiences in Indonesia and Japan, where there are many natural disasters. Community radio has played an important role as a "hub" for local information during times of disaster and recovery and reconstruction. In Indonesia, a community radio station will be established in the affected area under the leadership of the Community Radio Association, with civil society taking the lead. On the other, in Japan, in the event of a major disaster, local governments in the disaster-stricken areas set up temporary disaster broadcasting stations with the support of the Ministry of Internal Affairs and Communications and neighboring community radio stations hand. Both forms have advantages and disadvantages. In particular, in the case of Japan, there is little initiative from residents, and in the case of Indonesia, there is little involvement from the government. The chapter focuses on the experiences of Japan–Indonesia Joint program with the aim to enhance the functions of community radio, a public–private partnership to enhance the community-based disaster risk reduction capabilities. This chapter focuses on the installment of the Wakayama model to Boyolali, this paper examines a mechanism in which community radio is established with community initiative in the event of a disaster, and its activities can be continued until the period of recovery and reconstruction in cooperation with the government.

Chapter 4 focuses on role of social media in disaster response and recovery. It analyses several cases like 2010 earthquake in Haiti, the 2011 Tohoku earthquake and tsunami in Japan, the 2012 Hurricane Sandy in the USA, and a great number of crisis events ever since. Social media platforms are also increasingly used by a variety of actors—from ordinary residents, to local and international organizations, governments, and traditional media outlets—to a different degree and to different effects. Facebook, Twitter, Instagram, Youtube and others are now among the primary means for information dissemination, mapping and sending instant reports, organizing volunteers and help groups, connecting with family members, and donation gathering. Nonetheless, some concerns over personal data privacy, "fake" news, scams, misinformation and difficulties in outreach to older populations have also been identified. This chapter will provide a brief overview of the available literature on the role of social media for disaster management, and the types, uses, benefits and potential threats and challenges. A review of relevant case studies is included to identify some good and bad practices and derive lessons learnt. Finally, the chapter pinpoints some key takeaway messages for practitioners and policy-makers in an attempt to chart the way forward.

Chapter 5 focuses on the media that does not work at the time of calamity, but it works for the future. Records of disaster are useful information storage to raise awareness of disaster prevention among residents who live in places where disasters may occur again. It is very important to hand over the past records and lessons to the next generation. There are several effective forms of storage media such as books, stone monuments, videos, preserved relics and so on. However, the experiences felt by the victims are sometimes deleted from memory of the people who has psychological trauma. There are also various challenges in preserving damaged architectural structures. Example of efforts to record the experience by the children in the affected areas of the Great East Japan Earthquake showed the way to record their experiences in disaster media and absorb them into local culture. By comparing with the catastrophes of other countries like South Asia, this chapter will find that usage of relic is unique effort to Japan. The Atomic Bomb Dome in Hiroshima is a relic that tells the scale of destruction beyond generations. Its power as a media goes beyond video and language. The chapter highlights that it is necessary to consider how to preserve and use relic and remain sites as media for disaster mitigation.

Chapter 6 focuses on Indigenous and local knowledge (ILK) systems and practices have featured in agriculture, water resources management, forest management, disaster risk reduction, health risk management, disaster early warning, etc. in the Hindu Kush Himlayan (HKH) region. This area is one of the fragile ecosystems in terms of climate change and its impacts, which is reflected by the effect of both slow-onset and fast-onset disasters. Traditionally, this area has been a co-existence between nature and people. ILK could be an entry point for introducing appropriate adaptation know-how and practices through enhancement and customization in a cost-effective manner. However, communication is a challenge to the promotion and diffusion of potential ILK and practices for climate change adaptation (CCA). Lack of scientific assessments, inadequate documentation and their diversity are the key barriers for communicating the merits of ILK for CCA. In this chapter, the role of community radio networks in HKH is discussed as an effective vehicle to bridge the existing communication gaps in three ways. First, as a platform to share climate change impacts and ILK-based coping mechanisms among local communities. Second, share potential ILK-based solutions relevant to CCA across the local communities. Third, to connect with stakeholders beyond the community level (such as government, researchers and scientists, development partners) to disseminate information about local issues, financial and capacity needs, and mainstreaming of local practices into the region's CCA planning and implementation. A framework is proposed for the incorporation of community radio as a formal means of CCA communication.

Chapter 7 offers the diverse reporting experience of Asian journalists when covering major disasters in their countries for leading domestic and international media. Through their voices—as quoted in their personal contributions for this book—the reader is offered access to a special insider look into the intricacies of media reporting. In addition, this chapter opens a window into the varied topics covered by journalists before, during and after the disaster. A critical aspect of this section is the compilation of their recommendations based on their experience. We hope the information will contribute to the ongoing development of disaster communication practices and media research.

Chapter 8 focuses on community radio experiences from Indonesia and Haiti. Being governed and managed by the local people, community radios effectively serve for addressing local concerns in local language and cultural context. However, their sustainable operations during disaster situations are often interrupted due to technical issues like power blackouts, limited frequency range, etc. While contemporary research is focused on overcoming the social, financial and institutional challenges to community radio operations, this chapter mainly deliberates on overcoming the technological challenges. In that regard, digital technologies like mobile phones and internet are presenting newer means of information sharing that complement the community radio operations, helping cover a wider audience from within and beyond their geographical frequency range. The chapter discusses two selected case study examples of Jalin Merapi (Indonesia) and Signal FM (Haiti) based on literature review. Notably, the community radio operations in both the cases were restrained during disaster situation, however, the integration of digital technologies enhanced their effectiveness in disaster communication. The study derives key lessons from the selected cases and suggests feasible strategies for integrating digital technologies with community radio operations. To enhance the sustainability of community radio operations in long term, the study emphasizes enhancing community engagement and raising digital awareness.

Chapter 9 examines measures taken toward enabling media to report urban disasters. Bangladesh, a highly populated and disaster-prone country, has developed good response systems, especially focusing on coastal disasters where regular typhoons have led to widespread human and environmental destruction. But the emergence of deadly urban disasters with higher losses experienced in the country's cities has raised the urgent need to adopt and implement measures to strengthen urban resilience. The case study presented here outlines specific support is necessary for journalists to deepen their knowledge about disasters facing cities and the need to strengthen their Disaster Risk Reduction (DRR) reporting capacity to educate the public. Dhaka, the capital city with a 15 million population, is highly vulnerable to fires, urban floods and air pollution. Journalists participating in the training program focused on disasters in North Dhaka and were introduced to Japan's advanced reporting experience under the platform of learning from each other. Another prominent aspect of this study is the development of collaborative activities between journalists and communities to build disaster resilience in Dhaka. This network worked smoothly and facilitated the journalists to highlight DRR topics.

Chapter 10 focuses on disaster reporting and risk communication in China, which have played a critical role in face of the unexpected and catastrophic natural disasters, and even more so in the digital age. The innovative development of social media and new media technologies bring enormous potentials for exploring new paradigms of effective communication and reaching to the public proactively and effectively. It serves as a catalyst for not only disaster professionals but also media and science communication practitioners, even the lay population to engage in the communication. This chapter first introduces the diversified active players involved in the arena in the new media age. It then discusses the new media approaches and advanced technologies applied in practice. To further understand the tendencies, we summarize some of the new dynamics of risk communication in China. The chapter closes with discussions on how to contribute to effective risk communication with sufficient qualified professionals and quality contents.

Chapter 11 focuses on reporting and analyzing local disasters—usually smaller in scale in terms of fatalities and loss comparison to the major tragedies, which are usually ignored in the mainstream media. But, as a case study in Varanasi has illustrated, disasters occurring close to home have impacted local societies gravely by causing lasting destruction. Their occurrence tends to be regular and linked to seasonal changes and local reporters reporting the disasters to say their coverage is widely disseminated in the public and respected for providing crucial information. The case study also indicates news reports that capture the reality on the field have played a role in facilitating aid and assistance for the affected from outside. Journalists participating in the study further noted that when losses from local disasters have reached large proportions creating difficult political and economic consequences spreading beyond the area, local disaster reporting has gained the attention of the national media and central authorities.

Chapter 12 narrates a journalist's own experience in disaster reporting in ground zero. Disasters destroy critical infrastructures like rural roads and highways, bridges, power and water supply lines and communication infrastructure (including mobile towers) in and around Ground Zero. This makes it challenging for news correspondents to travel inside a disaster-affected zone and gather and transmit news from there. The unprecedented deluge in Jammu and Kashmir and the landslides that followed made it difficult for reporters to travel by road to Srinagar and other flood-affected areas for several days. Disasters also disrupt social processes: they create a social circle of fear in the affected areas, as the victims suffer from acute sense of loss of life and property around them. This makes it imperative for Reporters to develop a Protocol to manage risk and gather news in a climate of fear and insecurity. They also need to protect themselves from the possible outbreak of an epidemic in a given disaster zone. At a broader level, the chapter argues the outflow of credible information from a given disaster zone is largely conditioned by the ability of news correspondents to access and gather critical information in a disaster zone. Credible news reporting on the nature and scale of damages and the status of rescue and relief work in a disaster-affected zone can help direct relief and rescue operations in the right direction and also strengthen them. This is especially significant in situations where disasters impair the institutional flow of information from official channels, mainly because of the sudden collapse of communication structures.

Chapter 13 focuses on Japanese broadcasters' experiences, which have made great efforts to report disasters over the past 100 years. The role of broadcasting is not only to report the damage when a disaster occurs. When there is a risk of a disaster, to convey correct information and encourage rapid evacuation, to support the recovery and reconstruction of the affected area after a disaster, to deepen understanding of disaster risks in normal times and to raise awareness of disaster prevention. There are roles to be played before, during, after disasters and normal times. Since the Great East Japan Earthquake that killed more than 20,000 people on March 11, 2011, coverage of disasters in Japan has increasingly focused on hazard mitigation. Broadcasters have been making progress in improving both the software and hardware for encouraging early evacuation in disasters. This chapter describes the challenge and issues of disaster broadcasting in Japan in recent years.

Chapter 14 focuses on an important issue of information dissemination to foreign tourists and residents, the number of which is steadily increasing, which requires urgent attention in a strategic risk communication process. However, social infrastructure in Japan, including media communication, is not yet sufficient for foreigners due to lingual, cultural and social gaps. While the tourists need customized emergency information, foreign residents need more local risk information to enhance their daily life preparedness. To find an effective strategy, this chapter will analyze disaster awareness and risk communication of foreign tourists and residents in Japan through a first-hand survey, data analysis and interviews. The survey focuses on four language groups, Chinese, Portuguese, Vietnamese and Indonesian speaking communities, which have different historical and social background in Japan. This chapter also discusses countermeasures through a local activity, which involved foreign and Japanese residents and proved to be effective communication in the time of disaster.

Chapter 15 explains the experiences of NHK WORLD-JAPAN and elaborates the concept of "participatory coverage", inspired by "action research" in the academic world. "Participatory coverage" means that the media and citizens work together to improve society through the process of content production and by utilizing the content. This is especially important in the field of disaster preparedness, where taking action is indispensable to protect lives. The chapter also recognizes a TV program as an example of "participatory coverage", because the collaborators continue learning BOSAI on their own even after the program was over.

Reference

Hua J, Shaw R (2020) Corona virus "infodemic" and emerging issues through a data lens: the case of China. Int J Environ Res Public Health 17:2309. https://doi.org/10.3390/ijerph17072309

Chapter 2
Media Experiences of Asian Disasters—A Way Forward

Russell Isaac

Abstract During the second decade of the twenty-first century, members of the Asia Broadcast Union staff and associated consultants and trainers worked across the Asia–Pacific region on various training and consultation projects related to Climate Change and Disaster Risk Reduction programmes. Some of their experiences are highlighted in this paper, which is aimed primarily at outlining the lessons that have or should have been learned. Despite the logistic and practical challenges facing Asian and Pacific broadcasters and media outlets, the analysis offers a way forward regarding strategy and approaches that can be adopted for the development and improvement of mass audience awareness, safety and well-being.

Keyword Asia–Pacific Broadcast Union · Experiences · Challenges · Analysis · Developments

Having worked with broadcast media institutions across Asia for a decade, the challenges facing TV and radio in dealing with climate-related issues can be described as "substantial" but not beyond hope. Essentially, a change of attitude is required, not only from a journalistic perspective but also from the decision-making, editorial and managerial levels. A change in the approach of broadcasters to environmental programming has become a necessary step in the on-going and ever-growing campaign to address climate change and its consequences. Some of the following experiences and anecdotes serve to highlight the magnitude of the challenges ahead but also indicate routes toward positive actions. They are not scientifically verifiable solutions in themselves but point towards an approach that needs to be undertaken by governments, institutions and individuals alike, if the risks associated with natural disasters are to be reduced.

R. Isaac (✉)
Asia Pacific Broadcasting Association, Kuala Lumpur, Malaysia
e-mail: russell.isaac.sms@gmail.com

© Springer Nature Singapore Pte Ltd. 2021
R. Shaw et al. (eds.), *Media and Disaster Risk Reduction*, Disaster Risk Reduction,
https://doi.org/10.1007/978-981-16-0285-6_2

2.1   The Size of the Task

Given that Asia is a seismically active continent with a population of more than four and a half billion people and that many of the continents worst natural disasters have claimed more lives than any others in history, the role of the media is paramount in disseminating information, knowledge and guidance when natural events occur. This, however, has been seen as a reactive role which, under scrutiny and analysis, needs to become proactive by not only covering events as they occur and after they have occurred but also by becoming sources of warning and preparation before the occurrence of events.

There are 49 recognised countries that form the continent of Asia (UN 2011) and therefore their political, geographical, religious and economical differences make any homogeneous approach to dealing with media and climate issues virtually impossible to implement. Examples from various parts of the continent of media actions, in particular from TV and radio broadcasters, illustrate how organisations have shouldered their duties to their audiences, with differing degrees of success.

The magnitude of the Asian situation became apparent following an ABU Early Warning Broadcasting course conducted in Beijing in 2010. Twenty-five Chinese broadcasters were exposed to the theories and practices related to informing their audiences about procedures associated with impending natural events. The course included a visit to an earthquake simulation centre and introduced the participants to the work of national disaster management teams—experiences and meetings that had not hitherto been part of their journalistic/ broadcast education.

The immediate feedback from the participants led to an impromptu meeting with one of CCTV's senior news executives who praised the efforts of the ABU in initiating an Asian focus and perspective on Early Warning Broadcasting. His ambition was now to increase the exposure of this knowledge and guidance to more Chinese broadcasters. The question was asked regarding the number of broadcasters who would participate in these courses….. his answer was "Thirty Thousand!".

With the biggest population in the world, nearing one and a half billion and with a long history of massive, tragic natural disasters, this was an individual who realised that as national broadcasters, they had an obligation and a duty to their audience to inform and educate on vital issues. At the time, the undertaking of such a huge task was seen as impractical and costly and therefore was not pursued. A realisation of *what* is necessary is not therefore enough to secure actual development.

Effective risk communication across Asia is at best described as being approached in a piecemeal fashion. There is an imperative to create and establish a vision of the future based on how Asian audiences/viewers/listeners/users ingest and react to the news, information and factual output that "suppliers" offer them. This means that providers of information to mass audiences must utilise all means of mass communication that are available to them… traditional, new and developing.

2.2 The Complexity of the Task

With so many platforms and applications available across the continent, delivering vital, important or even useful information is fundamental if the increasing risks to our populations caused by environmental changes are to be reduced. The principle foundation of concentrating efforts on improving our Public Broadcast Service output related to DRR is that people, in general, are seeking reliable and trustworthy sources. The increase and proliferation of social media platforms have led to a situation where sources are not easily verifiable and where rumour and opinion are inextricably bound with some facts and some fiction—a dangerous cocktail for those seeking impartial advice and guidance in times of emergency or social uncertainty. The premise therefore is that a general public will turn to trusted sources when searching for reliable information. The need for all PBS outlets or significant independent media institutions, therefore, is to achieve loyalty among their audiences and this can only be achieved by implementing consistent reporting of issues quickly, effectively, impartially, professionally and more so using qualitative techniques and innovative styles. Compelling stories involving climate adaptation and processes to reduce high-risk situations need to be produced and distributed (via whichever means/platforms/devices) by content providers who know what they are talking about and who can achieve audience loyalty as they address locally relevant issues. Content must be produced by journalists/broadcasters who understand local perspectives and context—they report in means and ways that their audiences understand.

The demise of traditional TV and radio platforms has been grossly over-exaggerated (Television Expert Group 2007) in that advertisers are becoming more aware of the inconsistencies (false/fake news) of social media sites regarding vital information and are questioning their investments in platforms that cannot be trusted. In European surveys (research in Asia is not currently available), the trusted medium across inter-generational groups is still TV and radio—42%, compared to a 13% trust level for newspapers and publications and 5% for social media (News Media Association 2014).

In the UK, OFCOM's 2018 Media Report (OFCOM 2018) states that the most common source "for trusted news and factual programming" was Public Service Broadcasting ….. "73% value PSB most highly for the provision of news"; "63% state that "PSB helps me understand what's going on in the world"; and finally, "95% of affluent Europeans still watch TV daily".

Even though these statistics refer to Western audiences, the trends and patterns are likely to be similar on other continents, thus giving credence to the argument that the content providers need to be aware of their responsibilities; have a knowledge of the issues involving the environment and DRR; have the capacity to produce innovative and high-quality material and have the editorial and managerial backing to research and produce relevant stories and programmes.

Live and recorded linear viewing is still a mainstay source of information and guidance and therefore policies and projects that bring broadcasters, government departments, scientific institutions, Non-Governmental Organisations and other relevant stakeholders together to increase mass audience awareness, is vital. Valuable information and time-sensitive messages can only be securely delivered by worldwide networks working from shared experiences, utilising high quality, professional skill levels on multiple platforms.

2.3   Setting the Standard

The best possible example that can serve as a template for other broadcasters is the work of NHK Japan. They undoubtedly set "a gold standard" that others can only aspire toward. NHK are of course an extremely well-funded organisation (a government run "receiving fee" paid by television viewers) with resources that allow them to research, develop and innovate formats that appeal to mass audiences. However, the underlying success of NHK's approach to safeguarding the public is based on the responsibilities and duties undertaken by their management and staff. They are committed to increasing their knowledge and skills base; they have a healthy attitude toward the relationship between the environment and the people; their approach to communication is that of utilising a tool that enhances safety and security and that the means of communication must be constantly updated and amended so that they remain relevant and trustworthy.

One of the NHK's latest innovations is called BOSAI (NHK World 2020), which is a disaster prevention programme entitled "An Educational Journey"—essentially a collection of cross-generational ideas and practical proposals based on lessons learnt from past floods, earthquakes, the 2011 Tsunami and the Fukushima Daiichi nuclear disaster. It's Japan's message of help not only to their own people but also to the world. The 19,000 who died in the 2011 event devastated a country that was already operating an incredibly sophisticated disaster risk reduction programme (Rafferty and Pletcher 2011). The analysis of the effectiveness of their communication systems meant that they would increase their efforts to improve their service, proving to their audience that they cared and could be trusted in times of crises. An eminent and much-esteemed colleague at NHK, Akinori Hashimoto—former Executive Controller General Broadcasting Administration NHK—often stated that "Japan is the supermarket of natural disasters" and that the natural duty of the national broadcaster was to do its utmost to protect its people. This is the level of trust that other Asian broadcasters and indeed broadcasters across the globe should have in their sights.

The Philippines is another country that offers many examples of how broadcasters should approach the constant dangers facing their population. It has a well-designed and robust disaster risk management system in the National Disaster Risk Reduction and Management Council and the Office of Civil Defense (Rappler 2014). They also have an organisation named Pagasa (from the Tagalog language meaning "hope"), which is the Philippine Atmospheric, Geophysical and Astronomical Services Administration and is the National Meteorological agency mandated to provide protection against natural disasters. Since 1972, they have been tasked with ensuring the safety and economic security of their people by undertaking scientific and technological research and development of risk reduction policies (PAGASA 2020) (8).

A report prepared by the International Development Unit of the Australian Broadcasting Corporation following research conducted during 2014 offered some relevant observations of the Philippines media structure regarding their role in times of disaster (Australian Broadcasting Corporation (ABCID) 2014). The report stated that increasingly, the media was enabling citizens to interact with information providers about disasters and that media personalities and organisations had a strong following across the country. The following is a synopsis of that report's findings.

The Philippines has many organisations involved in the monitoring and management of disasters and the main approach is to manage incidents at the level of the 42,000 "barangays", or villages/suburbs, with escalation to a regional or national level as required. While this engages with citizens at a "grass roots" level, the performance of this decentralised management approach is dependent on the skills of people who, at a local level, are mostly elected to leadership positions and did not have any particular expertise or training in dealing with emergency situations.

Dissemination of information by disaster management organisations includes using short message service (SMS) and an early warning system. Communication by some departments to the public via the media is based on a traditional mix of scheduled bulletins and press releases, with some use of social media. Television and radio play a role in broadcasting information across the country as these platforms reach most areas. Mobile phone technology is of course becoming a key way for citizens to access information when and where they want it and the media has been described as "rowdy, vibrant, diverse and hugely profitable". The industry is highly competitive and increasingly being made up of conglomerates focused on income and controlling the production and distribution of content on multiple platforms. Internet usage is growing rapidly as basic literacy is almost universal in the Philippines according to their National Statistics Office (Philippine Statistics Authority 2020). Commercial and privately owned media, concentrating on entertainment, attracts larger audiences than government-operated stations. The report goes on to say "In the cities the focus of coverage is mostly about the magnitude of a disaster and any political ramifications, while in provincial areas media tends to engage more in disaster preparedness and delivery of basic information without much commentary. To get information, media organisations interact with disaster management authorities at a local and national level. A deeper working relationship has been formalised in some cases, with Albay Province held up as an example of how local partnerships involving the media and other actors can support more resilient communities".

Pagasa works in conjunction with Panahaon TV, which offers a syndicated daily weather news programme direct from the Pagasa Weather and Flood Forecasting Centre in Quezon City. The relationship between the source of scientific data and the messenger therefore is intrinsically close. According to a Time Magazine article in 2014 (Brown 2013), The Philippines is "the most exposed country in the world to tropical storms" and given that an average of 20 Tropical Cyclones will cross the Philippines annually, the public are in constant need of reliable information and guidance. Harsh lessons have been learnt in the aftermath of recent disasters.

The deadliest typhoon to impact the Philippines was Haiyan (known locally as Yolanda) in 2013 when over 7000 lives were lost as a result of storm surges and strong winds. Pagasa raised warning signals of the impending storm on November 6 2013— 2 days before the major impact occurred. Many thousands of people (750,000) took evasive action to avoid the storm but many also believed that they could withstand and survive the event. Relief and rescue efforts were underway by November 9 following days of power interruptions, landslides and flash floods but already more than 6,000 people had lost their lives, nearly 2 million were left homeless and more than 4 million were displaced. The brunt of the storm was funnelled into a bay where the densely populated city of Tacloban was situated. The questions remain regarding the reasons why so many people did not heed the warnings. Were the media explicit enough? Did people trust the media? Did the provincial governors (and their virtual autonomy within the regional context) lack the knowledge, the local preparation and necessary relationship with the media to influence the population?

Pagasa and other officials later admitted that the victims were unfamiliar with the term "storm surge" and in a county with many regional languages, the government and their communicators did not have the local terms to be able to correctly communicate with everyone. Following the disaster, the government agencies worked with linguists and various media outlets to craft simpler meteorological terms to ensure that the dangers posed by typhoons, floods, landslides and other climate-related events could be fully understood by all. In synthesis, the lack of an effective dissemination and communication of early warnings was a notable weakness in the run-up to the typhoon. Critical information was not clearly communicated to those who needed it and people were unaware of the severity of the hazard or did not react appropriately to the information given. One of the vital lessons to be gleaned from this example is the necessity to engage the media—and broadcasters in particular—as primary stakeholders within the disaster management framework, not just the messengers on behalf of others who will have their own particular area of expertise but not necessarily in the field of communication.

2.4   Working with the Science

At the World Meteorological Office conference held in Nanjing, China in April 2014 (World Meteorological Organization 2014), a presentation was submitted by the ABU to the gathered scientists offering a template for cooperation and understanding between the data gathering units of the WMO and the broadcasting departments of Asian media organisations. Whilst the collection and analysis of data are fundamental to understanding climate phenomena and their potential impacts, the dissemination and explanation of this information to a non-scientific public are of equal importance if action is to be taken to mitigate the effects of severe events or to devise adaptive processes to avoid disaster situations. The conference was a single event that was of value to those present but did not lead to a significant strategic or institutional change. However, WMO in its Communication Strategy 2017–2020 recognised that communication "has largely been performed on an ad-hoc basis, without a coherent framework (WCRP 2017). With a growing urgency to explain how our climate is changing, consistent branding and coherent messages are required". The 49-page document has gone a long way to increasing the communications system of the organisation internally and externally. It may seem obvious but necessary to state that all media organisations in Asia and beyond should establish a strong relationship with the WMO as a foundation for their work on climate and disaster-related issues. WMO by now is a media-friendly organisation and an essential part of the stakeholder communication jig-saw.

One intergovernmental organisation that is providing a significant contribution to the protection, the sustainability and the development of their region are SPREP—the Secretariat of the Pacific Regional Environment Programme based in Apia, Samoa (The Secretariat of the Pacific Regional Environment Programme 2020). Despite the fact that the organisation is not a broadcasting outlet, their work encompasses many aspects associated with the media,—training, up-skilling and generally including the media sector in the decision-making and policy implementation process. This inclusivity means that acclaimed scientific organisations such as CSIRO who are a key and influential data and analysis player in the Pacific Islands field of climate research (CSIRO 2020)—are focussed on turning knowledge into "actionable knowledge" into a "tangible, on-ground impact" (Evans et al. 2017). Through their increasing interaction with media outlets and practitioners, they can target the end-users who can adapt to climate change and mitigate the effects of potential on-coming disasters. Logically, this should be the approach of all those involved in current environmental issues in that a connected, interdisciplinary network of relevant stakeholders will lead to tangible improvements in reducing the effects of disasters.

A significant problem facing a joined-up, coherent approach to improving the situation is a lack of a coordinating umbrella organisation to arrange and help administer media action. There are literally hundreds of various courses, workshops and conferences that occur across the Asia–Pacific region annually. Whereas the variety and quantity of activities are to be commended, the outcomes are not as effective as they should be because of the lack of coordination between the organising bodies. During early 2019, for example, Fiji was the venue for a major Pacific Resilience Event at the University of The South Pacific in Suva but at the same time and unbeknown to each other, the ABU was conducting an intensive workshop for broadcasters from a number of Pacific Islands with the express objective of improving climate resilience. By the time the overlap was noticed, the organisers were unable to change any programme schedule although SPREP accommodated the workshop participants within the conference grounds and the workshop outcome was eventually a successful one. More than 25 broadcast items were produced from the conference and entire pilot programmes ("Tales of Resilience") were broadcasted on FBC Fiji (FBC Fiji 2019). However, last-minute adaptations of courses and conferences are not recommended if future strategies are to be optimised.

At the time of writing, a number of institutions are attempting to establish a mechanism that can map events associated with climate knowledge and action. Some of the bodies concerned include UNDRR, UNESCO, ABU, APDC, FAO, AMARC, with an aim of identifying the mechanisms that are in place, who the players are, what roles they play and what their needs are for improvement (Global Forum for Media Development (GFMD) 2020). The eventual and obvious aim of this project would be to produce a route map in order to prevent repetition, focus resources and generally improve the services and opportunities to develop the field. The complex nature, sheer size and diversity of the Asia–Pacific region make this an extremely difficult task to complete but one which appears necessary if a coherent approach is to be adopted.

2.5 High-risk Countries

The state broadcaster in the Maldives (Public Service Media, formerly MBC—Maldives Broadcasting Service) has reacted to advice and are more resilient to the effects of climate change than they were at the beginning of the last decade. The islands are recognised as within the high-risk category and are witnessing increased intensive rainfall and resulting flooding, cyclonic winds and storm surges. As a country, it is one of the lowest lyings in the world with its population living a few metres above sea level and most of its key buildings and institutions lying within 100 m of the coast. The continued warming of the planet will inevitably lead to sea level rises and even a metre rise will endanger the whole future of the nation. A comprehensive National Adaptation Programme of Action was implemented along with "The Safer Island Policy" to attempt to alleviate the serious existential threats that they face (Sovacool 2012) (18). The Government in conjunction with PSM embarked on an awareness campaign to understand the causes and effects of natural disasters such as tsunamis and flooding. The media led information campaign has led the comparatively high-density population of Male, where overcrowding has been prevalent, to rethink their livelihoods and residential requirements. Regional centres have been developed that encourage people to move from high-risk islands to safer locations where a more resilient infrastructure can lead to more sustainable homes and jobs.

MBC and subsequently PSM improved its relationship with the Meteorological services (MMS) and the National Disaster Management Centre (NDMC) following years of depending on a hap-hazard early warning communications system. A single Standard Operational Procedure guideline was adopted and staff were up-skilled to understand the necessity to keep their audience informed about environmental issues. Through the Green Climate Fund, the Government of the Republic of Maldives and JICA (Japanese International Cooperation Agency), a concept project was outlined in 2018 titled "Building Climate Resilient Safer Islands in Maldives" (Republic of Maldives and Japan International Cooperation Agency (JICA) 2018) (19). Under the heading, "Strengthening of Awareness of Climate Threats and Risk-reduction

Processes", JICA will provide an Integrated Services Digital Broadcasting-Terrestrial (ISDB-T) television network throughout the Maldives, making information more accessible to residents and reducing information disparities among islands. This further digital migration would enable the early warning system to spread throughout the nation, strengthening the awareness of climate threats through information provision on natural events including climate change impacts the most vulnerable outer islands. The Maldives is an outstanding example of the need for governmental and non-governmental stakeholders to embrace broadcast media as integral and essential partners in the development and implementation of risk-reduction policies.

Bangladesh Television (BTV) is the national channel of Bangladesh and is primarily financed through television licence fees. With the global proliferation and influx of digital content, the state-owned channel has lost its popularity during the past decade and faces a common problem within the global broadcast world of trying to maintain a loyal audience whilst producing content to attract a new generation who have not grown up viewing and listening to traditional media outlets. In their article "From Few to Many Voices: An Overview of Bangladesh's Media", Brian Shoesmith and Shameem Mahmud wrote that since the mid-1990s, Bangladesh has witnessed a proliferation of television broadcasters with terrestrial, satellite and transnational companies, all jostling for attention of the Bangladesh audiences (Shoesmith and Shameem 2014) (20). Surveys by NMS and Nielsen Bangladesh showed a persistent increase in TV consumption with viewership almost doubled from 42% in 1998 to 82.9% in 2016, slightly decreasing to 80% in 2017. There are 30 authorised TV channels in the county alongside a number of pirate channels. In an article written by M Abul Kalam Azad (21) "although a number of TV stations are now available, they are failing to provide quality news" (Azad 2019). A broadcasting void is being identified in some quarters therefore that need to be filled.

Environmental and disaster risk awareness courses have been conducted at BTV's studios in Dhaka under the guidance of ABU with positive responses from journalists, producers and at the managerial level. The Prime Minister of Bangladesh, Sheikh Hasina is an advocate of climate action stating "Bangladesh is one of the most vulnerable front-line countries.... and my government has mainstreamed climate actions and disaster risks reduction in its national plan" (Global Center on Adaptation 2019) (22). Given that BTV, as the only terrestrial channel is still seen as an effective means of communication, the channel now needs to embark on a structural support plan for DRR programming. The challenge ahead is to rebuild the trust levels that older generations had in state channel broadcasting—albeit on digital and social platforms—to ensure that knowledge, advice and guidance regarding natural events are understood and that means of mitigation and adaptation are acted upon.

Kazakhstan is another country where the Head of State, Nursultan Nazarbayev, gave his support a decade ago to an ambitious target of transforming the country to a green economy by 2050 (Ospanova 2014) (23). The country has an energy-intensive, petroleum-based economy and has embarked on a pathway towards a sustainable, low emission development. However, this environmental ambition is not necessarily reflected in its media output where TV is still the most popular medium. The concentration of news and factual programming that is produced via the Khabar Agency for example—one of the primary media outlets in Kazakhstan—is of a political and economic nature but there is currently no specific expertise or editorial impetus for promoting environmental knowledge and awareness (Kazakh TV 2020) (24). At the journalistic and research level, there is an appetite and an enthusiasm to incorporate a climate-based agenda into their factual output and at a managerial level, there is an understanding and awareness of the responsibilities that a state broadcaster should have towards its audience but as yet, as with the majority of Asian broadcasters, the transformation of understanding into tangible editorial and production action, has not yet happened.

2.6   A Detailed Case Study

Invariably, the tragic consequences of natural disasters lead to analysis and recriminations as the finger of blame is pointed—by those who have suffered or have been injured or bereaved—at those who they believe could have or should have prevented a tragic event. By detailing the time-scale and sequence of a disaster caused by a natural event, it is possible to trace a template that indicates how the media can become more responsible and more integrated into disaster risk reduction procedures.

In June 2014, at least 67 fishermen died as a result of a storm that hit Sri Lanka's southwestern coastal area. The homes of fishing families at Beruwala, Balapitiya and Hikkaduwa in the south, and Dehiwala, Ratmalana and Moratuwa in the western province, were also badly affected. According to the disaster management department, over 1,400 persons were displaced, 107 houses completely destroyed and more than 2,200 homes damaged (World Socialist Web Site (WSWS) 2013) (25).

Angry fishermen condemned the government for not providing a proper early warning system and safety facilities. Though the storm was a natural disaster, many lives could have been saved if people had been effectively alerted in advance.

The director of the meteorology department told reporters that his institute sent a warning to all agencies about weather conditions 3 days before the storm but he admitted that the department lacked sophisticated technology to observe sudden changes of the weather. His deputy later said the department was also short-staffed by 17 meteorologists and 77 technical officers, making it difficult to cope with storm events.

The government immediately blamed meteorology department officials and washed its hands of responsibility. An editorial in the "Island" publication stated: "What usually happens is that politicians employ such tactics to assuage and divert public anger at the expense of state officials and pigeonhole probe reports."

The government, under President Mahinda Rajapakse, appointed a committee to investigate the disaster and whether lapses occurred in the meteorology department. Some compensation (100,000 rupees $US800 plus funeral expenses) was also offered to the families of those who died.

A decade earlier, after the December 2004 Asian tsunami disaster, Rajapakse's predecessor, Chandrika Kumaratunga, pledged to establish a weather warning system as many fishermen were among the 40,000 people from Sri Lanka who perished. However, this system had not yet been tested to assess its effectiveness.

In 2011, the government promised to allocate funds to modernise the meteorology department but the Disaster Management Minister Mahinda Amaraweera admitted the plan was put off to 2014. This postponement was the result of government spending cutbacks.

About 1000 families lived in the Kadalamaththa area of Dehiwala between the sea and a railway line. Most of their houses were built from wooden planks. They had no basic facilities, such as running water and sanitation. The majority earned a living by fishing and fishermen are among the poorest layers of Sri Lankan society. Typically, three fishermen will go to sea in a small fibre boat fitted with a small engine and little else. Following the tragedy, surviving fishermen claimed that if the government had taken action and warnings had been issued some days in advance, many lives could have been saved. Most people died because their boats capsized near the shore on their return.

In their defence, the Meteorological Office claimed that they had sent weather warnings to media outlets but that these warnings had not been delivered in enough time to be effective. The media organisations in their defence claimed that the information received was unclear and had not been designated as urgent and therefore the appropriate warnings had not been given. In noting the sequence of events as recorded by the TV and radio newsrooms of the Maharaja organisation (one of Sri Lanka's most powerful broadcast institutions), the early warnings (up to 3 days prior to the storm) were broadcast but not using urgent language (UNESCO 2018) (27). On the day of the tragedy, further warnings were received but again they had been delivered to the broadcasters using scientific terms and data that were not interpreted by the journalistic intake to be of a severe nature. By the time the eventual weather warnings were transmitted (some 2 h after the meteorological information had been sent), the fishing fleet had already left their harbour and without appropriate safety equipment or on-board radios, the impending storm proved fatal.

The tale is a common one. A tragic series of events affecting the poorest people, in the most deprived areas, at the end of a sub-standard communication process. Despite the claims and counterclaims of all the parties concerned, eventual culpability lay in varying degrees, between all of the players. Following such a tragedy, the most important aspect is that the lessons learnt are developed into tangible solutions and safeguards for the future. The immediate reaction of the Maharaja programme department was to implement a joint scheme with the meteorological department to ensure that scientists, weather forecasters and journalists worked on means to improve the communication language and processes so that messages could be understood and delivered in better and quicker ways. The time of shipping and weather radio bulletins were brought forward so that information was transmitted before the fishing fleets left harbour. There was also an increase in multi-language weather warnings to improve communication with multiple ethnic origin groups involved in the fishing industry. Most indicators point towards a future increase in severe weather events such as cyclones and sea surges and therefore the requirement of media organisations to learn, adapt and to cooperate with other stakeholders is a logical progression.

The same principle is true for the "other" stakeholders, that is, to find solutions by incorporating the media at every stage of the risk reduction process.

2.7 Developments

Following the 5th ABU Media Climate Change Summit in Kathmandu (April 2019) and the launch of the UNESCO Handbook for Journalists reporting on Climate Change in Asia and the Pacific—"Getting the Message Across"—(UNESCO 2018) (27), a series of workshops were organised to train broadcasters utilising the suggestions, knowledge and specified targets established during the Nepal meetings. The first workshop was held in Suva, Fiji, with participants representing the Fiji Broadcasting Corporation (radio and television), Fiji Television, Radio Vanuatu and Vanuatu Broadcasting and TV Corporation.

As referred to earlier, running concurrently with the workshop in Suva was the Inaugural Pacific Resilience Meeting (PRM), organised by SPREP and facilitated by the University of South Pacific (USP) with more than 300 participants attending. The organisers kindly cooperated with the ABU to allow the workshop participants to attend the 3-day conference and to collect video and audio materials of the speakers and sessions—all related to Climate Change issues with an emphasis on community resilience.

The workshop itself concentrated on updating the participants on Climate Change broadcasting trends and imparting the necessary knowledge base to those working in the communication industry that would enable them to develop story and programme ideas.

From the UN Handbook, the missing elements from many Asian Broadcast outlets were discussed and the requirements for responsible Environmental reporting were recognised. Acknowledging the growing importance of climate-related issues in the Asia–Pacific region, the participants engaged in their past experiences of disaster situations (e.g. Cyclone Winston) and how the media should have been able to contribute more in the preparation of their audiences and been more effective during the post-disaster period.

As changes within the global environment affect us all, it was suggested that journalists involved in these issues should raise the profile of events such as campaigns and public global movements to underline the fact that the "environment" is becoming the fastest-growing source of news and factual programming. It was agreed that news editors and producers are slowly changing their agendas to reflect the changing global priorities but that more specialised reporting was necessary.

The production element of the workshop worked on a team-based principle of sharing experiences and production techniques with an editorial approach that would incorporate a series of interviewees and would ultimately reflect a wide range of contributors from across the Pacific Islands. The title of the final product was agreed as "Tales of Resilience—Pacific Stories". The workshop also included contributions from other key stakeholders such as the Red Cross Management Team who updated the participants on their activities and latest projects in the region. Up-skilling courses such as these are greatly enriched with contributions from various organisations but the Red Cross/Red Crescent never fail in delivering a current overview of practices and practical connections with disaster risk reduction exercises.

The product of the participants' practical efforts was a 25-min television factual programme and a series of radio inserts that managed to encapsulate the experiences and stories told at the PRM. Stories of resilience came from Fiji, The Marshall Islands, Kiribati, Tuvalu, The Solomon Islands and Bougainville and included contributions that highlighted disability challenges, the role of the Church, youth initiatives, renewable energy projects and new technology strategies and there were unused stories that would act as a source of material for further productions based on environmental issues and would be available to all participating media, free of copyright.

A long-time goal of the ABU as noted in each of their Climate Change Summits since (28) is to establish Correspondents of Expertise or where possible, Environmental Units within Broadcasting organisations across the Asia–Pacific region 2014 (ABU—Asia–Pacific Broadcasting Union 2020). Although some resource and staff allocation are required by broadcast organisations to implement such a target, the result of not undertaking this responsibility will ultimately affect the relationship between the broadcaster and the audience and cost the broadcaster in terms of diminishing levels of trust and follower numbers. As a result of this particular course in Fiji, the senior management team of FBC agreed that the establishment of such a unit within their structure was now very feasible and identified key individuals who could undertake those responsibilities. The unit began functioning immediately with regular broadcast (TV and radio) and online content being produced.

In conjunction with the use of the UNESCO Handbook, the next step was to conduct a series of webinars with the Fiji workshop participants working on follow-up environmental programme production and a similar course was then held in Samoa. The Apia workshop saw participants from Samoa, Fiji, Kiribati, Tuvalu, Tonga and Vanuatu taking part and was arranged to coincide with the ABU PMPC and the PMC (Pacific Meteorological Conference). Contributions during the course came from stakeholders such as UNESCO, UNICEF, FAO and the Red Cross to give further perspectives on reporting environmental issues and the interaction required between the media and the relevant organisations, non-governmental and governmental. Contributions from the PMC included speakers from SCIRO and SPREP highlighting the Next Generation Climate Projections, once again outlining the imperative need to cooperate and develop the work of scientists and to find ways to engage wider audiences using understandable language and to address issues that affect audiences at ground level. Interviews were also conducted at the PMC with various Meteorological Officers from across the Pacific for news outlets on Tonga, Kiribati and Vanuatu.

The results and outcomes of these initiatives were subsequently followed by an inter-continental Twinning Course organised by the ABU in Kuala Lumpur with broadcast journalists from 15 countries, representing Asia, Sub-Sahara Africa, and the Asia Pacific, participated in the ABU Twinning Workshop entitled "Getting the Message Across on Climate Change." The workshop (funded by the Malaysian

Government through "Malaysia Funds-in-Trust," and the United Nations Educational, Scientific, and Cultural Organization (UNESCO) workshop consisted of information sharing sessions with technical and media specialists from the Malaysian Meteorological Department, United Nations Disaster Risk Reduction, (UNDRR), International Federation of the Red Cross (IFRC), Intergovernmental Panel on Climate Change (IPCC), and Food Security. On location, the participants formed production teams and were able to film and record interviews with farmers, agricultural and food security experts, environmentalists, and providers of tourism services, on the issues and challenges of climate change, climate change adaptation, and specifically on Disaster Risk Reduction processes. The UNDRR highlighted the content and aims of the Handbook for African Journalists: "Disaster Through a Different Lens" which was the basis for the afore-mentioned Asian and Pacific Island Handbook "Getting the Message Across" (UNISDR 2011). Both publications serve as a tool for all "South by South" journalists and broadcasters and should be used as a reference point by those engaged in media-environmental issues.

The contribution from Professor Rajib Shaw explained the latest steps taken by the IPCC and the scientific community to address research issues and the continuing need to communicate relevant findings to wider audiences and particularly to those being affected by environmental events and climatic variations such as farmers, growers and fishermen. The subsequent "food security" presentation gave a perspective on how communities are attempting to adapt their traditional agricultural methods to compensate for fluctuating rainfall and temperature rises.

Two other major stakeholders from the Malaysian Meteorological Office and the International Federation of Red Cross and Red Crescent emphasised the need for improved interaction between media professionals and their respective organisations. Constant cooperation between governmental departments, key NGOs and environmental reporters again being underlined as an essential component of a responsible communications strategy. The result was that numerous features appeared or were heard on media platforms across 15 countries spanning Asia, Africa and the Pacific helping build local and national media dissemination and communication capacities on the critical and complex issues of climate change and efforts to successfully adapt to the ever-changing landscape.

2.8   Conclusions

The twinning experiment as described by the participants was "an outstanding event in the development of environmental reporting". The unanimous conclusion of the workshops and courses was that the exchange of ideas and experiences had improved their awareness of climate and DRR issues and given them a focus and impetus toward future productions.

The consistent call from the ABU Climate Change Summits has been to encourage media outlets to establish "Professional Approaches" and this is an initiative that a number of members are engaged in developing. It is recognised however that many organisations do not have the resources to fund dedicated units and correspondents as there are many other duties to be performed within their professional remit. In these circumstances, the participants agreed that an individual acceptance of an "extra" role of "environmental responsibilities" would at least go some way toward establishing a level of expertise and recognition amongst colleagues and stakeholders and would establish a foundation for further developments as climatic issues gain further traction and momentum.

The African members of DIRAJ involved in mainstreaming DRR content suggested that the African-Asian contact network established at the workshop could be extended and be of benefit to other African countries (Disaster Risk Reduction Association of Journalist (DIRAJ) 2020). A next step would be to fund a similar workshop in Africa that would strengthen and improve environmental reporting across the continent, again with Asian journalists contributing to the project.

Where the lack of resources prevents the establishment of small units or even dedicated reporters, it is believed that the initial workshops have established an awareness and an enthusiasm to undertake Climate Change and DRR features (across multi-platforms) along with a networking framework to share experiences and potential storylines.

The underlying problems requiring Behavioural and Organisational Change remain a challenge for all stakeholders—media and beyond. The next step should be to produce higher quality co-productions that are relevant across continents from local (not international) perspectives and to engage with other regions that have not yet been exposed to this initiative (e.g. Caribbean Islands, Central and South American countries, etc.).

The initial media workshops and courses have produced encouraging results but the challenge is to maintain a momentum and to secure organisational support for those individuals who have grasped the importance of responsible and engaging environmental reporting. But broadcasters cannot succeed alone and need the support of UN organisations and governments to achieve tangible and sustainable goals. UN organisations need TV and radio support to change the mind-sets and behavioural patterns of governments and individuals to advance the global agenda of climate change action, disaster risk reduction and sustainable development, which require a new approach from reporters and media outlets.

There is therefore a need for a massive capacity building programme addressing the weakest communication links to build resilient communities and UN organisations such as UNDRR, IPCC, ITU, WMO should help provide the support and capacity training that they urgently need.

The managerial levels of broadcast organisations need to be sensitised to the changing global concerns of their audiences and the editorial decision-makers need to be supportive of the new relationships being forged with their viewers and listeners. Journalists and producers of DRR content need to have institutional backing to promote innovative approaches to story-telling and programme construction.

In November 2019, leaders of ABU, ASBU, AUB and EBU met with the UN Secretary-General's Special Representative for DRR, Ms Mami Mizutori in Tokyo, Japan and agreed to support a long-term capacity building project for the unions' members on climate change adaptation and DRR. The organisations committed to develop a unified, detailed 3-year Action Plan to train broadcasters on disaster risk reduction and climate change. The plan aims at providing long-term sustainable outcomes rather than the piece-meal approach that is often used to engage media in Asia Pacific and Africa and a standardised content approach that will allow each broadcaster to be equipped with the necessary tools to ensure regular, accurate and timely DRR coverage.

The plan aims to strengthen the capacity of individual TV, radio and electronic media organisations who will be able to cover the complex issues of climate change adaptation and disaster prevention in a more regular and accurate manner in Asia, Africa and the Arab States. The plan also builds on the cooperation between UNDRR, UNESCO and World Broadcasting Unions, and in particular, the Asia–pacific Broadcasting Union (ABU) and the African Union of Broadcasting (AUB) that have accumulated considerable knowledge and expertise to develop and support training programmes that will equip reporters with the necessary tools to cover disaster risk reduction and climate change issues.

The purpose of the plan is to reinforce, at regional and national levels, the three main roles of broadcasters which are "to alert, inform and educate" so more TV and radio broadcasters from Africa, Arab States and Asia–Pacific can become effective partners in the early warning chain and decisive actors to advance the principles of Disaster Risk Reduction.

References

ABU—Asia-Pacific Broadcasting Union (2020) Events. https://www.abu.org.my/?doing_wp_cron=1602149815.6760690212249755859375. Accessed 19 July 2020

Australian Broadcasting Corporation (ABCID) (2014) Disaster information providers in the Philippines. https://www.abc.net.au/cm/lb/9223578/data/disaster-information-providers-in-philippines-data.pdf

Azad MAK (2019) Bangladesh—media landscapes, media lanscape. https://medialandscapes.org/country/bangladesh. Accessed 17 July 2020

CSIRO (2020) Our research. https://www.csiro.au/en/Research. Accessed 20 July 2020

Disaster Risk Reduction Association of Journalist (DIRAJ) (2020) Team archive. https://diraj.org/team/

Evans K, Terhorst A, Kang B (2017) CSIRO research publications repository—publication. Taylor & Francis. https://doi.org/10.1080/07352689.2017.1336047

FBC Fiji (2019) FBC news—latest Fiji news, sports, and weather. https://www.fbcnews.com.fj/. Accessed 19 July 2020

Global Center on Adaptation (2019) What Bangladesh can teach the world about climate change adaptation. https://gca.org/solutions/what-bangladesh-can-teach-the-world-about-climate-change-adaptation. Accessed 13 July 2020

Global Forum for Media Development (GFMD) (2020) Research, impact, and knowledge sharing. https://gfmd.info/gfmd-content/uploads/2020/06/MEDIAMAPPING-1.pdf

Kazakh TV (2020) News release. https://kazakh-tv.kz/en/view/news_release. Accessed 13 July 2020

News Media Association (2014) Home: reports. https://www.newsmediauk.org/. Accessed 20 July 2020

NHK World (2020) BOSAI—Radio—NHK WORLD-JAPAN—English. https://www3.nhk.or.jp/nhkworld/en/radio/bosaiweb/. Accessed 13 July 2020

OFCOM (2018) MEDIA NATIONS: UK 2018. UK. https://www.ofcom.org.uk/__data/assets/pdf_file/0014/116006/media-nations-2018-uk.pdf

Ospanova S (2014) Assessing Kazakhstan's policy and institutional framework for a green economy

PAGASA (2020) Philippine atmospheric, geophysical and astronomical services administration. https://bagong.pagasa.dost.gov.ph/. Accessed 24 July 2020

Philippine Statistics Authority (2020) Statistics of the Republic of the Philippines. https://psa.gov.ph/. Accessed 13 July 2020

Rafferty JP, Pletcher K (2011) Japan earthquake and tsunami of 2011 _ Facts & Death Toll _ Britannica. https://www.britannica.com/event/Japan-earthquake-and-tsunami-of-2011. Accessed 16 July 2020

Rappler (2014) Fast facts; the NDRRMC. https://www.rappler.com/newsbreak/iq/fast-facts-ndrrmc. Accessed 26 July 2020

Republic of Maldives and Japan International Cooperation Agency (JICA) (2018) Building climate resilient safer islands in Maldives. https://www.greenclimate.fund/sites/default/files/document/20490-building-climate-resilient-safer-islands-maldives.pdf

Shoesmith BP, Shameem M (2014) From few to many voices: an overview of Bangladesh's media. In: Brian Shoesmith JG (ed) Bangladesh's changing mediascape. Intellect Books Ltd, pp. 15–32. https://www.intellectbooks.com/bangladeshs-changing-mediascape

Sophie Brown (2013) The Philippines is the most storm-exposed country on Earth. Available at: https://world.time.com/2013/11/11/the-philippines-is-the-most-storm-exposed-country-on-earth/#:~:text=Situated in a vast expanse, the world to tropical storms. Accessed 13 July 2020

Sovacool BK (2012) Perceptions of climate change risks and resilient island planning in the Maldives, pp. 731–752. https://doi.org/10.1007/s11027-011-9341-7

Television Expert Group (2007) International comparison of TV ratings & TV audience measurement research boards and institutes—international. https://www.international-television.org/tv_audience_measurement_research_boards_and_institutes.html

The Secretariat of the Pacific Regional Environment Programme (2020) SPREP: events. https://www.sprep.org/events. Accessed 26 July 2020

UN (2011) United Nations—member states. https://www.un.org/en/members/. Accessed 26 July 2020

UNESCO (2018) Getting the message across. https://en.unesco.org/sites/default/files/getting_the_message_across_climate_change_asia_pacific_web_2018.pdf

UNISDR (2011) Disaster through a different lens: a guide for journalists covering disaster risk reduction. https://www.preventionweb.net/files/20108_mediabook.pdf

WCRP (2017) Communication strategy 2017–2020. https://www.wcrp-climate.org/JSC38/documents/WCRP_Communication_Strategy_2017-2020-draft.pdf

World Meteorological Organization (2014) Events and meetings. https://public.wmo.int/en/events. Accessed 20 July 2020

World Socialist Web Site (WSWS) (2013) Sri Lanka_ Storm kills dozens of fishermen—World S. https://www.wsws.org/en/articles/2013/06/14/sril-j14.html. Accessed 26 July 2020

Part II
Media Types and Its Role

Chapter 3
Community Radio Movement in the Promotion of Disaster Risk Reduction in Indonesia

Mario Antonius Birowo and Junichi Hibino

Abstract In Indonesia and Japan, where there are many natural disasters, community radio has played an important role as a "hub" for local information during times of disaster and recovery and reconstruction. In Indonesia, a community radio station will be established in the affected area under the leadership of the Community Radio Association, with civil society taking the lead. On the other, in Japan, in the event of a major disaster, local governments in the disaster-stricken areas set up temporary disaster broadcasting stations with the support of the Ministry of Internal Affairs and Communications and neighboring community radio stations hand. Both forms have advantages and disadvantages. In particular, in the case of Japan, there is little initiative from residents, and in the case of Indonesia, there is little involvement from the government. The Japan–Indonesia Joint program has been deployed in Indonesia since 2017. The aim of this project is to enhance the functions of community radio, a public–private partnership to enhance the community-based disaster risk reduction capabilities. The model is a public–private partnership in Wakayama, where the risk of a Nankai Trough Megathrust Earthquake is high. The community radio sectors in both countries continue to localize this model to several areas in Indonesia such as Boyolali, the location of Merapi Volcano, in Indonesia. This chapter focuses on the installment of the Wakayama model to Boyolali, this paper examines a mechanism in which community radio is established with community initiative in the event of a disaster, and its activities can be continued until the period of recovery and reconstruction in cooperation with the government.

Keywords Community radio · Risk · Disaster · Wakayama · Merapi · Boyolali

M. A. Birowo
Universitas Atma Jaya Yogyakarta, Yogyakarta, Indonesia

J. Hibino (✉)
FMYY Community Radio, Kobe, Japan
e-mail: hibijun@gmail.com

© Springer Nature Singapore Pte Ltd. 2021
R. Shaw et al. (eds.), *Media and Disaster Risk Reduction*, Disaster Risk Reduction,
https://doi.org/10.1007/978-981-16-0285-6_3

3.1 Introduction

Community is a backbone of the Disaster Risk Reduction (DRR) movement. Various studies have explained the role of communities on DRR. There are scientists who call it community-based disaster risk reduction/CBDRR, and there are also those who call it community-based disaster preparedness/CBDP. Both of them are the community's readiness in anticipating coming disasters. They take initiatives to reduce the risk of disaster. Studies on the role of communities on DRR have been carried out in various disasters (Allen 2006; Buckland 1999; Van Niekerk et al. 2017; Flint and Luloff 2007; Habiba et al. 2013; Hibino and Shaw 2014; Shaw 2016).

Community radio is generally considered to be media capable of playing the following roles in each phase of community-based disaster management, based on their experience in areas affected by large-scale disasters in Indonesia and Japan, such as the Great Hanshin-Awaji Earthquake, Tsunami Aceh, Mt. Merapi Eruption, and the Great East Japan Earthquake. In case of emergency phase, community radio played roles to communicate detailed disaster and relief information to the community; build a bridge between victims and their supporters; stop spreading rumors; heal the mind$_{heart}$ s of injured victims. While in recovery and reconstruction phases played roles to encourage dialogue between residents of different positions; stay close to the victims and connect with the community. In the case of normal situation (daily life), community radio played roles to communicate disaster experience and knowledge to the community.

This chapter discusses the people-to-people collaboration on DRR utilizing community radio between Indonesia and Japan. Both countries are similar in which both are prone to natural disasters, such as earthquakes, tsunami, volcano eruptions, floods, and landslides. These natural disasters are often unavoidable, but the risks can be reduced if the community and the government make good preparations to anticipate them. To support DRR, communities in both countries have initiatives to encourage policy advocacy, particularly in disaster communication and information systems. This chapter uses a case study from the local areas of both countries, Wakayama Prefecture (Japan) and the Boyolali Regency (Indonesia).

Since the UN World Conference on Disaster Risk Reduction in Sendai in 2015, natural disaster management has been launched from response to preparation, with the goal of reducing the significant loss of life and material (UNISDR 2015b). To achieve this goal, community participation is the center of Disaster Risk Reduction/DRR. Bearing in mind that communities are at the forefront in a disaster situation, both as victims or volunteers.

In many cases, community radio has shown its role in disaster management (Birowo 2011; Hadiyati et al. 2018; Hibino and Shaw 2014, b, 2015; Vaanoli 2017). This paper describes how public participation, especially the participation of community radio activists, in promoting DRR in Indonesia and Japan. These activists have been collaborating on the Emergency Radio for Resilient Community (Radar Tangguh) Program. This 4-year program (2017–2021) aims to campaign for DRR at the community level as well as policy advocacy at the government level.

Collaboration is one of the main features highlighted at Radar Tangguh program because through collaboration involved parties can learn about each other (share valuable knowledge). This is in line with what was driven by the Sendai Framework, in which the problems of natural disasters belong to all, not only the government but also the community. Disaster settlement needs to involve various parties because of its complex nature, thus it cannot be done partially; handling must be integrative (UNISDR 2015b).

3.2 Collaboration Between Indonesia and Japan

The collaboration of Indonesian and Japanese community radio at Radar Tangguh program is a result of similar collaborations since 2006. The meeting began since the 1st Association of Community Radio Broadcaster Asia Pacific (AMARC AP) Conference in Jakarta in 2006. At that time, a delegation of Japanese community radio attended the conference. Activists who have been active in community-based disaster radio stations in Japan and Indonesia have shared their experiences across borders at the World Conference of the World Association of Community Radio Broadcasters (AMARC) in Jordan, 2006. That was the first opportunity to learn mutual experiences. In the session "Community Radio on Disaster Risk Reduction" of the conference, the activities of FMYY which was the first community-based disaster radio station at the time of the Great Hanshin-Awaji Earthquake and the activities of the Aceh/Nias Reconstruction Radio Network (ARRNet) developed after the Aceh Tsunami were shared by the respective practitioners.

In 2007, with FMYY as a core, community radio activists in Japan organized AMARC Japan Working Group for the purpose of strengthening the network with community radio in the world. In particular, based on the experience of "Activities on Disaster Risk Reduction using community radio" that Japan has developed, and through mutual learning with Indonesia and other countries, it aimed to more clearly position the role of community radio, which contributes to DRR, in society. In 2007, FMYY Community Radio visited the Angkringan community radio in Yogyakarta and Lintas Merapi in Klaten, to exchange experiences in the use of community radio for information on natural disasters (Combine Resource Institution 2012). Then the Japanese community radio delegation was also present at the 2008 Training of Trainers Workshop on Poverty Alleviation and Disaster Management through Community Radio in Yogyakarta. This workshop was addressed to celebrate the 25 Years Community Radio Movement held by AMARC Asia Pacific (AMARC Asia Pacific 2008).

During the earthquake in West Sumatra in 2009, FMYY assisted community radio(s) in West Sumatra in responding to disasters (Rina 2010). Collaboration then continued in the Program Tanggap dan Siaga (Response and Readiness Program for Harmony) or called Tangguh Merapi Program. The program was implemented around the villages of Mt. Merapi focusing on DRR that took place in 2012–2016 (Combine Resource Institution 2012).

People-to-people collaboration can be seen as an understanding that DRR can be done effectively if it starts from the scope of the community. Those who were first affected and responded to the disaster that happened to him. Therefore, the community must be prepared to be resilient in the face of disasters (Combine Resource Institution 2010).

What is particularly noteworthy is that activists working on community radio stations in the areas affected by the Great East Japan Earthquake and other disasters, and members of the Indonesian Community Radio Network, which has led disaster radio station activities in Indonesia, participated in (1) a forum for sharing experiences on DRR and community radio, (2) visits to disaster radio stations in the areas affected by the Great East Japan Earthquake, and (3) visits to ministries and agencies responsible for community and disaster radio, in line with the United Nations World Conference on Disaster Risk Reduction to be held in Sendai in March 2015 (Japan Foundation 2019).

3.3 Community Radio in Indonesia

The fall of Soeharto in 1998 encouraged the people to change the political system that was maintained by the Soeharto era, especially with regard to centralization. In line with that, the push for decentralization has also affected the village government. The people saw that democracy must also be implemented at the village level. One of the intentions was that good governance (transparency, anti-corruption) must be present in the village administration. Community media was seen as one of the channels that could guard the village towards good governance. Not surprisingly, social activists at the village level began to pioneer community media. Henceforth, in various villages, community radio was founded as a part of balancing local power. They raised an issue of freedom of access to media and information. Additionally, some community radios were born out of a desire to care for local cultures such as the Pamor Community Radio FM and the Community Radio BalaiBudayaMinomartani FM in Yogyakarta (Birowo 2010b).

It can be said, along with political democratization, there is a similar desire for democratization in broadcast media (Masduki 2017). The combination of the democratization of politics and media is the presence of community radio. Several community forums then established community radio, such as Angkringan Community Radio and Panagati Community Radio (Yogyakarta), Kamal MuaraMuara Community Radio Forum (Jakarta), Cibangkong Citizen Forum Community Radio (FWC) and Majalaya Sejahtera Community Radio (MASE) in West Java (Jaringan Radio Komunitas Indonesia 2007). Generally, the establishment of those community radios was initiated by young people. In addition, community radio activists were dissatisfied with the performance of the mainstream media in serving the needs of marginal communities, especially in the villages. This dissatisfaction also departed from the mainstream media performances during the Soeharto government, which was considered to favor the government and commercialism rather than serving the public. So it is not surprising that the community radio movement is considered part of the counter-hegemony (Birowo 2004; Maryani 2011; Nugroho et al. 2013).

In fact, public broadcasting and private broadcasting were not happy with the presence of community radio. After going through heated debate, the advocacy efforts for the inclusion of community broadcasting into the Broadcasting Law were finally successful. Community Radio for the first time in Indonesian history was recognized by law, namely Broadcasting Law No. 32 of 2002. Along with advocacy to include community radio in the law, community radio activists established the Indonesia Community Radio Network (JRKI) on March 24, 2002 (Birowo 2010a, b; Sujoko 2013). This organization was actually founded by various radio elements outside of mainstream broadcast radio, such as campus radio, hobby radio, community radio and community forum radio (Jaringan Radio Komunitas Indonesia 2007). At present, JRKI has 457 members spread across 18 regions.

Even though community radio was recognized in the Broadcasting Law, it was not easy for community radio to sustain its existence. This uneasy situation appeared on the difficulty of community radio to obtain a broadcasting permit since permission procedures were treated similarly to private broadcasting institutions, for example licensing must be administered to Jakarta. It was considered heavy for community radio. Not surprisingly, the difficulty to get a license affected the number of licensed community radio. The latest data (2019) from SinamSutarno, Chair of JRKI, show that only 100 stations have licenses (Sutarno 2019b).

In this first phase, JRKI gained support from civil society networks (Prakoso and Nugent 2006). The interest of NGOs (foreign and domestic) and universities to support community radio was quite high. NGOs in their community empowerment programs have begun to involve community radio. At that time, the position of community radio was not the initiator of programs. Those programs were useful to promote the existence of community radio. One prominent NGO in the promotion of community radio was the Combine Resource Institution. This NGO has been supporting community radio since the early 2000s. Various programs were organized for community radio empowerment, related to the democratization of media, such as access to information, citizen journalism and disaster (Combine Resource Institution 2014; Gazali 2003; Prakoso and Nugent 2006). Combine's a large role in community radio has made this NGO as a place of learning for people interested in community radio in Indonesia. Combine is quite good at documenting community radio movements in Indonesia, including through the Kombinasi magazine. Some books have also been published.

During advocacy for the recognition of community radio in the Broadcasting Law, universities supported this movement by facilitating a place for a discussion forum on community radio. Academics saw community radio as a symbol of counter-hegemony against mainstream media controlled by the government and market. As a new phenomenon in the media system, academics also pay attention to study/research on the role of community radio in society. Several doctoral dissertations as well as bachelor and master degree theses took the topic of community radio. In the early 2000s, to strengthen support for the existence of community radio in Indonesia, NGOs and universities joined the Community Radio Support Network.

In the second phase (2012-until now), JRKI began to actively collaborate and fundraise through various parties, both governments, foreign institution and civil society. JRKI started to raise some issues according to the institutions invited to the collaboration. For example anti-corruption, protection of women and children, family planning, human rights, disaster (Sutarno 2019a, b). Collaboration with various parties, including government agencies, has a positive impact on the existence of community radio. These collaborations can be seen as a real recognition from other institutions toward community radio. The community radio gradually gained more confidence to participate in discussions in the national arena. They began to be involved in national issues, not only as invited parties but also those who took the initiative. They were increasingly actively lobbying for the benefit of organizing community radio, such as ease in the licensing process. The success of this lobbying indicated political recognition of the Ministry of Communication and Information. The ministry began to consider community radio in its policy. The JRKI National Congress in 2017, for example, received assistance to use the ministry building in Cisarua, Bogor. In another event, Minister of Communication and Information Rudiantara was present at the 2018 Asia Pacific Community Radio Conference at Universitas Atma Jaya Yogyakarta. At the conference, Rudiantara gave a statement of support for the presence of community radio in Indonesia, including in the ease of the licensing process, including radiofrequency for disaster emergency radio. The statement was said in front of 200 participants from the Asia Pacific region. Accordingly, that statement explicitly acknowledged community radio's contribution to the advocacy of government policy on disaster management.

3.4   Community Radio in Japan

The main features and purposes of community broadcasting in disaster management are community-based, citizen participation, disaster risk reduction, and disaster broadcasts. Among them, expectations for DRR and disaster broadcasts are high. In Japan, whenever a natural disaster occurs, such as the Great Hanshin-Awaji Earthquake in 1995, the Niigata-Chuetsu Earthquake in 2006, or the Great East Japan Earthquake in 2011, commuter radio stations provide the necessary information to local residents. In addition, the radio is highly regarded in DRR and in times of disaster a s it functions as mental support to heal the anxiety and fatigue of disaster victims.

Community radio meets the needs of local communities and plays an important role in providing information in the event of a disaster during the emergency and reconstruction process. This is because community radio can play an important role in DRR through awareness-raising and information sharing among various groups within the community. The need for community radio is growing in many parts of Japan, which are constantly hit by natural disasters. The number of community broadcasting stations continues to increase, and as of December 20, 2019, 322 stations were operating nationwide (JCBA 2019). These 322 stations, called Community

Broadcasting in Japan, are FM stations that provide "Low-power broadcasts by city, town or village", which was institutionalized in 1992. It has a maximum output of 20 watts and the broadcasting range of 15–20 km.

Community broadcasting stations are generally considered to be media capable of playing a leading role in each phase of disaster management, based on their experience in areas affected by large-scale disasters in Japan, such as the Great Hanshin-Awaji Earthquake, the Niigata Chuetsu Earthquake, the Great East Japan Earthquake, and the Kumamoto Earthquake.

According to the results of a nationwide survey on community broadcasting conducted by the Society for Study of Community Broadcasting in Japan in 2016, 92.5% of broadcasting stations have DRR and mitigation as their objectives, and 76.7% of them emphasize DRR and the environment in their news programs (Matsuura 2017).

3.5 Community Radio in Disaster Management

3.5.1 Experiences in Indonesia

Community radio in Indonesia since its existence in early 2000 has had great attention on community-based disaster management, starting from their involvement in the Aceh Tsunami emergency response. The earthquake that was followed by the tsunami in Aceh on December 26, 2004, became the turning point for the Indonesian people in handling disasters. The tsunami has struck the awareness of the Indonesian people that they live in a potentially catastrophic area called the ring of fire, located in the disaster area.

The earthquake measuring 9.3 Richter, which caused a tsunami that caused 180,000 people died, more than 500,000 people became refugees because their homes were destroyed. In addition, the destroyed area becomes isolated due to damage communication infrastructure. The Aceh disaster was then followed by other major disasters in 2006: two earthquakes in Java (in Bantul and Klaten districts on May 27) and a tsunami in West Java (Pangandaran Beach, 17 July), in which more than 5,000 people were killed (Birowo 2010a, b; Gaillard et al. 2008; Rafliana 2014).

The Aceh Earthquake and Tsunami changed the way the Indonesian people viewed Disaster Management. The government is starting to think about a Disaster Risk Reduction approach. This approach appears in the use of the term Disaster Risk Reduction in the Law on Disaster Management No. 27 of 2007.

For community radio, the 2004 disaster was also the starting point for its involvement. The involvement of community radio in Aceh originated from the AERNET (Aceh Emergency Radio Network) program initiated by the Combine Resource Institution (Hibino and Shaw 2015; Ndolu 2013; Sutarno 2019b). The program continues with the ARRNET (Aceh Nias Reconstruction Radio Network), which consisted of community radio in Aceh and North Sumatra. The radio was intended for rehabilitation and reconstruction after the 2004 Aceh Tsunami (Buckley 2011; Prakoso and Nugent 2006). At that time, the communication infrastructure was destroyed by the tsunami, so that people had difficulty in obtaining information about the current situation in their area, including logistical problems, searching for missing families and access to disaster assistance from the government. Some community radio volunteers invited by Combine to assist the operation of community radio to deliver that information.

Earthquakes in Aceh and Nias provided valuable experiences for those volunteers, in turn, they could immediately respond to natural disasters that occurred after the Aceh Tsunami. Several natural disasters responded by community radio, including Yogyakarta earthquake (2006); Merapi eruption, Yogyakarta & Central Java (2006); the Pangandaran earthquake, West Java (2006); Padang earthquake, West Sumatra (2009); Merapi eruption, Yogyakarta and Central Java (2010); Sinabung Volcano, North Sumatra (2013); Jemblung Landslide, Central Java (2014); Agung Volcano, Bali (2018), Lombok earthquake (2018), and Palu earthquake and tsunami (2019) (Birowo 2010a, b, 2011; Sutarno 2019a).

The spirit of community radio to respond to disasters is quite interesting. In the mid of limited equipment and funds, they were quite quickly present in the disaster response. The spirit of volunteerism is the foundation of their activities to help people in the disaster area. The speed of the community and solidarity in responding to disasters is a confirmation that community movements are important in disaster management. The Merapi eruption in 2010 became one of the phenomenal events describing the role of community radio in disaster management. At that time, community radio around the slopes of Mount Merapi became the driving force for the creation of volunteer solidarity from various places in Indonesia. They used JalinMerapi (which was formed during the 2006 Merapi eruption) to become the center of the humanitarian movement to deal with the disaster of the Mount Merapi eruption. JalinMerapi was able to maximize communication and information systems by combining broadcast media, websites, Facebook, Yahoo Messenger, Twitter, Email, SMS, CCTV, fixed-line telephone, citizen band and handy talkie (Birowo 2011; Hadiyati et al. 2018; Wardyaningrum 2017). This solidarity movement succeeded in bringing together 3000 volunteers, who carried out their activities based on trustworthiness (Birowo 2011; Gultom 2016; Sutarno 2019a).

3.5.2 Experiences in Japan

In Japan, the first disaster radio station named "FMYY" was established immediately after the Great Hanshin-Awaji Earthquake in 1995. At the time of the Great East Japan Earthquake in 2011, 30 temporary disaster broadcasting stations were established in the affected areas, and temporary disaster radio stations were established whenever a major disaster occurred in Japan. In Indonesia, 40 community radio stations were set up in Aceh as a temporary measure in response to the Indian Ocean tsunami off the coast of Sumatra. Since then, there has been a growing trend to use community radio to disseminate information and disseminate knowledge about disaster prevention (Hibino J, Matsuura S, Shaw R 2012).

On the other hand, the temporary disaster radio station called Temporary Disaster Broadcasting Station was institutionalized in Japan immediately after the Great Hanshin-Awaji Earthquake in 1995. The first temporary disaster broadcasting station was established in Hyogo Prefecture in February 1995. Since then, a total of 55 stations have been set up in the 24 years up to the time when temporary disaster broadcasting stations were set up in the areas hit by Typhoon No. 19 in 2019. Temporary disaster broadcasting stations are radio stations that can be temporarily established by local governments in disaster-hit areas by obtaining a license from the Ministry of Internal Affairs and Communications. Compared with the establishment of a community radio station, the establishment of a temporary disaster broadcasting station requires a simple procedure to obtain a broadcasting license. The license is issued upon a telephone application from a local government to the Ministry of Internal Affairs and Communications, and payment of frequency usage fees is not required. The maximum broadcast output is 150 W, which is wider than community broadcasting stations. After the Great East Japan Earthquake, many local governments obtained licenses by converting existing community FM stations to temporary disaster FM stations.

The Great East Japan Earthquake (2011) also severely damaged communications networks, making it impossible for disaster victims to access television and the Internet, and many affected areas needed radio broadcasts to provide detailed information to disaster victims. However, the tsunami-hit areas were particularly extensive in Iwate, Miyagi, Fukushima, and Ibaraki prefectures, and existing community radio broadcasts alone were only able to deliver information to victims in those limited broadcast coverage areas. As a result, as many as 30 temporary disaster broadcasting stations were launched. The use of 30 temporary disaster broadcasting stations by disaster-stricken governments and local communities aiming for restoration and reconstruction shows how community radio stations and temporary disaster broadcasting stations are needed for disaster relief, recovery, and reconstruction That was also announced to the whole country.

However, the establishment of a temporary disaster broadcasting station did not proceed smoothly. Most local governments in the disaster-hit areas did not know it. According to a survey conducted by the Ministry of Internal Affairs and Communications of the Tohoku Telecommunications Bureau on 24 local governments in 7 local governments in Iwate Prefecture, 11 local governments in Miyagi Prefecture, and 6 local governments in Fukushima Prefecture, there were only 5 local governments that knew about the system of the temporary disaster broadcasting station at the time of the earthquake (Ohuchi 2018). Some stations were set up by citizens who knew about the system of temporary disaster broadcast stations from neighboring community radio stations and NGOs, and who knew about the establishment of temporary disaster broadcast stations by other local governments through TV and newspapers. There are also temporary disaster broadcasting stations established with the support of neighboring community radio stations and NGOs that are aware of the system of temporary disaster broadcasting stations, and temporary disaster broadcasting stations established by citizens who learned through television and newspapers that other local governments have established temporary disaster broadcasting stations and appealed to local governments to establish them. In addition, it was not easy to get broadcasting equipment and to secure broadcasting staffs with experience in the operation of radio stations, and program production. Local governments and communities in the affected areas did not have the operating funds to continue broadcasting. For this reason, the cooperation of support organizations outside the affected areas (NGOs, community radio stations, commercial radio stations, etc.) was indispensable, and it took time to establish a temporary disaster broadcasting station.

The broadcasting activities of the temporary disaster broadcasting stations that were established in the areas affected by the Great East Japan Earthquake took a long time. Of them, 15 stations continued broadcasting for more than 1000 days, with 7 stations broadcasting for more than 2000 days (Ohuchi 2018). Why did the activity of the temporary disaster radio stations last so long? This is because the role of broadcasting has changed from the communication of information in the emergency phase to the mental care of disaster victims, and to the communication of diverse voices of the victims and the building of bridges among the victims. The temporary disaster broadcast stations that continued broadcasting until the reconstruction period were those that established and operated the radio stations in cooperation with local governments and residents.

On the other hand, the government has taken the initiative to set up a disaster radio station, which does not allow broadcasting of information other than administrative information, or which has a system in which the government strictly checks the contents of broadcasts and the right to edit information is completely controlled by the government. Community radio stations are generally distinguished from public radio and should not be completely under the control of the government even in times of disaster (Hibino and Shaw 2015). This is a question that always accompanies temporary disaster broadcast stations in Japan.

The establishment of 30 temporary disaster broadcast stations in response to the Great East Japan Earthquake has made the existence of temporary disaster broadcast stations widely recognized by society. However, in the case of the Great East Japan Earthquake, it took at least 1 week, and in the longest case, more than 1 year, from the occurrence of the disaster to the establishment of the temporary disaster broadcasting station.

In order to resolve the problem of delays in the establishment of temporary disaster broadcast stations highlighted by the Great East Japan Earthquake, the Ministry of Internal Affairs and Communications deployed the broadcasting equipment necessary for the establishment of temporary disaster broadcast stations to regional Telecommunications Bureaus and completed the deployment to all of 10 regional Telecommunications Bureaus in June 2019 (MIC 2019).

The procurement of broadcasting equipment is not the only effort to make the broadcasting of temporary disaster broadcasting stations more beneficial to the entire affected area. In Wakayama Prefecture, where the Nankai Trough earthquake is highly likely to strike, the "Disaster Information Council" was established in January 2019 so that temporary disaster broadcasting stations can be established quickly in the affected areas of the prefecture. The Disaster Information Council is composed of: the Kinki Bureau of Telecommunications, Ministry of Internal Affairs and Communications; local governments in the Wakayama area; media (Community radio stations, NHK) that can support the establishment and operation of temporary disaster broadcast stations; wireless communities; and experts in these fields.

Specifically, the members have carried out activities such as (1) conducting training for establishing temporary disaster broadcasting stations in areas where tsunami is expected to hit, (2) holding seminars to disseminate disaster information, and (3) simulating the allocation of frequencies in the event that a large number of temporary disaster broadcasting stations are established at the same time. In order to facilitate the establishment and operation of temporary disaster broadcasting stations, the capacity and network are being strengthened through cooperation between the public and private sectors.

3.6 The Effort of Installment of Boyolali Model

3.6.1 Japan–Indonesia Collaboration Has Been Developed from Experience in Aceh

As mentioned above, after the Tsunami in Aceh in Indonesia, many community radio stations were set up to provide information for the purpose of rehabilitation and reconstruction in the affected areas. Many existing community radio stations have also provided detailed information during disasters to the affected people. The power of civil organizations such as JRKI and CRI has greatly contributed to this. However, a problem analysis conducted in March 2015 revealed that (1) most community radio stations do not have cooperative relationships with administrative agencies such as village offices and prefectural disaster prevention bureaus; (2) stakeholders involved in community disaster prevention activities other than village offices and prefectural disaster prevention bureaus do not fully understand the role that community radios can play in disaster prevention; and (3) even though there are voluntary DRR groups in which residents participate, community radio stations do not participate so much and do not fully utilize the disaster response potential of community radio.

Learning from field experiences, references, and discussions, JRKI concluded to swift its approach. The involvement of community radio, which was initially responsive, has now developed to be anticipatory for DRR. The experience involved in managing various natural disasters is useful for building JRKI's active capacity on DRR. Through these activities, the experiences of practitioners and supporters of disaster radio stations have been shared in Japan and Indonesia, and the functions of community radio, which contribute to disaster prevention and mitigation, have been further enhanced in Japan and Indonesia. At the same time, a platform has been formed for Japanese and Indonesian activists to work together (FMYY, which has a base in Indonesia, and the Indonesian Community Radio Association) to establish an Indonesian version of disaster radio station system based on the system of the temporary disaster radio stations in Japan.

One community radio initiative in DRR was carried out with Radar Tangguh program. This program is a consortium of JRKI, FMYY, Combine Resource Institution, AMARC Asia Pacific and Universitas Atma Jaya Yogyakarta (UAJY). JRKI is an association established to strengthen the social role of community radio by networking community radio stations spread throughout Indonesia. More than 500 community radio stations all over Indonesia are members of JRKI. It is engaged in the following activities in cooperation with subordinate organizations in 17 states throughout Japan.

The Combined Resource Institute is an NGO based in Yogyakarta, Indonesia that has been conducting international cooperation activities with FMYY to enhance disaster prevention capabilities of community radio stations in volcanic eruptions and sediment-related disasters in central Java, Indonesia since 2009. In 2014, in cooperation with FMYY and JRKI, two disaster radio stations were set up in a volcanic eruption area in North Sumatra, Indonesia.

UAJY is known for its community radio research in collaboration with JRKI and CRI and contributes to the popularization of community radio from an academic standpoint. It also provides a place for students to learn the social significance of community radio through practical activities.

The program has a working period from 2017 until 2021. The program aims to encourage people living in disaster-prone areas to have DRR awareness and encourage the government to bring policies that support DRR, specifically related to communication and information aspects. Through a bottom-up approach, Radar Tangguh supports community radio to become a backbone of community participation on DRR.

Community radio initiatives for DRR policy advocacy require a long process because they have to change the mindset of the community and the government from reactive-oriented to anticipatory-oriented ones such as DRR. JRKI activities are a combination of practical and lobbying activities. To support its mission on DRR, JRKI plays its role not only community empowerment at the grassroots level but also at the advocacy of regulations at the government level both KementerianKomunikasi dan Informatika/Kominfo (Ministry of Communication and Informatics) and Badan Nasional PenanggulanganBencana/BNPB (The National Disaster Management Agency). With Kominfo, JRKI made a lobby for special broadcasting frequency, which will be used in emergency situation. While BNPB is interested in the use of community radio as a hub for coordination among volunteers. During encounters between JRKI and BNPB-related natural disaster issues, there were dialogues to find solution on reduce disaster risk in community. Good practices of community radio involvement in some natural disaster areas are advantageous for JRKI to do a collaboration with the government in promoting DRR. BNPB made communication with JRKI in Bali when Mt. Agung Volcano eruption, Lombok earthquake in 2018 and Central Sulawesi earthquake and tsunami in 2018. Also, every year since

2015, JRKI participated in events of PeringatanBulanPenguranganRisikoBencana (Commemorations month of Disaster Risk Reduction) held by BNPB. Those interactions become an entry gate to collaborations and mutual understanding between JRKI and BNPB. Lobbying not in national level but also in local level. JRKI also created networking with Badan Penanggulangan Bencana Daerah/BPBD (The Local Agency for Disaster Countermeasure). In the frame of Radar Tangguh Program, JRKI visited and made dialogues with some BPBDs, such as Karo Regency, Kediri Regency, Boyolali Regency. As a result of those activities, BNPB was welcome with efforts of JRKI in participating on DRR campaign.

3.6.2   Localizing Japanese Model into Indonesia

One effort to build disaster management from the perspective of DRR was to conduct a study on DRR in Wakayama Prefecture, Japan. This study was elaborated on Wakayama Prefecture in anticipating Nankai Trough quake, a mega earthquake that is predicted to potentially occur within the next 30 years (Nagata 2017). Based on the prediction, the Japanese government has made a policy for preparing all sectors to do efforts related to disaster management. At the local level, Wakayama Prefecture also has been making preparation to anticipate the Nankai Trough Earthquake. This preparation involves various parties so that there appears to be a synergy between the government and the community, including the community radio sector. Those efforts of Wakayama are called Wakayama Model. On the other hand, there is a regulation of temporary disaster broadcasting station in Japan, and many community radio stations have their operating organizations under the leadership of local governments and broadcast their programs with the main purpose of disaster prevention (Matsuura 2017).

Many local governments have included the use of community radios and the establishment of temporary disaster broadcasting stations in their disaster prevention plans. When the Broadcast Law in Japan was revised in 2011, community radio was incorporated into basic broadcasting, and it became necessary to fulfill the social responsibility of disaster prevention measures within the system. But "How to fulfill the social mission of disaster prevention by operating with a limited number of staff is a major challenge." (Matsuura 2017). It can be said that community radio is becoming an administrative radio in the name of disaster prevention measures.

Besides studying Wakayama Model, JRKI also got an inspiration from the Sendai Framework for Disaster Risk Reduction 2015–2030 (Sendai Framework). JRKI attended the 3rd UN World Conference on Disaster Risk Reduction in Sendai 2015. Sendai Framework emphasizes four priority actions (UNISDR 2015a): Understanding Disaster Risk, Strengthening Disaster Risk Management to Manage Disaster Risk, Investing on DRR for Resilience, Supporting Disaster Preparation for Effective Response and "Build Back Better" on Recovery, Rehabilitation, and Reconstruction.

Based on the Sendai Conference, United Nations Office for Disaster Risk Reduction/UNDRR (formerly known as United Nations International Strategy for Disaster

Reduction/UNISDR) encourages the implementation of the four priority actions carried out at various levels, including the local level. JRKI wanted to bring Sendai Framework and Wakayama Model into Boyolali Regency. Cooperating with the Boyolali Regional Disaster Management Agency (BPBD) and the Forum PenguranganRisikoBencana/FPRB (DRR Forum) volunteers, JRKI developed the operationalization of DRR concept, especially the Boyolali Communication and Information Disaster Cluster (KKIB).

Volunteers have a reason to implement DRR in Boyolali Regency. Considering Indonesia, which is located in the ring of fire, has many natural disasters. BNPB data say there are 3,768 natural disasters that occurred during 2019. From these figures, the impact of fatalities due to the disasters, 478 people were killed, 109 missing, 6.1 million displaced and 3,419 injured (BNPB 2019). Among natural disasters, Indonesia has 127 active volcanoes. One of the most active volcanoes is Merapi Volcano, which is located in four regencies, namely Sleman (Yogyakarta Province); Magelang, Boyolali, and Klaten (Central Java Province). As previously stated, in 2006 and 2010, Merapi erupted violently (Jimawan et al. 2018; Kementerian Energi dan Sumber Daya Mineral Badan Geologi (2014); Marfai et al. 2012). Merapi on October 26, 2010 experienced its first eruption and continued until early November 2010. The eruption event was the largest disaster compared to the five previous eruptions that occurred in 1994, 1997, 1998, 2001, and 2006. Results from the BNPB in 2010 were reported that the impact eruption of Mount Merapi on October 26, 2010, resulted in 347 fatalities and 258 injured (Susilo and Rudiarto 2014).

3.6.3 Standard Operation Procedures of Communication and Information for DRR

Based on those data, JRKI enforces the creation of standard operation procedures (SOP) of communication and information for DRR in Merapi Volcano. As mentioned before, this advocacy inspired by Wakayama Model, therefore this advocacy is called Boyolali Model. The conceptual flow of the process of formulation Boyolali Model can be seen as follows:

Merapi Volcano received special attention because of its activity and location, which is full of residents. It has potential major damage for people living on its surroundings (Indonesian Institute of Sciences, 2012). According to records from the Institute for Investigation and Development of Geological Disaster Technology (BPPTKG), Merapi erupted between 2 and 7 years with an average of every 4 years. Since the twentieth century, 1987 souls died due to the eruption of Mount Merapi consisting of 1909 people caused by hot clouds and 78 people caused by lava. In the 2010 eruption, the number of refugees was 200,000, 388 dead (BPPTKG Yogyakarta 2019).

As regency located on the slopes of Mount Merapi, Boyolali is very concerned about the catastrophic eruption of Merapi Volcano. According to the Merapi Hazard

Zoning Map issued by The National Agency for Disaster Countermeasure (BNPB) November 14, 2010, there are three districts in Boyolali Regency, which occupy the Merapi threat zone. These districts are Selo, Cepogo and Musuk Districts. All three are within a radius of 10–15 km from the crater. Therefore, the threat of the eruption of Merapi against its inhabitants is quite large (BPPTKG Yogyakarta 2019).

Based on its potential hazards to inhabitants, in the framework of DRR, Boyolali disaster volunteers and Boyolali BPBD initiated community-centered DRR. This model has a comparison with the Wakayama Model mentioned earlier. Boyolali model cannot be made instantly since it needed people's participation. Although advocacy to make Boyolali model is still an ongoing process, but it can be traced back. The process was indicated by a strong involvement of community and civil society. There are several steps in this making: creating a forum, formulating an idea, examining the idea, creating policy.

The first step is, creating a forum. Boyolali Regency has a Disaster Risk Reduction Forum consisting of volunteers in the field of disaster. Community radio activists on the slopes of Merapi Boyolali participated in this FPRB. Some have key positions as the Presidium Board and Coordinator of the Emergency and Disaster Preparedness Bureau of the Boyolali District FPRB establishment on November 25, 2015. The outcome of the FPRB Congress I was the formation of an organizational structure divided into five bureaus. FPRB administrators come from various components of society and government. Current arrangement, activists of community radio in Boyolali Regency are driving forces behind the FPRB.

The First Congress recommended work programs for DRR, including Development of a media center and disaster information system in Boyolali district; Management of communication media between volunteers throughout Boyolali; Management of multi-platform information media for publication of Boyolali FPRB activities such as Website, FB Account, Twitter, Instagram, Radio Streaming; Production of creative content for disaster awareness education; Making database of Boyolali Regency Disaster Risk Reduction Forum (FPRB) members; Documentation of various disasters and efforts to reduce disaster risk and disaster response in Boyolali; Explores the source of knowledge about the disaster that happened in Boyolali.

3.6.4 Expected to Be a Model for Developing Standards and Procedures for Contingency Plans

To carry out its activities, FPRB then formed various clusters, including the Communication and Information Cluster. Community radio activists participate in this cluster. From this cluster, an initiative was born to develop operating standards and procedures (SOP) to anticipate disasters. Keiko Murakami, a researcher at NHK Broadcasting Culture Research Institute, said that it is too late to think of emergency response if a disaster has occurred. She proposed that emergency response should be made long before the disaster occurs. Therefore, it is very important to do preparedness. Accordingly, FPRB volunteers, in collaboration with Radar Tangguh, conducted SOP of communication and information systems for the Merapi eruption. The basis of the SOP is Merapi Eruption's Contingency Plan, created by BPBD of Boyolali Regency. This SOP is expected to be a model for developing SOPs for contingency plans for other types of disasters as well as for other regions in Indonesia. Advocacy at the national level will be discussed later on.

Second step: formulating an idea. The making of this SOP is carried out within the framework of Participatory Action Research through a participatory process in collaboration with BPBD as the authorized party in handling disasters in Boyolali. The making process went through phases to gather various aspirations of the volunteers. First, JRKI and Radar Tangguh compiled good practices that JRKI has done when handling disasters in various places as well as relevant references from other institutions, showing the activities carried out by the government and community radio in Wakayama in response to data about potential disasters (major earthquakes) that will occur. Those materials were then presented by JRKI and Radar Tangguh at the seminar as triggers of discussion among volunteers of the FPRB, the Communication and Information Cluster. The various responses in the seminar are processed into material for discussions (Focus Group Discussion) at later stages. Wakayama's experience was then reflected in the context of Boyolali, specifically the potential hazard of the Merapi eruption.

Most discussions were held in the BPBD Boyolali office, since the office can be accessed easily by participants, including staffs of BPBD. The use of the office is also strengthening collaboration among civil society and the BPBD, as a representation of the local government, which will be useful on DRR, since DRR belongs to all. Additionally, the involvement of the BPBD is strategic since the BPBD will lead actions during disaster response and recovery. In turn, when there will be Merapi eruption, the policy will be implemented by the government.

The stages of the discussion included mapping of problems, mapping of actors involved in disaster management, the role of actors, formulation of coordination channels, formulation of procedures, and formulation of policy concepts. Since Communication and Information Cluster consists of various groups of volunteers, there was a need to create a guideline of consolidation (SOP) in order to make their future activities will continue smoothly. In the process of drafting the SOP, the framework for consolidation was thought out in detail. Every action needed during a disaster response was discussed. The ease in preparing community-based SOP was those participants had knowledge about the map of actors, their roles and their environment. As a result, they could share real ideas to find problems and solutions. Some points generated in this long process for the Cluster of Communication and Information of the Merapi Eruption Boyolali Regency (KlasterKomunikasi dan InformasiBencana/KKIB) are: The speed and accuracy of information are very important in the DRR; the speed and accuracy of information require neat coordination between various parties; each component of the volunteer has an important role in the process of communication and information on the DRR; sharing roles in neat coordination will make KKIB work well; Making standard operating procedure (SOP) to ensure each role is carried out properly; SOP consists of steps that are chronological activities (stages) that must be done to complete a task effectively and efficiently. For example, the forming of the mechanism of the media center establishment, they discussed "Who will be responsible for making decisions?", "When will the media center be effectively working?", "Who will be persons in charge to operate the media center?", "Where will the media center be located?", "How will gather relevant information?", "What will be the flow of information?", and "How will the information be delivered to people."

After the draft of SOP at the local level was obtained, the next step is to disseminate (sounding) at the national level. For this purpose, on December 12, a national seminar was held at the Office of the BNPB in Jakarta, which was attended by various parties related to the disaster. This activity is a part of national policy advocacy based on good practices from the community. The participatory approach, from the community to the government, shows that DRR is the business of all parties.

The SOP cannot be stopped only as a concept on paper but also can be implemented in the field. The SOP should be trialed on a large scale such as simulation in the disaster-prone area. The simulation will give valuable inputs for bettering SOP.

It is a long process to make DRR in Boyolali as a model that belongs to all its stakeholders there. A participatory approach can be seen in this process, then it can be expected that if the eruption of Merapi occurs, people and the government will hand in hand to manage the problems caused by the disaster.

3.6.5 Participatory Communication

Community participation is a potential component to support DRR. It is related to the capacity for disaster mitigation. This participatory initiative is a result of a long-term process that is influenced by the social closeness of the community. They built solidarity in facing their common problem living in the disaster-prone areas on the slopes of Merapi volcano.

They learned from experiences about Merapi eruption 2006, 2010. Step by step, they learned to implement disaster management. In the first phase, they focused on emergency response. They learned from the pass and used it as their knowledge to react to disaster.

At the second phase, they improved their capacity to deal with the risk of disaster. It was not only based on their own experiences but also others' experiences to solve their problem regarding the disaster. As shown in Boyolali, after 2010, volunteers had opportunities to get knowledge from outside the regency since they were exposed by dialogues, workshops, seminars, and visits, which enabled them to recognize new approaches in disaster management. Some volunteers were facilitated by JICA to develop people-to-people cooperation, especially in community radio sectors. They were invited to visit conferences and some community radio stations in Japan. Otherwise, they were visited by community radio volunteers from Japan. These people-to-people encounters became forum of dialogues among participants. Dialogues allowed them to learn from each other in equal situations. They shared their experiences in how they acted when a disaster occurred. The unique experience of each party is a useful lesson learned to enrich each party.

These encounters helped them to enlarge their references for disaster risk reduction. Sendai Framework has enriched its vision to build a resilience community. That framework endorsed them to understand the importance of preparedness to anticipate disaster. In Boyolali, for example, by mixing references and experiences they started to develop their approach to create a model, namely the Boyolali model. By the model, they go hand in hand with the Government of Boyolali Regency to arrange Standard of Operation Procedure (SOP) of the Eruption of Merapi volcano.

3.7   Conclusion

Boyolali model describes a participatory approach in community-based DRR in dealing with Merapi Volcano Eruption. Community radio activists play their role to initiate policy in making the best preparation for anticipating disaster. They use their own field experiences, Sendai Framework, Japan Community Radio, and Wakayama Model as references to create SOP of communication and information cluster. Creating the SOP as a tool for smooth and neat collaboration is a part of efforts to make the Boyolali Regency capable to manage disaster coming from Merapi eruption. This concept will be proposed by JRKI as a model of DRR at the national level. To support that goal, JRKI is supported by its networking such as FPRB, Radar Tangguh, BPBD, and BNPB.

Community radio is a non-profit radio station that serves the interests of the community and actively encourages local people to speak and participate (Suzuki 1997). In other words, community radio, both on a daily basis and in times of disaster, can contribute to the social interests of the community through the participation of local people. As described above, temporary disaster broadcasting stations in Japan are basically established under the initiative of local governments, and the national government's guidance in disaster management by community radio stations has been strengthened. The involvement of local governments and external support from the government and NGOs are essential for community-based disaster risk reduction. However, effective and successful disaster reduction initiatives are often attributed to the spontaneous participation of the communities and involvement of the people (Rajib 2003). As Mr. Zane Ibrahim (founder of Bush Radio), known as the father of South African community radio, said, "community radio is made up of 90% community, 10% radio"; community radio uses the radio for community creation. In the same way, community radio uses the radio for support activities and recovery/revitalization activities (Hibino and Shaw 2014).

One of the features of Boyolali model is that the main players are members of the community. In this model, community radio plays a role as a device to encourage local people to participate and participate in local activities. Even if community radio does not work in the event of a disaster, if this people-to-people platform works, temporary

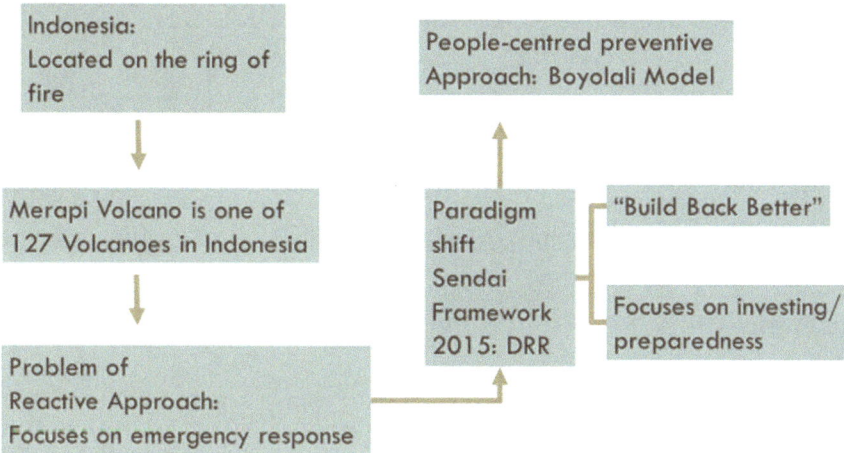

Fig. 3.1 The conceptual flow of the process of formulation Boyolali model

radio stations and other community media can also be used to inform residents about how to survive the disaster. This is community resilience in communication and information on DRR.

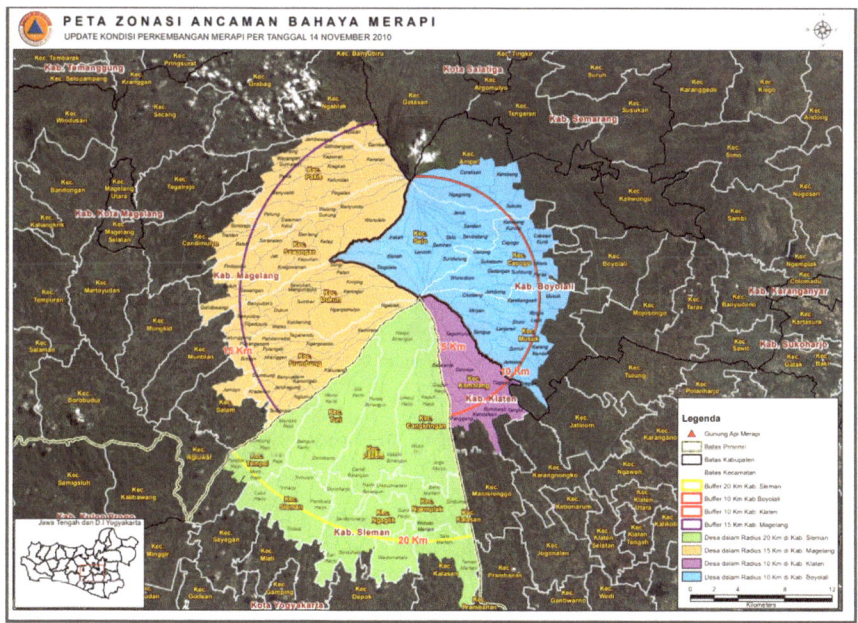

Fig. 3.2 Zoning Map of the Merapi Hazard Threat (2010 Eruption). *Source* (National Disaster Management Agency, 2010)

Table 3.1 Number of residents in the Merapi Threat Zone in Boyolali Regency in 2018

Kecamatan (Sub-regency)	Jumlah Desa (Number of villages)	Penduduk (Population)		
		Male	Female	Total
Selo	10	15.058	14.119	29.177
Cepogo	15	29.570	29,354	58.924
Musuk	10	15.999	15.875	31.874

Source DisdukcapilKab. Boyolali 2018 (Central Bureau of Statistics of Boyolali Regency, 2019)

References

Allen KM (2006) Community-based disaster preparedness and climate adaptation: local capacity-building in the Philippines. Disasters 30(1):81–101

AMARC Asia Pacific (2008) Celebrating 25 years of community radio Movement-Newsletter-Year 4 No. 6 content. https://www.asiapacific.amarc.org

Birowo MA (2004) Melawan Hegemoni Media dengan Strategi Komunikasi Berpusat pada Masyarakat. Jurnal Ilmu Komunikasi 1(1):37–72. https://ojs.uajy.ac.id/index.php/jik/article/view/246/335

Birowo MA (2010a) Community radio and grassroots democracy: a case study of three villages in Yogyakarta Region, Indonesia (Curtin University). https://hdl.handle.net/20.500.11937/1846

Birowo MA (2010b) Community radio and the empowerment of local culture in Indonesia. In: Politics and the media in twenty-first century Indonesia: decade of democracy, pp 49–66. https://doi.org/https://doi.org/10.4324/9780203840429

Birowo MA (2011) Community media and civic action in response to volcanic hazards. In: Crisis information management: communication and technologies. https://doi.org/10.1016/B978-1-84334-647-0.50008-4

BNPB (2019) Video Kaleidoskop Bencana 2019. https://bnpb.go.id/video-kaleidoskop-bencana-2019

BPPTKG Yogyakarta (2019) Rapat Kerja Gunung Merapi Kabupaten Boyolali 19 November 2019. Balai Penyelidikan dan Pengembangan Teknologi Kebencanaan Geologi, Boyolali

Buckland J (1999) Community-based disaster management during the 1997 Red River Flood in Canada. Disasters 23(2):174–191

Buckley S (2011) Community media: a good practice handbook. https://unesdoc.unesco.org/ark:/48223/pf0000215097

Combine Resource Institution (2010) Annual report 2010. https://www.combine.or.id/cdn/doc/07a10576-ad30-4b86-b1a8-151fe85c539d-Annual-Report-2010.pdf

Combine Resource Institution (2012) Desa "Tangguh" Merapi Dimulai. Retrieved January 8, 2020, from https://www.combine.or.id/article/Desa-Tangguh"-Merapi-Dimulai__%23__90

Combine Resource Institution (2014) Annual report 2014, vol 3. https://doi.org/10.35799/jm.3.1.2014.3912

Flint CG, Luloff AE (2007) Society & natural resources community activeness in response to forest disturbance in Alaska. Soc Nat Resour 20(5):431–450. https://doi.org/10.1080/08941920701211850

Gaillard JC et al (2008) Ethnic groups' response to the 26 December 2004 earthquake and tsunami in Aceh Indonesia. Nat Hazards 47(1):17–38. https://doi.org/10.1007/s11069-007-9193-3

Gazali E (2003) Negotiating public and community media in post-Suharto. The Public 10(1):85–100

Gultom DI (2016) Trustworthy and participatory community-based disaster communication : a case study of Jalin Merapi in the 2010 Merapi eruption in Indonesia

Habiba U, Shaw R, Abedin MA (2013) Community-based disaster risk reduction approaches in Bangladesh. In: Shaw R (ed) Disaster risk reduction approaches in Bangladesh, pp 259–279. https://doi.org/10.1007/978-4-431-54252-0_12

Hadiyati S, Hafida N, Setiawan B, A, R. A. (2018) The effectiveness of community radio infrastructure to support disaster preparedness (case study of community radio in Merapi Volcano, Yogyakarta, Indonesia). MATEC web of conferences 04004:6–11. https://doi.org/10.1051/matecconf/2018229

Hibino J, Matsuura S, Shaw R (2012) The role of community radio in disasters. Church World. https://www.preventionweb.net/publications/view/29931

Hadiyati S, Hafida N, Setiawan B (2018) The effectiveness of community radio infrastructure to support disaster preparedness (case study of community radio in Merapi Volcano, Yogyakarta, Indonesia). In: MATEC web of conferences, 04004, 6–11. https://doi.org/10.1007/978-4-431-54255-1_20

Hibino J, Shaw R (2014) Roles of community radio in disaster management: reflections from Japan. In: Shaw R (ed) Community practices for disaster risk reduction in Japan. Disaster risk reduction (methods, approaches and practices), pp 121–132. Springer. https://doi.org/10.1007/978-4-431-54246-9_7

Hibino J, Shaw R (2015) Establishment and sustainability of emergency radio in Tohoku: implications and key lessons. In: Shaw R (ed) Tohoku recovery. Disaster risk reduction (methods, approaches and practices), pp 147–164. Springer. https://doi.org/10.1007/978-4-431-55136-2_11

Japan Foundation (2019) Sharing of experiences of community radio on disaster management in Japan and Indonesia. https://grant-fellowship-db.jfac.jp/ja/grant/pp1431/. Consulted on 23rd December 2019

Jaringan Radio Komunitas Indonesia (2007) Tentang JRKI. Retrieved from Jaringan Radio Komunitas Indonesia website: https://jrki.wordpress.com/about/

JCBA (2019) List of community broadcasting stations. https://www.jcba.jp/. Consulted on 22nd December 2019

Jimawan ON, Stephanie S, Aurelia P, Jimawan ON, Stephanie S, Aurelia P (2018) Probabilistic and statistical analysis of historical activity of Merapi Volcano, Indonesia. In: International symposium on Earth hazard and disaster mitigation (ISEDM) 2017, 020067. https://doi.org/10.1063/1.5047352

Kementerian Energi dan Sumber Daya Mineral Badan Geologi (2014) G. Merapi - Sejarah Letusan. Retrieved November 9, 2019, from Kementerian Energi dan Sumber Daya Mineral Badan Geologi website: https://www.vsi.esdm.go.id/index.php/gunungapi/data-dasar-gunungapi/542-g-merapi?start=1

Marfai MA, Cahyadi A, Hadmoko DS, Sekaranom AB (2012) Sejarah Letusan Gunung Merapi Berdasarkan Fasies Gunungapi Di Daerah Aliran Sungai Bedog, Daerah Istimewa Yogyakarta. Jurnal RISET Geologi Dan Pertambangan 22(2):73. https://doi.org/10.14203/risetgeotam2012.v22.59

Maryani E (2011) Media dan Perubahan Sosial: Suara Perlawanan Melalui Radio Komunitas. Remaja Rosdakarya, Bandung

Masduki (2017) Public broadcasting reform in the transitional society : the case of Indonesia. Jurnal Komunikasi Indonesia, VI(2). https://journal.ui.ac.id/index.php/jkmi/article/viewFile/8916/pdf

Matsuura S (2017) Community broadcasting in Japan-Nihon no Community Housou. Koyoushobou

MIC (2019) Ministry of Internal Affairs and Communications press release "Completed deployment of "Equipment for emergency disaster broadcast stations" for disaster response". https://www.soumu.go.jp/menu_news/s-news/01ryutsu09_02000238.html

Nagata K (2017) The Nankai Trough Earthquake Information : an interim measure in transition from "The Tokai Earthquake Prediction". https://cais.gsi.go.jp/UJNR/12th/document/abst/O-23.pdf

Ndolu F (2013) The roles of broadcasters in disaster reportage: a lesson learned from tsunami reportage in Indonesia. Tsunami Response Systems and the Role of Asia's Broadcasters. https://www.jamco.or.jp/en/symposium/21/5/

Nugroho Y, Putri DA, Laksmi S (2013) Mapping the landscape of the media industry in contemporary Indonesia. Retrieved from Centre for Innovation Policy and Governance website: https://cipg.or.id/wp-content/uploads/2015/06/MEDIA-2-Media-Industry-2012.pdf

Ohuchi N (2018) Media called temporary disaster broadcasting Station—Rinjisaigaihousoukyoku Toiu Media. Seikyusya

Prakoso I, Nugent N (2006) Community Radio in Indonesia A Study for the World Bank October 2005 Imam Prakoso, Combine Resource Institution Nicholas Nugent, Broadcasting Consultant. World Bank, Washington

Rafliana I (2014) Pengurangan Risiko Bencana: Sebuah Restrospeksi Pasca-Tsunami Aceh 2004. EMPATI: Jurnal Ilmu Kesejahteraan Sosial 3(1):48–60. https://doi.org/10.15408/empati.v3i1.9762

Rina S (2010) Women role in disaster information management in West Sumatra's earthquake. Retrieved January 8, 2020, from facebook website: https://www.facebook.com/notes/sabarrina/women-role-in-disaster-information-management-in-west-sumatras-earthquake/243912141401/?comment_id=10156470949986402&notif_id=1578542942212833&notif_t=note_reply

Shaw R (2016) Community-based disaster risk reduction. Oxford Research Encyclopedia of Natural Hazard Science (November):1–21. https://doi.org/10.1093/acrefore/9780199389407.013.47

Sujoko A (2013) A model of civil society empowerment through community radio

Susilo A, Rudiarto I (2014) Analisis Tingkat Resiko Erupsi Gunung Merapi Terhadap Permukiman Di Kecamatan Kemalang Kabupaten Klaten. Teknik Perencanaan Wilayah Kota 3(1):34–49

Sutarno SM (2019a) Radio Komunitas : Membangun Komunikasi Dan Informasi Partisipatif Di Masa Tanggap Bencana Melalui Radio Darurat. Retrieved January 6, 2020, from Jaringan Radio Komunitas Indonesia website: https://jrki.or.id/radio-komunitas-membangun-komunikasi-dan-informasi-partisipatif-di-masa-tanggap-bencana-melalui-radio-darurat/

Sutarno SM (2019b) Radio Komunitas Mengudara untuk Masyarakat Tangguh. Jakarta

Suzuki M (1997) For those who study media literacy. Media literacy wo manabu hitonotameni. Sekaishiousya

UNISDR (2015a) Sendai framework for disaster risk reduction 2015–2030 1.

UNISDR (2015b) The Sendai framework for disaster risk reduction 2015–2030: the challenge for science. Royal Society Meeting Note 9. A/CONF.224/CRP.1

Vaanoli K (2017) Media Asia community radio and crisis communication : a study on the reach and effectiveness community radio and crisis communication: a study on the reach and effectiveness of Peridar Kaala Vaanoli 107.8 MHz

Van Niekerk D, Nemakonde L, Kruger L, Genade K (2017) Community-based disaster risk management. In: Handbook of disaster research, pp 1–45. https://www.researchgate.net/publication/317411922_Community-based_Disaster_Risk_Management

Wardyaningrum D (2017) Perubahan Komunikasi Masyarakat Dalam Inovasi Mitigasi Bencana di Wilayah Rawan Bencana Gunung Merapi. Jurnal ASPIKOM 2(3):179. https://doi.org/10.24329/aspikom.v2i3.69

Chapter 4
Social Media in Disaster Management

Aleksandrina V. Mavrodieva and Rajib Shaw

Abstract The role of social media in disaster response and recovery is becoming more and more prominent, as it was seen during and after the 2010 earthquake in Haiti, the 2011 Tohoku earthquake and tsunami in Japan, the 2012 Hurricane Sandy in the USA, and a great number of crisis events ever since. Social media platforms are also increasingly used by a variety of actors—from ordinary residents, to local and international organizations, governments, and traditional media outlets—to a different degree and to different effects. Facebook, Twitter, Instagram, Youtube and others are now among the primary means for information dissemination, mapping and sending instant reports, organizing volunteers and help groups, connecting with family members, and donation gathering. Nonetheless, some concerns over personal data privacy, "fake" news, scams, misinformation and difficulties in outreach to older populations have also been identified. This chapter will provide a brief overview of the available literature on the role of social media for disaster management, and the types, uses, benefits and potential threats and challenges. A review of relevant case studies is included to identify some good and bad practices and derive lessons learnt. Finally, the chapter will pinpoint some key takeaway messages for practitioners and policy-makers in an attempt to chart the way forward.

Keywords Social media · Disaster management · Fake news · Twitter · Facebook safe alert

4.1 Introduction

The Sendai Framework for Disaster Risk Reduction (SFDRR) specifically mentions using social media, among other communication channels, with the aim of raising awareness and strengthening public education on disaster risks. It urges governments to promote their national strategies through online networks, as well as to use those

A. V. Mavrodieva · R. Shaw (✉)
Graduate School of Media and Governance, Keio University, Fujisawa, Japan
e-mail: shaw@sfc.keio.ac.jp

for sharing data and for risk communication, in line with Priority Action 1: Understanding Disaster Risk (24 (m); 25 (c)). Usage of social media for sharing risk data and improved preparedness also directly links with Target G of the Sendai Framework, which focuses on increasing communities' access to early-warning systems, risk information and assessments (UNISDR: SFDRR 2015).

Ever since the terrorist attacks of 9/11 in 2001 in the USA, social media has shown that it has a prominent role to play in crisis response (Reuter and Kaufhold 2017). In the past 20 years, social media platforms, such as Facebook, Twitter, Instagram, YouTube, blogging tools, websites, as well as mobile apps, have been used for vital disaster management functions, such as sharing information on shelters, safe routes and supplies, for connecting families, for damage and needs assessment, as well as for fundraising and providing moral support. At times, social media is the only available communication channel during disasters, when infrastructure and telecommunications are destroyed or disrupted (Peary et. al. 2012).

Social media also has the benefit of providing respondents with the most up-to-date information from the ground during disasters, as it is the affected people themselves who are sharing content. This capability has proved to be crucial in disaster response, as it was evident from a number of past events, such as the 2010 earthquake in Haiti, the 2011 Tohoku earthquake and tsunami in Japan, and the 2013 typhoon Haiyan, among others.

In recent years, social media has practically become a part of everyday life for a large number of people worldwide. In the last quarter of 2019, Facebook had 2.5 billion monthly active users, Twitter—330 million (by mid-2019), and Whatsapp— more than half a billion (Statista 2020a, b, 2019). Overall, by the beginning of 2020, 3.8 billion people were actively using different social media platforms every day (Kemp 2020).

Humanitarian organizations and governments have taken notice of the vast outreach and the multiple benefits of social media platforms and have started to use these channels in all stages of the disaster management cycle. What is more, residents are now expecting respondents to pro-actively share disaster information on social media, prompting emergency managers to consider new working practices and policies that would be able to accommodate both the needs of the communities they serve, and the challenges that inevitably come with sharing sensitive content online (Alexander 2013).

The present chapter aims to provide a brief overview of the available literature on the role of social media for disaster management, and the types, uses, benefits and potential threats and challenges. A review of relevant case studies is included to identify some good and bad practices and derive lessons learnt. Finally, the chapter will pinpoint some key takeaway messages for practitioners and policy-makers in an attempt to chart the way forward.

4.2 Brief Literature Review

Extensive literature on the topic of utilizing social media platforms in disaster management has emerged in the past 20 years, with researchers focusing on various aspects of their application.

Giroux et al. (2013) provide an overview of the opportunities and risks in which governments should consider in relation to using social media in the pre-disaster, response and recovery phases of the disaster management cycle, and Dragović et al. (2019) compile a comprehensive list of case studies with a view to exemplify how social media was used in practice during the different phases. That said, Ngamassi et al. (2016) note that social media is mostly used in the response phase of disasters and underused in the other phases, which is seen as a gap.

Hong et al. (2018) analyze data collected from Tweeter during 18 snowstorms in Maryland, USA, revealing some insights on how information changes based on the rural–urban divide or the severity of the snowstorms, and suggest that local governments should adapt their messages to the public to match the context and the specific needs of the communities they serve. Olteanu et al. (2015) evaluate information collected from Twitter, concerning 26 crisis events between 2012 and 2013, concluding that the type of messages shared by the public changes according to the type of crisis situation at present. Liu et al. (2008) pay special attention to imagery information uploaded by citizens to the photo platform Flickr in times of a crisis and Peters and De Albuquerque (2015) take the 2013 floods in Saxony, German, as a basis to assess the usefulness of posting images for situational awareness.

A number of papers are focused on a specific country or on an incident. Ambinder and Jennings (2013) thoroughly describe the activities by citizens during super-storm Sandy, which hit the USA in October 2012, and how they managed to organize a huge support network using social media. Cheong and Cheong (2011) analyzed Tweets to made deductions on the types of online communities and identify active online players during the 2010–2011 floods in Australia, and Ehnis and Bunker (2012) looked into the ways the Queensland Police Service utilized social media to engage with the public and tackle false rumors during the same crisis. Kongthon et al. (2014) analyzed posts on Twitter and other social media to understand the role online platforms played during the 2011 Thai floods, and Gunawong and Jankananon (2013) provided gender-segregated data extracted from Twitter and Facebook to identify how men and women reacted to the same event, which could have important implication for disaster response.

Peary et al. (2012) look at the 2011 Tohoku earthquake as a case study to analyze which, to what extent, and how useful different social media platforms were during and after the disaster.

Sakurai and Murayama (2019) provide some specific examples of how information technology, including social media, could be used during the different disaster phases, focusing on Japan. They underlined the need for developing a more holistic approach to using such technology in all disaster phases, as well as setting data standards for information sharing among the various information systems and stakeholders.

The importance for governments to set up frameworks and guidelines, in order to adequately utilize social media tools, has also been highlighted by Chan (2013) who identifies three key capabilities in which governments need to develop: mechanisms for early detection through community engagement on social media; optimized task handling through dedicating resources; an integrated public alert and feedback system for improved two-way communication.

Ehnis (2018) specifically explores useful ways of integrating social media into the day-to-day activities of emergency and disaster management organizations, including in their internal organization communication, as well as with other similar organizations, or with the public and media outlets. Mauroner and Heudorfer (2016) pay attention to how volunteer groups and organizations are formed through social media around disaster events, such as the 2013 floods in Germany and typhoon Haiyan in the Philippines in the same year. The authors showcase that public participation is evolving, but at the same time caution that such activities can only be one part of strategies for disaster response and early warning and not the whole strategy.

Reuter and Kaufhold (2017) present a summary and analysis of the previous 15 years of research on social media in emergencies, emphasizing usage patterns and types of interactions and users. The authors further differentiate perception patterns of both authorities and the public, and conclude that the use of social media in crises has matured in recent years and will continue maturing in the future.

The above-mentioned studies represent only but a tiny portion of the available research on social media uses in disaster management. As social media platforms develop and data mining and analysis technology improves, such studies will only multiply to showcase new possibilities as well as new threats in the field.

4.3 Social Media Overview

4.3.1 Types, Uses and Benefits

Chan identifies four main functions of social media: (1) information sharing; (2) planning and training (e.g. with games); (3) collaborative decision making through crowdsourcing and analyzing information from different social platforms; and (4) information collection, utilizing information and footage shared by the public (Chan 2013). The Global Disaster Preparedness Center of the International Federation of the Red Cross and Red Crescent Societies gives a more in depth description of the possible uses of social media at the household, the community organization, and the local and national government levels. According to the Center social media could be utilized as an emergency management tool: apart from raising awareness about risks it could be used for monitoring and early warning, for providing specific instructions and real-time alerts to populations, for mobilizing volunteers, to support search and rescue operations through identifying risk areas and survivors and victims, to support fundraising activities, to improve the lessons learnt process and to disseminate information on recovery and reconstruction. If properly used, social media could also assist in building trust between different stakeholders and between respondents and the communities, as well as could be used to counter inaccurate or false information that might spread during crises (GDPC 2017).

At the household and community organization levels, crowdsourcing platforms, such as Ushahidi, Sahana foundation, and Geeks Without Bounds, provide the opportunity for ordinary citizens to assist in crisis management in different parts of the world. Ushahidi, for instance, was developed by volunteers who wanted to map and report incidences of violence after the 2008 elections in Kenya. The platform received messages from the communities via SMS or online. The reports helped to improve situational awareness and assisted people in identifying safe zones. In that first instance of using the platform, more than 40,000 reports were sent and verified by a team. Since then, the platform was developed further and now exists as a service, having been deployed in approximately 160 countries and having accumulated more than 50 million reports related to different crisis events. In 2015 the platform was used to help coordinate aid activities after a 7.8 earthquake struck Nepal on 25 April. As there were no established formal ways for people to report their condition and needs to authorities, the platform was used to collect voices on the ground, to the result of improved needs assessment and better coordination of relief activities (Ushahidi Website 2020).

During and immediately after the 2011 Tohoku Earthquake in Japan, Twitter became one of the main information channels for people to share and receive updates, with 1200 related Tweets posted every minute (Akhgar et al. 2013). Twitter, Facebook and local networking social platforms, such as Mixi, were widely used to provide support in the affected area—to locate affected people, to provide information on damages, to record needs, and to coordinate efforts. In the aftermath of the disaster, these platforms were also offering moral support to the affected and were used for organizing fundraising campaigns and a multitude of other volunteer initiatives (Peary et al. 2012).

In 2016, during the Kaikōura Earthquake in New Zealand, residents started uploading content, pictures and videos from affected areas, which assisted respondents in identifying priority zones and in organizing their response actions (Fakhruddin et al. 2019). One of the advantages of this method is that while satellite imagery is effective, it may not always provide such detailed information as could photos and videos on the ground, or may simply not be available. Utilizing both satellite and social media information simultaneously could provide a more comprehensive picture of what is truly happening in affected areas (EKU online 2020).

This and other such instances have provided insight into the benefits of using data obtained from social media and more and more big data analysis tools are being developed for improved assessment of public opinion, trends and needs. Big data analysis can also assist agencies and organizations in early prediction and forecast of disasters, as well as in identifying areas of higher risk or vulnerable communities (Ayers 2018).

Organizations, local and national governments have largely tapped into using social media to reach out to populations, creating their own social media accounts and pages. This has allowed for two-way communication between decision-makers and citizens: while citizens receive the opportunity to voice their needs and worries, public institutions have the opportunity to inform communities of their activities, to better understand their environment and to counter false rumors around important events or in times of crises (Giroux et al. 2013). Thus, for instance, the US Centers for Disease Control and Prevention has more than 1.9 million followers on Twitter and is using its account to send out useful information and instructions to improve early warning and preparedness related to public health, as well as to assist response efforts during disease outbreaks, such as the current spread of the COVID-19 virus. The social media channels, which the organization is using, are updated and monitored by trained specialists and follow a detailed information dissemination process (Giroux et al. 2013; Twitter 2020).

A number of social media platforms have developed functions and services in response to the increasing number of disaster events across the world. Facebook, for instance, has embedded a function that allows people to mark themselves safe and thus inform close ones in times of crisis and has also released a Disaster Maps tool, which shows the location of users and their movement patterns. This feature has been used to identify places, which needed supplies of respiratory masks during the 2017 Southern California Wildfires. The tool was also used to show Internet and cellular phone network coverage during disasters in several instances, such as during Hurricane Maria which hit Puerto Rico in 2017 and after the eruption of the Alotenango volcano in Guatemala in 2018. Google has added a Crisis Map tool to its functions, where users can find emergency updates, including satellite images, weather-related information, evacuation routes and shelters, etc. This service is still limited to a small number of countries and areas, but has the potential to expand (ITU 2019).

Apart from instant messaging platforms, such as Twitter or Instagram, there are also various other information outlets, which provide space for more elaborate discussions between groups and sub-groups: the social network Reddit; different blogging platforms, such as Blogger or Wordpress; the crowd-sourced information page Wikipedia; or platforms providing free or cheaper calls, such as Skype and WhatsApp. Such outlets could be used also in the mitigation and preparedness phases of disasters, sharing content on climate change impacts, possible disaster risks, basic emergency response measures or warnings about expected disaster risks; as well as in the recovery phase of a crisis event to support coordination and community engagement in recovery activities, to connect affected persons, helping them share their experiences, as well as to keep a record of the events, thus facilitating the lessons learnt process. Table 4.1 shows some of the possible benefits of utilizing different types of social media in the different phases of the disaster cycle.

Social media was extremely useful in spreading alert messages in the pre-disaster phase of Hurricane Sandy, which hit large areas in the USA in 2012. A great amount of

Table 4.1 Possible uses of social media during the different disaster phases. *Source* Authors; adapted content from GDPC (2017)

Social media/ Crisis phase	Pre-crisis	During crisis	Post-crisis
Facebook	News are shared through the platform—awareness raising; early-warning messages	Facebook safety check function is activated, real-time updates; links people	Crowd-funding and other initiatives
Twitter	News and messages are shared through the platform—awareness raising; early-warning messages	Real-time updates and coordination; links people	Could be used for crowd-funding and other initiatives
YouTube	Informative videos for awareness raising	Live footage and updates, information sharing	Record of events and visual information on post-crisis efforts
Google Maps/Docs	–	Real-time updates and coordination	Coordination of relief efforts
Interactive mapping tools (Ushahidi, Sahana)	Can be used to map high-risk areas and resources	Real-time updates and coordination; used for search and rescue	Coordination of relief efforts
Mobile apps	Disaster risk games for improving awareness and preparedness	Real-time updates and coordination; links people	Link people, could provide psychological and other assistance
Blogs	Awareness raising and public discussion; early-warning messages	Public discussion, updates, analysis	Discussion and analysis, could be used for crowd-funding and other initiatives
Websites and social network websites	Awareness raising and public discussion; early-warning messages	Public discussion, updates, analysis; coordination of efforts	Discussion and analysis, could be used for crowd-funding and other initiatives; could provide psychological and other assistance

evacuation information was posted on different platforms and the National Hurricane Centre kept updating its Facebook page with the location and movement of the storm in order to warn citizens to evacuate on time (Dragović et al. 2019).

During the devastating bushfires in Australia in 2019 and 2020, social media has been widely utilized by both citizens and authorities to share images and information as well as for fundraising. More than one million people and a number of popular figures donated funds in support of the efforts by firefighters and other respondents. The Australian comedian Celeste Barber raised more than 50 million dollars through a campaign on Facebook, and a group of professional tennis players managed to raise approximately 5 million dollars in a day. Religious groups such as members of the Jewish and Islamic communities also used social media to coordinate volunteer initiatives and to offer support through providing shelter and meals (Sokolov 2020).

During and in the aftermath of the disastrous 2010 earthquake, which took the lives of more than 250,000 people and displaced more than 5 million people in Haiti, a plethora of social media platforms were used to support relief and recovery efforts (World Vision 2019). The Ushahidi platform was used to crowd-source volunteer assistance to create an interactive map. Among the volunteers were many people of Haitian descent who were helping translate messages in Creole, which sped up search and rescue activities (Wendling et al. 2013). In the weeks and even years to follow, social media platforms such as Facebook, Twitter and the messaging mobile application Whatsapp played a big role in connecting Haitians in the country with the diaspora abroad, which was offering donations and psychological support (Bojarski 2020).

These examples come to show many benefits in which social media could bring to each phase of the disaster cycle. In the next few paragraphs, two more case studies have been described in greater detail, in order to showcase the specific steps that were taken by residents and respondents, as well as to identify some gaps and lessons learnt.

4.3.2   2013 Typhoon Haiyan (Yolanda), the Philippines

Typhoon Haiyan (also known as Yolanda) was a Category 5 storm, which hit the Philippines on 8 November 2013 and which affected more than 14 million people across 44 provinces. Over 6,000 people lost their lives and approximately 4.1 million were displaced. More than a million houses were destroyed and the overall economic loss amounted to $5.8 billion (Reid 2018).

All telecommunication networks in the affected areas were destroyed and there were no electricity, telephone or Internet connections until 20 November. The typhoon also destroyed essential infrastructure such as hospitals which significantly limited the access to healthcare providers. The World Health Organization (WHO) Representative Office in the Philippines did not traditionally use social media for sharing information with communities prior to the disaster but decided to include social media components in its response strategy to disseminate important public health messages (Cool et al. 2015).

The UN International Telecommunications Union (ITU) provided the WHO with satellite phones with GPS to support the search and rescue efforts of the organization, and set up Inmarsat Broadband Global Area Network terminals to restore Internet connectivity in the affected zones. At that time over 37 million people, or 36%, in the Philippines were Internet users (over 105 million people total population), of whom 34 million were active Facebook users. By 27 November, the WHO established a social media team, created a Facebook page, and started sharing useful information on the crisis (Claravall 2015). In the following days, the organization also set up Twitter and Instagram accounts. It was assessed that among the social media platforms used in the Philippines, Facebook had the highest penetration, especially in rural areas, and was therefore prioritized by the respondents (Cool et al. 2015).

In the beginning, the messages contained mostly text and pictures focused on the WHO emergency response activities but over time, with the increased demands of the affected people, those changed to messages which urged people to follow public health advice. Illustrations and infographics we used to provide easy to understand and remember information (Cool et al. 2015).

As the WHO had no prior experience in actively using social media for disaster response and recovery, the only evaluation tools available at the time were the Facebook and Twitter analytics sites. The respondents could assess the number of viewers, posts and re-posts but could not assess to what extent this effort had practical implication on people's behavior. This became one of the lessons learnt for the WHO and the organization updated its emergency risk communication (ERC) strategy to include new evaluation methods. The methods included conducting surveys on the ground and monitoring change in behavior to determine if messages on social media had an impact in real life (Cool et al. 2015).

The second important lesson was that social media presence and strategies should be developed before emergencies strike, which would allow for outreach activities, gaining a wider follower base and assessment on which types of messages are most useful. Finally, the WHO underlined the need for effective cooperation and coordination among partners, as different groups had different priorities, which they wanted to share with the communities. Existing social media outreach cooperation mechanisms were also deemed necessary for improved response (Cool et al. 2015).

In the aftermath of the disaster, relief teams from across the world joined the efforts, introducing new ways of using social media to reach out to and localize victims. Real-time maps were created to identify what was needed where and by whom. A volunteer platform called MicroMappers was checking content posted on social media and assessing the validity of the messages and giving them identifying tags depending on the content (does it contain image, is it a request for help, etc.), after which they were forwarding relevant information to aid workers on site. The platform-assisted respondents in obtaining situational information related the level of destruction of infrastructure and supplied them with up to date maps from rural areas that were previously unavailable (Mackenzie 2013). Hundreds of volunteers joined the initiative. For quality control purposes, every post or picture was validated and tagged by three different volunteers. A special task force team was then performing a second-level assessment before finalization. The MicroMappers team significantly assisted humanitarian agencies in making sense of the huge amount of social media content, which allowed for timelier and more adequate response actions (Howard 2013).

4.3.3   2015 Chennai Floods, India

In November 2015, Chennai, the capital of the Tamil Nadu state in India, received 1,049 mm of rain in that month alone generated by an annual northeast cyclone influenced by El Nino. Towards the middle of the month large areas of the city were flooded, killing over 500 and displacing more than 1.8 million people. Shortly after, on 1 December, heavy rains hit the city once more, leading to over 60% power cuts, and a number of schools and hospitals closed doors (Lal 2017; Nair et al. 2017; Janardhanan 2015). Supply of basic goods was disrupted and prices increased manifold in the days after the floods. The army and police dispatched rescue teams and emergency telephone numbers were set up and promoted. Several telecom companies offered free calls and messaging but the lines were soon overloaded (Express Web Desk 2015).

As official response was slow and insufficient some ordinary citizens turned to social media to seek and provide information and to reach out to their stranded friends and relatives. They were quickly followed by others and between 1 and 4 December Twitter saw conversation volume of approximately 1.4 million Tweets (Express Web Desk 2015). The Tweets contained various types of messages—weather forecast, safety instructions, helpline phone numbers, transport updates, updates from specific areas as well as messages to friends and relatives (@sowmyarao_ 2015).

Seeing the massive flow of information a few citizens realized the potential of using the platform to share and receive up-to-date information and to coordinate efforts among volunteers. A simple spreadsheet was created that was linking people who could offer shelter and assistance with people in need and it was shared online. Twitter India promoted three main hashtags: #ChennaiRainsHelp, #ChennaiRescue, and #ChennaiVolunteer that were used each according to the type of the message the user was posting, which helped in distinguishing between the Tweets and organizing activities faster. Two social groups: @ChennaiCares and @ChennaiRainsOrg were also set up in order to link seekers with providers of help and for raising funds in support of the affected communities. Over 100,000 people used this social media channel during and in the aftermath of the floods and hundreds of volunteers joined the efforts from around the world. People on the ground could receive instant updates and send immediate feedback as well (@sowmyarao_ 2015).

Twitter and other social media platforms were also used by organizations, NGOs, and popular figures to express and provide support and to ask for donations. During the disaster, Facebook activated a "Chennai Flooding safety check" feature which allowed people to mark themselves safe and thus let their contacts know they are well. Set-up online payment systems also played a role in collecting donations when ATMs became unusable (Pradnya 2015).

In 2016, Twitter India organized a workshop and meetings to discuss lessons learnt and how response could be improved in the future. The use of standardized hashtags was identified as a good practice, which helped quickly organize and link information in a logical flow. On this occasion, volunteers and citizens acted according to unwritten agreement to be responsible and honest in their conduct but this is not the case in all disastrous events and some there should be mechanisms for information verification in place. Also, online social media platforms were still available when emergency landlines were overloaded but still they can only be used in areas with higher level of ICT penetration, which is usually urban areas, such as Chennai (ITU 2019; @sowmyarao_ 2015).

The examples above show that social media could be a powerful tool, capable of improving disaster response activities. That said, there are also certain challenges and threats related to using social media in emergency contexts, which respondents and authorities should consider.

4.4 Threats and Challenges

Research conducted after the 2011 Tohoku earthquake in Japan revealed that while social media substantially assisted people in connecting with their close ones and in coordinating activities, there were also many hoax calls for help. A wide spread of inaccurate or misleading information also became an issue but there was not enough response from the government or the mass media to try to counter such messages (Peary et al. 2012). In 2016, false information spread during the Kumamoto earthquake, Japan, about a lion escaping the local zoo. The Tweet was reposted more than 20,000 times and the zoo received a multitude of phone calls and inquires, after which they filed a complaint with the police. Such fraudulent or misleading information could create mass panic and prompt authorities to mobilize resources in vain (Sakurai and Murayama 2019; JapanToday 2016).

Another challenge lies in the ability and capacity to extract and analyze relevant and reliable information out of the noise in social media and from different dynamic content platforms at the same time. The majority of information is conversational in nature and might not contain useable data on the given disaster. Twitter, for instance, is also limited to messages of 140 characters that are usually written in informal way and using multiple abbreviations or jargon words, which makes the effective assessment of the information rather difficult. During the 2015 Nepal earthquake, the abbreviation "KTM" was used by residents on social media when sharing posts about the situation in Kathmandu. Intelligent algorithms and information analysis tools need to be able to pick up such specificities. This task becomes even more challenging when different languages are involved. Objectivity of the reported information is also questionable, as it reflects the user's personal perception of the risk. A Tweet by a user describing the water level during a flood based on their height (e.g. at knee level), for example, could be unintentionally misleading or inaccurate (Ghosh et al. 2018; Alie and Ogie 2018).

Social media platforms and mobile application could have a limited outreach to users. Facebook, for instance, is not widely used in a number of countries and content is filtered according to the user's preferences and shared among the users friendship list, which could have some negative effects in relation to people's perception regarding the response to a disaster or in relation to disaster risk awareness and preparedness efforts. At the same time, initiatives by citizens organized through social media could be very helpful in times of a crisis or in the rebuilding phase but could also unintentionally obstruct or duplicate efforts by authorities and respondents, if not coordinated in advance (Peary et al. 2012; Giroux et al. 2013).

Millions of bots and spam Tweets are generated every day, as well as fake or fishing accounts, which use the same hashtags and keywords as official accounts but might be aiming to collect users' personal information, or to promote certain products, to change public perceptions on a topic, or could have other malicious intent. Approximately, 50% of the Twitter accounts created in 2014 were identified as spamming or fraudulent and suspended by the platform, revealing the huge amount of potential misleading profiles on social media (Nazer et al. 2016).

Social media could also exacerbate existing ethnic, racial or religious tensions in times of disasters or other crises when certain groups are targeted and the negative messages are widely shared (Ghosh et al. 2018). It is worth noting that the most vulnerable groups in societies might be exactly the ones who have the least access to technology and social media channels. Divisions could exist along the lines of race, class, gender, age, and culture among other factors. The majority of social platform users across the world still is typically more economically stable, male, and living in urban environments (Alexander 2013; Larsson 2017).

Last but not least, as identified by Watson and Rodrigues (2017), there is a multitude of risks and challenges related to personal data privacy, which policy-makers and respondents should take into consideration. If issues such as cybersecurity, surveillance and unrestricted or unauthorized collection of personal information are not addressed it could lead not only to grave consequences for individuals and for the society as a whole but also to diminishing trust in public institutions and organizations (Watson and Rodrigues 2017).

One of the risks in this relation is that people could be photographed or taken videos of without their knowledge and/or consent. Even if those were taken with a good cause in mind it might harm the person, if the image or video are used for different purposes. As posts are usually public is it very difficult to predict the possible second uses of online content. To add to this, users are unaware of actors involved in data mining and analytics. Apart from governments, such actors could include also civil society organizations, private companies, and even private individuals, who could all have different intentions. The unregulated collection of sensitive data of persons affected by disasters, cyber-attacks and system failures also pose severe risks related to data leakage and misuse, or intrusion into private life (Watson and Rodrigues 2017).

4.5 Takeaway Messages for Practitioners and Policy-Makers

A study by Sakurai and Murayama (2019) on the implementation of information technologies, which include social media, indicated that local governments in Japan had no comprehensive strategy on the use of specific technologies for specific crises and there was no clear division of responsibilities among staff. According to an official report, in 2017, 941 (54%) out of 1741 local governments in Japan were using social media channels for disaster response. Nonetheless, most of the offices used social media only to share information and only 22 of them were also collecting situational information from online posts. Sakurai and Murayama (2019) further explain that even though there has been an effort from the central government to develop an ICT (Information and Communications Technology)-Business Continuity Plan (ICT-BCP), officials were finding it difficult to implement social media strategies, as well as to commit human resources to the task.

Giroux et al. (2013) reiterate on the importance of establishing coherent social media policies and strategies by governments and organizations, adding that in this time and age failing to provide regular information through social media channels and following up on comments by residents might put the credibility of such institutions in danger. This could be particularly problematic if there is not enough trained staff during disasters, when there are sudden peaks of information flow and requests for assistance coming through social media. The authors recommend allocating time and funds for hiring and training staff that would have the responsibility to lead the social media presence of organizations. They also mentioned that one way of managing expectations would be for institutions to release public statements, in order to clearly delineate their possibilities and limitations in relation to what they could provide in reaction to messages from social media. Realistically, organizations cannot respond to each and every inquiry or request by users, especially amidst a crisis situation (Giroux et al. 2013).

Allocating human and financial resources for social media maintenance, however, might be challenging for a great number of institutions and organizations. One possible way to address this issue could be through collaborating with or nurturing crowdsourcing initiatives. Open-source platforms such as the OpenStreetMap and Sahana could be used for every phase of the disaster cycle. More and more private sectors are also tapping into data mining and assessment. That said, a more sustainable way, which would support community resilience, would be to reach out to the communities themselves and engage young people and the academia in order to grow local networks of social media teams who are trained in advance. This will allow for an improved understanding of the local context and situation on the ground and would raise awareness in the society. All such efforts should be envisaged in national and local long-term strategies to ensure continuity and institutional memory and follow-up.

Respondents should also be very clear and specific in their social media posts so that residents can easily understand what the message is about and what is expected from them. Updates on the results of activities should be shared so that transparency can be ensured and trust is built. The work of volunteers and partners should also be recognized publicly so that networks can grow (Kaul 2016).

An important aspect of social media strategies is educating the public on how to relay messages during disasters, e.g. to use specific hashtags or words, or combination of words, that could be caught by analytical systems. For instance, simply using "Chennai" might give a multitude of results, which could be related to other events or tourism promotions, etc., which would pollute the data and make the analysis more difficult. At the same time, other messages with relevant content might not be picked up by the systems if not tagged in a certain way. Engaging the public early on could improve responses (Maron 2013).

Even though large social media platforms, such as Facebook and Twitter are increasingly working together with governments and organizations and have started to detect and regulate false content, rumors and incorrect or outdated information are still very difficult to catch immediately before they spread widely. The US Federal Emergency Management Agency (FEMA) has dedicated a special page on its website under the name "Rumor Control" in order to prevent misinformation during crisis events (Maron 2013). Another good practice would be to have a team of trained staff or volunteers who can quickly pick up false messages and counter them through regularly sharing credible information. Coordinating social media activities with other organizations, local governments, and trusted individuals, could significantly support these efforts. Establishing preliminary agreements with partners before a disaster strikes would immensely speed up coordination afterwards. Working together with traditional media, such as radio and television, would make information shared on social media appear much more credible and would reach out to more social and age groups (DHS 2018).

An April 2011 survey, conducted among 1,891 individuals who were using social media during the Tohoku earthquake, showed that 63.9% of people who used Twitter during the disaster felt that the platform was useful in providing information and 30.7% felt it did not help them in any particular way. In relation to Facebook, 34.7% provided positive feedback about the application and 49.4% provided negative feedback. The local social network platform Mixi received 26.0% positive and 57.9% negative responses (Peary et al. 2012). Following this and many other examples in the literature, it is evident that even though social media could be highly beneficial, it should not be the only, or the main, communication channel of governments and organizations.

Giroux et al. (2013) also warned about the risk of sending out mixed messages. Even though organizations and respondents could and should use different social media platforms, adjusting the language to fit the specific platform and the targeted group, all posts should essentially transmit the same message. As users from the public might react to those messages, the official responses should also be coordinated among platforms and institutions (Giroux et al. 2013).

Another take-away message that was identified is that instead of using written messages and instructional materials only, agencies could use more engaging methods to reach to the communities, such as streaming videos or activities on channels such as YouTube, Instagram and others. These could, for instance, be short videos introducing local staff members and "behind the scenes" activities presented in humane or even humorous ways, while also including essential information. Different initiatives could be created to target different age groups—e.g. these could be in a cartoon format for the youngest. Such measures could be especially useful in the mitigation and preparedness phases of disasters, addressing an important gap in the disaster cycle, when there is enough time to develop such programs and collect feedback from viewers. In this respect, the power of crowdsourcing could be used as well, for example, through asking people to comment on the result of emergency drills and sirens, thus also checking if systems are operating properly in all areas (Crowe 2012).

A major issue is ensuring the security of social media accounts and the protection of data. If people with malicious intentions manage to hack the accounts of disaster management agencies it could have disastrous effects for hundreds of affected people (Giroux et al. 2013). Watson and Rodrigues (2017) suggest that organizations should include guidelines in their national and local plans and strategies on using social media in a transparent way, and establish mechanisms for lawful and accountable monitoring of social media in times of disasters. Further on, rules and standards should also be developed to regulate the monitoring and data analysis done by private sectors and third parties. Privacy and data protection impact assessments should be conducted in regular intervals to allow identifying gaps and readjustments of policies and practices (Watson and Rodrigues 2017).

Another suggestion by the authors is to encourage the principle of "Privacy by Design" which would mean certain security breaks and measures would be in-built in the design of information and communication technologies (ICT) from the start (Watson and Rodrigues 2017). This recommendation is reiterated by De Stefani (2017) who considers that data mining and analytical software tools should be sophisticated and flexible enough to accommodate a wide range of legal and institutional specificities and context-related characteristics in their design. The purpose is to ensure that in the process of collecting and retaining personal information, no human rights are being violated, and that tools are built based on a preliminary analysis of the legal codes and social norms of the communities where they are going to be used (De Stefani 2017). A number of organizations and bodies have already developed guidelines and principles in this area. The International Committee of the Red Cross (ICRC) has published a comprehensive Handbook on Data Protection in Humanitarian Action, dealing with the issues of data collection, processing, retention and sharing, which could be a useful reference by bodies, which have still not developed their own strategies (ICRC 2017).

Finally, new and more complex tools for data collection and analysis have appeared on the scene in recent year and keep evolving. For instance, the Qatar Computing Research Institute (QCRI) has released an Artificial Intelligence for Digital Response tool (AIDR), which is capable for processing large amount of data in real time during disasters. The system classifies messages through combining machine computation with human intelligence through machine learning. One more example is the European Media Monitor (EMM) tool, which monitors news from traditional and social media across the world, using sources in more than 70 languages, classifying the information according to the subject. The tool is updated every 10 min. Still, cultural differences, linguistic specificities, reliability and completeness of data, machine learning, big data processing and timely geographical coverage remain among the challenges yet to be solved (Mugnai et al. 2018; EU Commision 2020).

References

@sowmyarao_ (2015) Guest post: online activism for #ChennaiRainsHelp on Twitter. Twitter blog. https://blog.twitter.com/official/en_in/a/2015/guest-post-online-activism-for-chennairains help-on-twitter.html. Accessed 05 April 2020

Akhgar B, Fortune D, Hayes RE, Guerra B, Manso M (2013) Social media in crisis events: open networks and collaboration supporting disaster response and recovery. In: Conference paper: technologies for homeland security (HST), 2013. https://doi.org/10.1109/THS.2013.6699099

Alexander DE (2013) Social media in disaster risk reduction and crisis management. Sci Eng Ethics (2014) 20:717–733. DOI: https://doi.org/10.1007/s11948-013-9502-z. Springer Science+Business Media, Dordrecht

Alie AU, Ogie R (2018) Social media and disasters: highlighting some wicked problems. Technology and Society. https://technologyandsociety.org/social-media-and-disasters-highlighting-some-wicked-problems/. Accessed 31 March 2020

Ambinder E, Jennings DM (2013) The resilient social network @OccupySandy #Supperstorm-Sandy. Homeland Security Studies & Analysis Institute. https://www.documentcloud.org/doc uments/1357203-the-resilient-social-network.html. Accessed 14 Oct 2019

Ayers R (2018) How Big Data assists in disaster relief and preparedness. Dataconomy. https://dat aconomy.com/2018/12/how-big-data-assists-in-disaster-relief-and-preparedness/. Accessed 23 March 2020

Bojarski S (2020) Social media and its role connecting earthquake survivors with the diaspora. Pulitzer Center. https://pulitzercenter.org/reporting/social-media and its role connecting earthq uake-survivors-diaspora. Accessed 12 April 2020

Chan JC (2013) The role of social media in crisis preparedness, response and recovery. Vanguard, RAHS Think Centre. https://www.oecd.org/governance/risk/The%20role%20of%20Social% 20media%20in%20crisis%20preparedness,%20response%20and%20recovery.pdf. Accessed 20 March 2020

Cheong F, Cheong C (2011) Social media data mining: a social network analysis of tweets during the 2010–2011 Australian floods. In: Seddon PB, Gregor S (eds) Proceedings of the 15th Pacific Asia Conference on Information Systems (PACIS), Brisbane, Australia, 2011, 46

Claravall MCL (2015) Social media in natural disasters: lessons from Typhon Haiyan (presentation). The WHO. https://www.itu.int/net4/wsis/forum/2015/Uploads/S/233/WHO-C7eHealth-25May2 015-Disasters-Claravall.pdf. Accessed 08 April 2020

Cool CT et al (2015) (2015) Social media as a risk communication tool following Typhoon Haiyan. West Pac Surveill Response J 6(Suppl 1):86–90. https://doi.org/10.5365/wpsar.2015.6.2.HYN _013

Crowe A (2012) 6 ways to utilize social media before a disaster strikes. Government Technology. https://www.govtech.com/em/disaster/6-Ways-Utilize-Social-Media-Disaster.html. Accessed 04 April 2020

De Stefani P (2017) (2017) Using social media in natural disaster management: ahuman-rights based approach. Peace Human Rights Govern (PHRG) 1(2):195–221. https://doi.org/10.14658/ pupj-phrg-2017-2-3

Dragović N, Vasiljević Đ, Stankov U, Vujičić M (2019) Go social for your own safety! Review of social networks use on natural disasters—case studies from worldwide. Open Geosciences 11(1). https://www.degruyter.com/view/journals/geo/11/1/article-p352.xml?tab_body=fullHtml-69327. Accessed 04 April 2020

Ehnis CF (2018) Social media within emergency management organisations—a case study exploring social media utilisation for emergency and disaster management. A thesis submitted in fulfillment of the requirements for the degree of Doctor of Philosophy, The University of Sydney Business School, Australia. https://ses.library.usyd.edu.au/handle/2123/17938. Accessed 02 April 2020

Ehnis C, Bunker D (2012) Social media in disaster response: Queensland Police Service-public engagement during the 2011 floods. In: Lamp J (ed) ACIS 2012: location, location, location. Proceedings of the 23rd Australasian conference on information systems, Geelong, Australia, 2012

EKU online (2020) 4 ways Big Data is Revolutionizing emergency management. Eastern Kentucky University. https://safetymanagement.eku.edu/blog/4-ways-big-data-is-revolutionizing-emergency-management/. Accessed 23 March 2020

European Commission website (2020) EMM—European media monitor. https://ec.europa.eu/knowledge4policy/online-resource/emm-european-media-monitor_en. Accessed 12 April .2020

Express Web Desk (2015) Chennai struggling to return to normalcy after raging floods. The Indian Express. https://indianexpress.com/article/india/india-news-india/live-chennai-hit-by-heaviest-rains-in-a-century-normal-life-thrown-out-of-gear/. Accessed 14 March 2020

Fakhruddin B, Chu E, Li G (lead authors) (2019) Next generation disaster data infrastructure. A study report of the CODATA Task Group on linked open data for global disaster risk research. CODATA, IRDR, Chinese Academy of Sciences and Tonkin & Taylor. https://reliefweb.int/sites/reliefweb.int/files/resources/White-Paper_HR.pdf. Accessed 23 March 2020

Ghosh S, Ghosh K, Ganguly D et al (2018) Exploitation of social media for emergency relief and preparedness: recent research and trends. Inf Syst Front 20:901–907. https://doi.org/10.1007/s10796-018-9878-z

Giroux J, Roth F, Herzog M (2013) Using ICT & social media in disasters: opportunities & risks for government. Background document: 3RG special report. Center for Security Studies (CSS), ETH Zürich, Switzeland. https://www.researchgate.net/publication/255723714_Using_ICT_Social_Media_in_Disasters_Opportunities_Risks_for_Government. Accessed 22 March 2020

Global Disaster Preparedness Center (GDPC) (2017) Social media in disasters. https://www.preparecenter.org/topics/social-media-disasters. Accessed 14 Oct 2019

Gunawong P, Jankananon P (2013) Social network reactions to a flood situation. In: Conference paper: the technology innovation and industrial management conference (TIIM), at Phuket, Thailand, May 2013. https://www.researchgate.net/publication/291747206_Social_Network_Reactions_to_a_Flood_Situation. Accessed 04 April 2020

Hong L, Fu C, Frias-Martinez V (2018) Information needs and communication gaps between citizens and local governments online during natural disasters. Inf Syst Front 20:1027–1039

Howard BC (2013) Scanning social media to improve Typhoon Haiyan relief efforts. National Geographic. https://www.nationalgeographic.com/news/2013/11/131108-typhoon-haiyan-philippines-crisis-mapping/. Accessed 08 April 2020

International Committee of the Red Cross (ICRC) (2017) Handbook on data protection in humanitarian action; Kune C, Marelli M (co-edit) Geneva, Switzerland. file:///C:/Users/user/Desktop/4305_002_Data_protection_and_humanitarian_action_low.pdf. Accessed 12 April 2020

International Telecommunication Union (ITU) (2019) Disruptive technologies and their use in disaster risk reduction and management 2019. https://www.itu.int/en/ITU-D/Emergency-Telecommunications/Documents/2019/GET_2019/Disruptive-Technologies.pdf. Accessed 4 Oct 2019

Janardhanan A (2015) Now Chennai struggles to lay its dead to rest. The Indian Express. https://indianexpress.com/article/india/india-news-india/now-chennai-struggles-to-lay-its-dead-to-rest/. Accessed 11 March 2020

JapanToday (2016) Man arrested for posting false tweet claiming lion on the loose after Kumamoto quake. https://japantoday.com/category/crime/man-arrested-for-posting-false-tweet-claiming-lion-on-the-loose-after-kumamoto-quake. Accessed 24 March 2020

Kaul M (2016) Twitter for crisis and disaster relief. Twitter blog. https://blog.twitter.com/official/en_us/a/2016/twitter-for-crisis-and-disaster-relief.html. Accessed 10 April 2020

Kemp S (2020) Digital 2020: 3.8 billion people use social media. WeAreSocial. https://wearesocial.com/blog/2020/01/digital-2020-3-8-billion-people-use-social-media. Accessed 12 April 2020

Kongthon A, Haruechaiyasak C, Pailai J, Kongyoung S (2014) The role of social media during a natural disaster: a case study of the 2011 Thai flood. Int J Innov Technol Manag 11(03), May 2014. https://doi.org/10.1142/S0219877014400124

Lal A (2017) How social media showed its unique power of crowdsourcing during the Chennai floods. Scroll.in. https://scroll.in/article/859304/how-social-media-showed-its-unique-power-of-crowdsourcing-during-the-chennai-floods. Accessed 11 March 2020

Larsson N (2017) How technology can help disaster response. The Guardian. https://www.theguardian.com/global-development-professionals-network/2017/jan/25/the-future-of-technology-in-disaster-response. Accessed 18 Jan 2020

Liu SB, Palen L, Sutton JN, Hughes AL, Vieweg S (2008) In search of the bigger picture: the emergent role of on-line photo sharing in times of disaster. In: Information Systems for Crisis Response and Management, ISCRAM, Proceedings of ISCRAM 2008—5th International Conference on Information Systems for Crisis Response and Management, Washington, DC, United States (4 May 2008—7 May 2008)

Mackenzie D (2013) Social media helps aid efforts after Typhoon Haiyan. NewScientist. https://www.newscientist.com/article/dn24565-social-media-helps-aid-efforts-after-typhoon-haiyan/. Accessed 04 April 2020

Maron DF (2013) How social media is changing disaster response. Scientific American. https://www.scientificamerican.com/article/how-social-media-is-changing-disaster-response/. Accessed 10 April 2020

Mauroner O, Heudorfer A (2016) Social media in disaster management: how social media impact the work of volunteer groups and aid organisations in disaster preparation and response. Int J Emerg Manag 12(2):196. https://doi.org/10.1504/IJEM.2016.076625

Mugnai F, Fonio C, Annunziato A (2018) Social media in crisis management: outcomes of the 7th JRC ECML crisis management technology workshop. European Union. https://publications.jrc.ec.europa.eu/repository/bitstream/JRC104806/jrc104806_online.pdf. Accessed 12 April 2020

Nair MR, Ramya GR, Sivakumar PB (2017) Usage and analysis of Twitter during 2015 Chennai flood towards disaster management. In: 7th International conference on advances in computing & communications, ICACC-2017, 22–24 August 2017, Cochin, India. ScienceDirect, Elsevier B.V—Procedia Computer Science 115 (2017) 350–358. https://www.sciencedirect.com/science/article/pii/S1877050917319038?via%3Dihub. Accessed 11 March 2020

Nazer TH, Liu H, Xue H (2016) Information filtering in social media during disasters. Middle East Institute. https://www.mei.edu/publications/information-filtering-social-media-during-disasters#_edn4. Accessed 30 March 2020

Ngamassi L, Ramakrishnan T, Rahman S (2016) Examining the role of social media in disaster management from an attribution theory perspective. Short paper—social media studies. In: Proceedings of the ISCRAM 2016 conference—Rio de Janeiro, Brazil, May 2016. https://pdfs.semanticscholar.org/39d4/f7860c69d16d5951ba127d35fdfa8b375ffa.pdf%20-%20?. Accessed 02 April 2020

Olteanu A, Vieweg S, Castillo C (2015) What to expect when the unexpected happens: social media communications across crises. CSCW 2015, March 14–18, 2015, Vancouver, BC, Canada. https://www.academia.edu/13371040/What_to_Expect_When_the_Unexpected_Happens_Social_Media_Communications_Across_Crises. Accessed 05 April 2020

Peary BDM, Shaw R, Takeuchi Y (2012) Utilization of social media in the East Japan earthquake and tsunami and its effectiveness. J Nat Disaster Sci 34(1):3–18

Peters R, De Albuquerque JP (2015) Investigating images as indicators for relevant social media messages in disaster management. In: Conference paper: Proceedings of the ISCRAM 2015 conference—Kristiansand, May 24–27, At Kristiansand, Norway. https://www.researchgate.net/publication/275153042_Investigating_images_as_indicators_for_relevant_social_media_messages_in_disaster_management. Accessed 05 April 2020

Pradnya (2015) How social media helped during chennai floods as a disaster management tool. Digital Vidya. https://www.digitalvidya.com/blog/how-social-media-helped-during-chennai-floods-as-a-disaster-management-tool/. Accessed 05 April 2020

Reid K (2018) (updated) 2013 Typhoon Haiyan: facts, FAQs, and how to help. World Vision. https://www.worldvision.org/disaster-relief-news-stories/2013-typhoon-haiyan-facts. Accessed 08 April 2020

Reuter C, Kaufhold MA (2017) Fifteen years of social media in emergencies: a retrospective review and future directions for crisis informatics. J Conting Crisis Manag 26(1):41–57. https://doi.org/10.1111/1468-5973.12196

Sakurai M, Murayama Y (2019) Information technologies and disaster management—benefits and issues. Prog Disaster Sci 2, July 2019, 100012. https://doi.org/10.1016/j.pdisas.2019.100012

Sokolov M (2020) Social media as a force for good: the case of Australian bushfires. The Drum. https://www.thedrum.com/opinion/2020/02/17/social-media-force-good-the-case-australian-bushfires. Accessed 04 April 2020

Statista (2019) Twitter: number of monthly active users 2010–2019. https://www.statista.com/statistics/282087/number-of-monthly-active-twitter-users/. Accessed 12 April 2020

Statista (2020a) Number of Facebook users worldwide 2008–2019. https://www.statista.com/statistics/264810/number-of-monthly-active-facebook-users-worldwide/. Accessed 12 April 2020

Statista (2020b) Daily active users of WhatsApp Status 2019. https://www.statista.com/statistics/730306/whatsapp-status-dau/. Accessed 12 April 2020

Twitter (2020) https://twitter.com/. Accessed 22 March 2020

US Department of Homeland Security (DHS) (2018) Countering false information on social media in disasters and emergencies. https://www.dhs.gov/sites/default/files/publications/SMWG_Countering-False-Info-Social-Media-Disasters-Emergencies_Mar2018-508.pdf. Accessed 10 April 2020

UNISDR (2015) Sendai framework for disaster risk reduction 2015–2030 (SFDRR). Geneva, Switzerland. https://www.preventionweb.net/files/43291_sendaiframeworkfordrren.pdf. Accessed 18 March 2020

Watson H, Rodrigues R (2017) Bringing privacy into the fold: considerations for the use of social media in crisis management. J Conting Crisis Manag March 2018, 26(1), 89–98. https://doi.org/10.1111/1468-5973.12150

Ushahidi Website (2020) Case studies. https://www.ushahidi.com/impact-report/case-studies. Accessed 20 March 2020

Wendling C, Radisch J, Jacobzone S (2013) The use of social media in risk and crisis communication. OECD Working Papers on Public Governance No. 24. OECD-publishing. https://read.oecd-ilibrary.org/governance/the-use-of-social-media-in-risk-and-crisis-communication_5k3v01fskp9s-en#page1. Accessed 12 April 2020

World Vision (2019) (updated) 2010 Haiti earthquake: facts, FAQs, and how to help. https://www.worldvision.org/disaster-relief-news-stories/2010-haiti-earthquake-facts. Accessed 12 April 2020

Chapter 5
Relic as Record Media in Japan

Hiromi Hirose

Abstract It is generally thought that the role of media played in disasters is to give alerts and reduce damage with information on affected areas. Media such as televisions, radio reports and newspaper articles provide this kind of information as soon as possible. In other words, these media work at the same time as disaster occur and spread. The media, on the other hand, this chapter focuses on does not work at the time of calamity, but it works for the future. Records of disaster are useful information storage to raise awareness of disaster prevention among residents who live in places where disasters may occur again. It is very important to hand over the past records and lessons to the next generation. There are several effective forms of storage media such as books, stone monuments, videos, preserved relics and so on. However, the experiences felt by the victims are sometimes deleted from the memory of the people who have psychological trauma. There are also various challenges in preserving damaged architectural structures. How is Japan, disaster-prone nation, addressing these issues? Example of efforts to record the experience by the children in the affected areas of the Great East Japan Earthquake showed us the way to record their experiences in disaster media and absorb them into local culture. By comparing with the catastrophes of other countries like South Asia, this chapter will find that the usage of relic is unique effort to Japan. The Atomic Bomb Dome in Hiroshima is a relic that tells the scale of destruction beyond generations (Shimakawa 2012). Its power as a media goes beyond video and language. It is necessary to consider how to preserve and use relic and remain sites as media for disaster mitigation.

Keywords Relic preservation · Disaster record · Media for the future · Residents' awareness · Japanese culture and tradition

H. Hirose (✉)
Broadcasting Culture Research Institute, Japan Broadcasting Corporation (NHK), Tokyo, Japan
e-mail: hiromi.hirose@gmail.com

Center for South, Asian Studies of Gifu Women's University, Gifu-shi, Gifu, Japan

© Springer Nature Singapore Pte Ltd. 2021   75
R. Shaw et al. (eds.), *Media and Disaster Risk Reduction*, Disaster Risk Reduction,
https://doi.org/10.1007/978-981-16-0285-6_5

5.1   Introduction

Disasters are a painful experience for the parties. For this reason, disaster records tend to lean toward erasure rather than preservation, especially in people's awareness of disaster prevention. On the other hand, preparing for disasters is also a lesson that must be passed on to generations. In communities affected by the Great East Japan Earthquake that struck in 2011 in Japan, local communities were divided on whether to preserve architectural remains. The feelings of victims and families who did not want to remember the tsunami were observed.

At the same time, there was opinion that records of the scale and nature of the disaster should be kept for future generations. For example, large ships in various places like Kyoei-Maru (Kesennuma, Miyagi Prefecture) have been removed. Meanwhile, some ruins of buildings like Taro Kanko Hotel (Miyako, Iwate Prefecture) have been preserved. It has a duality and dilemma.

To overcome this dilemma, efforts have been made by school children to record memories of the tsunami and earthquake in the form of haiku (Japanese style of poem in 17 letters). They engraved their experiences on stone monuments (Kurosawa and Nishino 2014). How students in Onagawa Town, Miyagi Prefecture managed to pass on memories to the future? They had to use various kinds of media, and relics are one of the record media. It was necessary to mix these media into local disaster prevention culture. As a disaster-prone nation, Japan often pass on disaster preparedness in the form of lore, songs and festivals. Media as means of communication recognizes the lessons learned from the catastrophe and the tragic situation of the disaster. It passes on important information to future generations. The case of Onagawa children is ongoing effort to store the memory of victims.

5.2   Classification and Needs of Records

The word "media" usually has two meanings. One is a means of communication. In mainstream media such as radio, newspapers, and television that value current news, there are many reports at the time of the disaster, but the amount of information reported in these media decreases dramatically after the disaster. Articles are published only in the form of the anniversary stories.

On the other hand, the "media" also means a storage medium like an external storage device such as a magnetic disk or an optical disk. Regarding disaster, record media have important role, because human life span and memory are limited. It is often said that large-scale disasters occur once every 100 years or once every 1000 years. These time spans exceed human longevity. These non-mainstream media discussed in this chapter has a role as media that tells the situation of the disaster, irrespective of people's memories and interests.

Therefore, stone monument is used to convey lessons generation to generation. They are made as means of data storage. They function during the period longer than human life. Remains of disaster such as half-broken buildings have also important role to convey messages to reduce the damage caused by disaster (Kitahara et al. 2012).

It is necessary to classify media related to disasters.

The first major category is media as communication. These include newspapers, television, radio, SNS, publicity announcements by government agencies and disaster observation agencies such as the Meteorological Agency. The characteristic of this is that the time at which information is transmitted functions almost simultaneously with the time when a disaster occurs.

The second major classification considered in this chapter is, as I noted before, communication with the future. There are 5 types of storage media.

1. BOOK
2. STELE
3. VIDEO
4. RELIC
5. CE

BOOK is represented books, papers, observation data, etc. It also includes testimonies of disasters. Records are made mainly with words and sometimes pictures.

STELE is stone monument that inscribes relatively short message and often build in the affected area or historical site.

VIDEO is visual images. It includes moving images such as home video and films as well as static images like paintings and photographs.

RELIC is broken structures like half-destroyed houses and buildings. They are man-made structures. Sometimes they are natural and not damaged by the disaster. Anything that shows the magnitude and seriousness of the damage is in this category.

CE (cultural event) is local festivals and anniversary events. Songs, legends folklore traditional culture are also in this category. The record of the disaster customs and traditions sometimes is not shown in obvious form.

Each of these five media has characteristics as storage medium and can be valued with following criteria,

(a) the ability to preserve information for a long time without loss,
(b) the ability to appeal to the residents' awareness of disaster prevention,
(c) the superiority in the physical quantity of the storage medium,
(d) Evaluate on the four criteria of the feasibility of producing a storage medium.

(1) BOOK: It is a traditional recording medium and has high preservation power. The general public, however, does not necessarily have many opportunities to come into contact with books. Professional description may be difficult to reach for the public. There have many quantities. Publishing opportunities are limited.
(2) STELE: It has high preservation capability, because it is made of stones, etc. The number of characters that can be written on a stone is inferior to a book.

Table 5.1 Disaster records media (good = 3 fair = 2 not good = 1)

	Conservation	Appeal	Quantity	Feasibility
BOOK	3	2	3	2
STELE	2	1	1	1
VIDEO	2	3	3	3
RELIC	1	3	1	1
CE	2	3	1	2

Sometimes it is difficult to decipher due to deterioration of surface of stele. Public place where it can be built is limited. The quantity is not large.

(3)   VIDEO: It has become easier to save due to the development of recording technology. There are not many photos or videos of old disasters. The power to appeal on resident's disaster prevention awareness is great. The quantity is large because general residents can take photos and videos. It is easy to copy them and spread on the Internet.

(4)   RELIC: Preservation power is small because it is damaged by the disaster and can be removed as wastes after the disaster (Cabinet Office Japan 2016). As it is real thing, appeal to residents' disaster prevention awareness is extremely large. Storage costs a lot because damaged structures pose safety concerns. Small in quantity,

(5)   CE: In some cases, even if cultural events are inherited, the connection with disaster prevention is not clear and the preservation capacity is limited. The appeal is great because the residents participate in events. The quantity is not large. It takes time to form culture.

The following is a matrix of general evaluations by me (Table 5.1).

Through the above matrix, it can be observed that RELIC, despite having appealing power, lacks conservation ability, quantity and feasibility. For this reason, it is meaningful to explore the possibility of utilizing RELIC as a disaster recording media.

5.3   Records in Words

5.3.1   Witness Report in 17 Characters

The school children of Onagawa-Cho, Miyagi Prefecture, which were affected by the Great East Japan Earthquake, are building monuments called "Onagawa Stone Monument of Life" (Fig. 5.1). First, let us look at the role of words for disaster prevention and reduction.

In the stone monument they carve 17 Japanese characters in the form of haiku recording of the memories of those affected by the tsunami caused by 2011 off the

Fig. 5.1 Onagawa stone monument of life

Pacific coast of Tohoku Earthquake on March 11, 2011. At the time of the tsunami, they were sixth graders.

They planned to build or install them to protect the lives of later generations (ONO 2012).

After the disaster, students began to work on the earthquake disaster mitigation starting from social studies classes. A student committee to consider future tsunami countermeasures was formed and they summarized in "Three tsunami countermeasures we consider." The contents were: (1) deepening the bond, (2) creating a town that could be evacuated to a hill, and (3) leaving a record.

For this above (3), they described their own experiences of the disaster in words, such as "The Great Earthquake that Only Dreams Couldn't Break." The students stood on the street to raise 10 million-yen, 450,000 yen per unit, and called for donation at school excursions. Parents, motivated by the children's will, managed the funds and supported them.

Examples of children's haiku are as follows,

"The Great Earthquake That Couldn't Break Dreams"

YumedakehaKowasenakattaDaisinsai (in Japanese consisted of 17 sounds)

This is the haiku Inscribed on the first stele built in the school grounds of Onagawa Junior High School.

"I can't hear the voice I want to hear right now"

TadaimatoKıkıtaıKoegaKıkoenaı (same as above)

This haiku describes the feelings of a friend who has lost his family.

"If you look up, you will climb over the rubble."

Miagereba Garekino Ueni Koinobori

This haiku records the scene 2 months after the earthquake. He saw the carp streamers over the rubble. Carp is traditional symbol of people's strength.

"What color does Onagawa look like now?"

Onagawawa Ima Naniironi Miemasuka?

This is a short monologue talking to the grandfather who has gone to heaven. Onagawa, fishery town full of natural beauty turned into earthy color by the turbulent tsunami. She is asking whether it has regained its original vivid color.

These are 17-character straight expressions felt by the children. March 11 was a time for children to approach junior high school soon. Students who became junior high school students shortly after the disaster exchanged opinions about tsunami-counter measures. They summarized the best plan to build resilient area. Their plan was to "creating a town where people can evacuate to higher ground." They decided to build monuments higher place than the tsunami reached. On each stone monument they engraved different haikus and lessons from their experiences to protect lives of future generation from disasters.

There are 21 beaches in Onagawa-Cho, so 21 monuments will be set up by the day of their coming-of-age ceremony. This project received a Grand Prix at the 2013 "Bosai Koshien."

The installation of "Onagawa Stone Monument of Life" recorded the actual disaster in the words of the victim and witness of earthquake. The stele became medium for preserving the record and communicating it to the future. More importantly, it was achieved not only by the efforts of children but also by the support of parents, residents and communities, and those who supported the children's movement.

5.3.2   Function of Stele

Before the Great East Japan Earthquake, there were stone monuments in Onagawa-Cho that recorded damage of the old tsunami (Uchida and Tan 2012). But they did not function in a limited way as record media on 3.11. The "Tsunami Damage and Tsunami Stone Monument Information Archive" created by the Tohoku Regional Development Bureau of the Ministry of Land, Infrastructure, Transport and Tourism has the details.

Three major tsunamis of the Meiji Sanriku Earthquake Tsunami, the Showa Sanriku Earthquake Tsunami, and the Chile Earthquake Tsunami. The remaining stone monuments are about 300 in the three prefectures (Aomori, Iwate, Miyagi) of Tohoku. Of the 300 tsunami stone monuments in the three prefectures of Tohoku, 198 stone monuments have inscriptions. 61% of the inscriptions are engraved with lessons about tsunami signs, evacuation, and residence, 38% are marked with dire damage. The stone monument says, "Don't let your guard down if there is an earthquake," "If you are chased by the tsunami, go up to a higher place," " Build a house lower than here."

However, in the case of the Great East Japan Earthquake, the scale of the tsunami was larger than expected. So, the role played by monuments in mitigating the disaster was in some places limited (Sato et al. 2017). For this reason, the "Onagawa Stone Monument of Life" was built higher than the tsunami reached. The monument was with massage calling direct action to "flee to a higher place." It describes the strong feelings of survivors immediately after the disaster.

5.4   Records in Relic

5.4.1   Like Hiroshima Atomic Bomb Dome

There are also thoughts that monuments are not enough. Torahiko Terada, a famous pre-war physicist and essayist, wrote the phrase, "Natural disasters will come when you forget them." He wrote about the Sanriku Tsunami in Showa. In his essay "Tsunami and humans," he wrote, "When the monument is buried in weed, the next tsunami will be ready soon." Torahiko warns that human can easily forget the past.

In the group of "Onagawa Stone Monument of Life," the students started to think that there was something missing to leave the record. More else is left in addition to installing stone monuments.

In Onagawa-Cho, the buildings on the coastline were pushed down by the tsunami. The collapse of a concrete building indicates the great energy of the tsunami. They wanted to keep these on the site. They wanted to leave it as a message that conveys an unforgettable reality. One of the members reported "I want to keep it like an Atomic Bomb Dome." Some of the children's documents state that they want to preserve it: "The real thing has sorrow and power that cannot be conveyed by video alone."

However, many local people did not actually need the remains. In a questionnaire given by the students, only 20% thought that the building should be preserved and 50% said that it should be demolished. It was hard to preserve relic. They claim that it would cost much for maintenance, and broken buildings hinder recovery of the town. In Onagawa-Cho, the outflow of the population continued, and, in my own hearing, I heard that reconstruction was more important than memory.

In communities affected by the Great East Japan Earthquake, local communities were divided on whether to preserve architectural remains. The feelings of victims and families who did not want to remember the tsunami were observed. At the same time, there was opinion that the scale and nature of the disaster should be documented to leave them to future generations.

Large ships at various places like Kyoei-Maru (Kesennuma, Miyagi Prefecture) has been removed and dismantled as they would never leave.

Meanwhile, some ruins of buildings like Taro Kanko Hotel (Miyako, Iwate Prefecture) have been preserved for a quick glance at the height of the tsunami.

What to preserve is a very difficult issue. Because the remains are objects, they do not speak by themselves. It is humans who read and give meaning to them, and there are various thoughts and ways of thinking depending on the circumstances they have. That idea can change over time. There is no single answer on it.

In the case of Onagawa-Cho, one of the three major earthquake disasters affected building, Onagawa police box, was preserved due to the movement of the children, but the other two were demolished (Fig. 5.2). Onagawa police box (Fig. 5.3) was second floor structure made of reinforced concrete, and the foundation part was pulled out by the tsunami. It was a rare case in the world where a reinforced concrete building collapsed due to a tsunami and was worth explaining the power of the tsunami. The police box, as a public facility, met the official purpose of preservation.

Fig. 5.2 Steel frame building (demolished)

Fig. 5.3 Onagawa police box (preserved)

5.4.2 Disaster Relics and Remains in Asia

Let us look at examples from other countries in Asian major catastrophe to see what happened to the remaining of buildings and houses and how the damage was recorded at the disaster site. Disasters that I filed news report for NHK visiting the area are as the Indian Ocean Tsunami (2004), the Great Nepal Earthquake (2015), the Gujarat Earthquake (2001), and the Kashmir Earthquake (2005). The gap between the country's awareness of disaster prevention and the progress of reconstruction varies by countries, and relic of disaster varies as well.

INDONESIA: In the aftermath of the Indian Ocean tsunami, a museum was built in Aceh, the largest stricken area, to preserve the remains of the earthquake. However, the actual number of visitors to the museum was limited, and shortly after the museum opened, it began to suffer from a shortage of visitors. Although it was used as a park, but it was to some extent difficult to play a fundamental role in retaining memories of the disaster in detail. In the Indian Ocean tsunami, the affected area was widespread, and the shores were cut off in the coastal area. People had to start rebuilding their households while many residents were willing to return to the affected areas (Hirose 2008). It reflects the Asian view of nature, which has no border between natural disasters and human activities. In famous literary work of Pearl Sydenstricker Buck" Tsunami" was based on real tsunami in Japan. In Indonesia, there were some popular songs that called for vigilance against the tsunami (Suciani et al. 2017). Some songs emphasized only the fear of the tsunami and did not encourage specific evacuation actions. There is a record that the damage was increased on the island where this song was transmitted. On the other hand, there was almost no damage on the island where the song "Smong," which recorded tsunami sightings and provided a method of detecting disasters and prompting specific evacuation routes, was left.

NEPAL: In the case of Nepal Earthquake that destroyed many historic buildings, post-earthquake remains were rarely observed. For historical heritage, protection is an incentive for restoration. The Dharahara Tower, a cylindrical white tower located in Kathmandu, dates from 1832, with an exact height of 61.88 m, built by Nepalese Prime Minister Bhimsen Thapa, accordingly the tower has another name Bhimsen Tower. The Kathmandu Valley, including the tower, is a UNESCO World Heritage Site. It was rebuilt after a collapse in the 1934 Bihar-Nepal earthquake. It had been closed off for many years, but since 2005 it has been open to the public and has become a tourist attraction with a panoramic view of the city. However, it collapsed again in the earthquake on April 25, 2015. It is regrettable that it was not rebuilt after earthquake collapse in 1934 as a highly earthquake-resistant one. If not, it could have functioned as a record media.

INDIA: In India, buildings were destroyed in the major earthquake in Gujarat. Many buildings were totally or partially destroyed, so many buildings were left as remains of the earthquake disaster. However, what was left in the stricken area was a park without buildings.

The 2001 Gujarat earthquake, also known as the Bhuj earthquake, occurred on 26 January, India's 52nd Republic Day, at 08:46 am IST. The epicenter was about

9 km south–southwest of the village of Chobari in Bhachau Taluka of Kutch District of Gujarat, India. The intraplate earthquake reached 7.7 on the moment magnitude scale and had a maximum felt intensity of X on the Mercalli intensity scale. Smriti Van Memorial was supposed to be a natural monument to the victims of Gujarat earthquake. However, it is difficult to know at a glance its own scale and destructive power because there are not many remains of the earthquake in this park. In particular, foreigners who did not know about the Gujarat earthquake and young people born after the earthquake would not be able to feel the earthquake deeper if they had no real objects to relive the earthquake experience as well as the fear felt by people. In case of this, park focus is rather to tell the magnitude of earthquake. Stress is more on turning desert land into greenery area by planting trees.

KASHMIR: The Kashmir earthquake of 2005 occurred in Azad Kashmir at 08:50:39 PST on October 8. The earthquake in a Kashmir Pakistan governing zone destroyed many houses in mountainous area. There are a limited number of buildings that could be left untouched, and few people inherit the disaster prevention culture. Damage was concentrated near the city of Muzaffarabad and has also affected Pakistan's Khyber Pakhtunkhwa Province and Jam and Kashmir. The quake also affected countries in Afghanistan, Tajikistan, and in surrounding areas trembling was felt. The severity of the damage caused by the quake is due to heavy push-ups. It is considered the deadliest earthquake that has hit South Asia since the 1935 Quetta earthquake. Most of the stone houses collapsed, roads were broken by collapses. In this kind of areas, it is necessary to convey not only the wisdom for earthquake resistance and evacuation but also lessons to live after disaster. Measures to secure water and food should be handed down to the next generation as wisdom for survival in isolation after the disaster. In this special environment of mountainous areas, it is also important to consider the role religion. In areas where there are many Muslims, Islamic mutual aid organizations played a major role in helping victims. Because there was also fight among victims for support supplies and the deprivation of merchandise from stores were seen.

It is natural that the characteristics of disaster prevention are different from place to place because the characteristics of disasters are different. In Japan, it may be easier to preserve the relic of the earthquake than in major disaster areas in South Asia. In disaster-stricken areas in South Asia, a lot of people who have witnessed the disaster lost their lives and few people who survived are suffering from poverty and health problems. Consciousness to disaster prevention is relatively lower than Japan. It is important to exchange wisdom based on each culture, climate and experience.

5.5 Records in Tradition and Culture

5.5.1 Events Symbolizing Evacuation

In Japan, whether it is a stone monument or a post-earthquake manuscript, the dilemma of "don't forget but want to forget" remains. In this context, we need to pay attention to ways to preserve the lessons of disaster prevention as invisible and tacit cultural events such as songs and festivals. This culture of disaster prevention can lead to the revitalization of young and old, men and women, victims and others, and sometimes the local community itself.

In Onagawa-Cho, an event called "Tsunami Revival Man" custom was made. It tells the lessons of evacuation to a hill when the tsunami hits. It is a festival in which people inside and outside the town run up from the town hall to the height to Hakusan Shrine. Participants compete the speed to reach the goal. Mothers and adult runners with children in strollers also participate widely. The first-place winner will be given the title of "Onagawa Revival Man." This event has been held every year since 2013 to make the tsunami disaster prevention tradition an annual event.

The start time is set at 3:32 pm when the tsunami of the Great East Japan Earthquake reached the town. It is a reminder to evacuate to high places, not just a running race. Participants run up the road against the sea with the shout of "Run away!" The townspeople who gathered along the road send cheering ales.

The prototype of this "Tsunami Revival Man" can be found in Nishinomiya, Hyogo Prefecture, the area affected by the Great Hanshin-Awaji Earthquake (Tachibana and Hirata 2013). At Nishinomiya Shrine, the annual festival "Toka Ebisu" is held at 6:00 am on January 10, every year. When the sound of a large drum is played, the Omotesando (front gate registered as national cultural property) open, hundreds of people who spent the night in front of the gate run about 230 m to the main shrine at a stretch. The first person in the main hall is praised as "First Man." "Tsunami Revival Man" at Onagawa-Cho, which serves as an evacuation drill, has been officially recognized by Nishinomiya Shrine since 2014.

There are three merits as an event of "Tsunami Revival Man." First, the tsunami survivors can tackle the traumatic experience with bright and energetic mood. The second point is that the evacuation moves to a hill lead to a very simple and important action. Third, the bonds between local communities can get deeper during the festival. At the preparation stage, local people can get to know each other and raise awareness of disaster prevention as local culture.

What kind of disaster record media Kobe has? In the stricken area of the Great Hanshin-Awaji Earthquake (1995), it was difficult to preserve the remains of the earthquake, because it was a disaster in an urban area. Partially collapsed buildings at risk of collapse needed to be demolished immediately for the safety of the area. In order to promote the redevelopment of the city, it was difficult to leave relic in places where many people gather.

"Kobe Wall (Kobe no Kabe)" is an example of a few earthquake disaster relic, but it was moved to Hokudan Earthquake Memorial Parkfrom its original location. It is a concrete fire wall (7.3 m high, 13.5 m wide, 23 cm thick) built around 1927 as a public market fire wall and was left behind after a large fire that hit Kobe's Nagata Ward. It survived two major fires, the Kobe bombing of 1945, the earthquake of 1995. It can be said that the emphasis is not only the strength of the earthquake but also the strength of the surviving people.

"Kobe Luminarie" is annual illumination event to remember the earthquake. In consideration of the feelings of the victims' families, no lively disaster reproduction is made in this event. After 25 years memory is still in their mind. In order to know the actual situation of the damage directly, it is necessary to visit facilities such as a museum or memorial. The number of opportunities for ordinary citizens to look back on past experiences through relic in town scenery is relatively small compared to the area affected by the great earthquake in Tohoku.

It is important to consider the role of archeological sites as a media for transmitting messages across generations. Monument relics and popular culture such as songs sometimes play more effective roles than mainstream media such as newspapers, radio and television.

5.5.2   On the Coast of "Fire of Inamura"

In disaster-prone Japan, there are many intangible cultural heritages that deal with disasters. A famous example in Wakayama is the "Fire of Inamura (Inamura no Hi in Japanese means The Burning of the rice Field)."

The description of "Fire of Inamura" tells the lesson of need for evacuation to higher places to mitigate the damage.

In the case of "Fire of Inamura" story in Wakayama, all five media that record disasters, BOOK, STELE, VIDEO, RELIC, and CE, are related each other. As a result, it functions in a hybrid manner to raise awareness of disaster prevention. Let us compare the case with Onagawa efforts to know the power of recording words of the victims.

Fig. 5.4 Statue of Hamaguchi Goryo

In Yuasahiro Village, Arita-gun, Kishu (Wakayama Prefecture), the earthquakes occurred on November 4 and 5 and on December 23, 24, 1854, Kaei Period. A series of massive earthquakes occurred. The first earthquake occurred around 10 am on December 23. The tsunami swept from the Boso Peninsula on the Pacific coast to Tosa, Shikoku, killing 600 people and damaging 9,000 homes. At around 4:00 pm on 24th, a massive earthquake called the Ansei Nankai Earthquake occurred. A massive earthquake swept through causing severe damage. Era name was changed from Kaei to Ansei to avoid the misfortune. It is said that approximately 60,000 buildings were destroyed, and the number of dead exceeded 3,000.

At that time, Hamaguchi Goryo (Fig. 5.4) had been operating the soy sauce manufacturing industry in Kishu (Wakayama). Around 10 am on the 23rd of the first earthquake, Hamaguchi evacuated the villagers to the grounds of Hirohachiman Shrine on a hill. The villagers who spent the night at the altitude returned home. The following day around 4:00 pm, another big earthquake hits the village again. The sea surface was swelling and flooded the houses. Water went up the Hiro Rivers that flow on both sides of river and destroyed the village.

Hamaguchi fired rice field to push the villagers to higher places. The record of Hamaguchi's lighting of rice spots is recorded in "Ansei-Monroku" at Yogenji Temple in Hirokawa-Cho.

There is also an inscription left by Katsu Kaishu (Japanese statesman and naval engineer during the late Tokugawa shogunate and early Meiji period), a friend of Hamaguchi, at Hirohachiman Shrine. It records as "The Ansei Tsunami broke out at night, so we couldn't know where to flee and escape. At that time, you (Hamaguchi) evacuated everyone loudly to a high place. He saved people's lives."

Hamaguchi's story was inherited to Lafcadio Hearn's book "Gleanings in Buddha-Fields," which was simultaneously published in Boston and London in 1897. In 1934, the Ministry of Education of Japan put this story into elementary school teaching materials.

In the case of "Fire of Inamura," the tsunami was described as "sea" instead of "wave". That is the witness testimony of the tsunami experienced by the victims, and it is handed down through the words and story of "Fire of Inamura."

I have visited Hirokawa Town and noticed that it is not only words and images that record the tsunami. In Hirokawa, facing the sea, the history of the people remained as a 600-m long embankment. The guide notes for Hiromura embankment, which is designated as a national cultural property, is as follows.

"Hirokawa Town has been hit by tsunami many times since ancient times. In particular, the massive tsunami of 1717 in 1874 and 1854 of the first year of Ansei caused so much damage to the wide area. Hamaguchi Goryo witnessing the tsunami of the first year of Ansei, planned to build a stone bank five meters high, twenty meters wide. The construction of a large levee embankment, which started in February 1855, took three years and ten months, and the private expenditure. It took 56, 736 people, and was completed in December of the fifth year of Ansei."

The land remembers the tsunami and establishes itself as a traditional climate of the region. Human memories have been merged into the land through the act of resettlement. If you escape, the experience of the tsunami will disperse. The connection between nature and humans left a record of the tsunami on land through the act of staying in the same place.

5.6   Role of Media and Records

The great disaster like tsunami occurs almost every 100 years. Since human life is usually shorter, the memory of the tsunami in the minds of the parties disappears every 100 years like the tsunami disappears into the sea. When the generations change and people forget the horror of the tsunami, they come back again. It is like waiting timing people become careless. If we do not keep it on record, humans will soon forget it. Japan is a country surrounded by the sea. Crustal movements are continuing at the depth of the earth. Japan has experienced many tsunamis in the past, and it may be easy to forget that if a tsunami occurs somewhere in the Pacific it can reach Japan.

With the lapse of time since the disaster, there is little recollection of the fears felt by the victims and little to be reported on mainstream media about the disaster-stricken area after the disaster. Certainly, powerful images of the tsunami have been left, we can watch it anytime while at home on the internet, however, only a small part of the tsunami appears in the video. There is no real feeling of the party who experienced the tsunami there. There is no picture of the tsunami that continues to live in the human heart. None of the footage was shot with the eyes of the dead. It should not be forgotten that only a part of the things can be recorded for reference to the future generation.

The role of relic as media is important. It is more important to remember, however, that this only works with the effective use of local communities sharing a disaster prevention culture.

The message that Onagawa Junior High School students were trying to convey was "the preciousness of life." In the stricken areas where reconstruction is delayed, the earthquake is still is not a thing of the past (Reconstruction Agency of Japan 2019). The act of building a stone monument is becoming a tradition, custom and is becoming established as a local culture.

5.7 Conclusion

In this chapter, I saw the role of relic as media for recording and communicating. In Onagawa's case, verbal witness in the form of haiku was attempted. In addition, the act of leaving relic was observed. The dilemma of "don't forget but want to forget" remains.

In order to overcome the contradiction, Onagawa's case was able to confirm that they would pass on lessons in cultural event.

Japan's community can be said to be distinctive in disaster culture. Further media studies should be conducted in comparison with examples in areas other area to find commonalities in media role in disaster-stricken area.

The focus has been on communication and recording performed by media. These two overlap each other and cannot be separated. However, without a record, it will not be possible to pass on the awareness of disaster prevention to the next generation. Human life is often shorter than the intervals between different catastrophes, so it is important to leave it as a physical medium, not in the consciousness of an inhabitant. In that sense, relic plays an important role. Especially in Japan, traditional events such as rituals also have the function of raising awareness of disasters and remembering past disasters. 5 types of storage media are also connected each other. Their functions as the recording media will be limited unless measures are taken to make the most of their respective characteristics to complement each other and amplify fully.

There are some themes not covered in this chapter. It is also an issue to consider the records in the local community rituals as well as family history, disaster records in anecdotes and parables. The functions of paintings art, poetry and folk songs should be studied. It is also necessary to make an international comparison of disaster death recognition as well as the role of religion in a disaster. In order to consider the long-term mental problems of the victims, it is also necessary to verify that erroneous dogmas d o not hinder proper evacuation behavior.

References

Cabinet Office Japan (2016) Effective use of disaster-proof relics. White paper disaster management in Japan 2016, Nikkei Insatsu, Tokyo, p 44

Hirose H (2008) KAIJINSYURAI Indian Ocean Tsunami Testimony of survivors. Soshisya ,Tokyo

Kitahara I, Uhana M, Ohmura J (2012) The rediscovery of tsunami monuments: a survey and study of tsunami monuments preserved in Miyagi prefecture. Stud Disaster Recover Revital 4:25–42

Kurosawa S, Nishino A (2014) Transformation in affection for the sea and hometown observed in haiku composed by junior high school students in the "Haiku-Renku School Program" after a tsunami. Graduate School of Psychology Mejiro Journal of Psychology, 2014, vol 11

Matsuoka M (2020) New tourism issues based on Earthquake ruins: a case of ruins of the Great East Japan Earthquake Sendai Arahama Elementally School. Association of Japanese Geographers, AJG, Tokyo

Ministry of Land, Infrastructure and Transport (2020) (accessed) Tsunami damage and tsunami monument information archive

Okamoto1 M (2012) Disaster archives—current situation and problem. JSIK vol 22–4 Academic Resource Guide, Inc., pp 308–315. Yokohama

Onagawa Town (2015) Report on the earthquake remains preservation plan in Onagawa

Ono S (2012) Haiku of Onagawa Daiichi junior high school students: from that day. Hatori, Tokyo

Reconstruction Agency of Japan (2019) Regarding the summary of reconstruction measures after the Great East Japan Earthquake Working group field survey report Appendix 8. Reconstruction Agency, Tokyo

Sato S, Hirakawa Y, Okumura M, Imamura F (2017) Statiscal analysis for effectiveness of casualty reduction due to tsunami tradition media : focus on tsunami monuments and place name stemming from tsunami disasters in affected areas of the 2011 Great East Japan Earthquake

Shimakawa T (2012) Changes in the residents' will on the preservation process of disaster as a tourism resource and role of mayor and city council: the case of the Atomic Bomb Dome. Proc Jpn Found Int Tour 19. JAFIT, Tokyo

Suciani A, Islami ZR, Zainal S, Sofiyan, Bukhari (2017) "Smong" as local wisdom for disaster risk reduction. In: IOP conference series: earth and environmental science

Tachibana T, Hirata F (2013) Present situation and issues of parks and facilities which transmit memories of the Great Hanshin-Awaji earthquake disaster. Lands Res Jpn 76–5:517–520. Japanese Institute of Landscape, Tokyo
Uchida N, Tan Y (2012) Value of earthquake disaster remains in earthquake disaster reconstruction. Jpn J Ergon 48:138–141. JES, Tokyo

Part III
Examples and Issues Related to Role of Media

Chapter 6
Adaptation Communication of Indigenous and Local Knowledge: Can Community Radios Be Mobilized in the Hindu Kush Himalaya Region?

Binaya Raj Shivakoti, Suman Basnet, Rajib Shaw, Osamu Mizuno, and Dhrupad Choudhury

Abstract The Hindu Kush Himalaya (HKH) region is one of the fragile ecosystems in terms of climate change and its impacts, which is reflected by the effect of both slow-onset and fast-onset disasters. Traditionally, this area has been a co-existence between nature and people. Indigenous and local knowledge (ILK) systems and practices have featured in agriculture, water resources management, forest management, disaster risk reduction, health risk management, disaster early warning, etc. ILK could be an entry point for introducing appropriate adaptation know-how and practices through enhancement and customization in a cost-effective manner. However, communication is a challenge to the promotion and diffusion of potential ILK and practices for climate change adaptation (CCA). Lack of scientific assessments, inadequate documentation, and their diversity are the key barriers for communicating the merits of ILK for CCA. In this chapter, the role of community radio networks in HKH is discussed as an effective vehicle to bridge the existing communication gaps in three ways. First, as a platform to share climate change impacts and ILK-based coping mechanisms among local communities. Second, share potential ILK-based solutions relevant to CCA across the local communities. And third, to connect with stakeholders beyond the community level (such as government, researchers and scientists, and development partners) to disseminate information about local issues, financial and capacity needs, and mainstreaming of local practices into the region's CCA planning and implementation. A framework is proposed for the incorporation of community radio as a formal means of CCA communication.

B. R. Shivakoti (✉) · O. Mizuno
Institute for Global Environmental Strategies (IGES), Hayama, Japan
e-mail: shivakoti@iges.or.jp

S. Basnet
World Association of Community Radio Broadcasters Asia Pacific (AMARC AP), Kathmandu, Nepal

R. Shaw
Graduate School of Media and Governance, Keio University, Fujisawa, Japan

D. Choudhury
International Center for Integrated Mountain Development (ICIMOD), Kathmandu, Nepal

© Springer Nature Singapore Pte Ltd. 2021
R. Shaw et al. (eds.), *Media and Disaster Risk Reduction*, Disaster Risk Reduction, https://doi.org/10.1007/978-981-16-0285-6_6

Keywords Adaptation communication · Climate change adaptation · Community radios · Hindu Kush Himalaya · Indigenous and local knowledge

6.1 Introduction

Although adaptation and mitigation of climate change are equally important, much of the discussion and deliberation surrounding them has been concentrated on mitigation, and specifically greenhouse gas emission reductions and sinks. Recently, however, there has been a surge of attention towards climate change adaptation (CCA) in the face of increased incidence of natural disasters caused by abnormal weather patterns in many parts of the world, most of which have been attributed to climate change. While the need for CCA is undisputable, definitive answers regarding its operational implications are lacking. What CCA stands for and how it looks like in the real-world situation is still hard to comprehend and communicate. There are no universal definitions on how countries or communities could interpret CCA.

The Intergovernmental Panel on Climate Change (IPCC) defines adaptation as the process of adjustment to actual or expected climate and its effects (IPCC 2014). Further, the IPCC stresses the importance of actions and strategies involving human deliberation, whether is it a social or natural system, as opposed to "adaptation", which is more of a continuous process happening over time in response to the changing environment. The process of adjustment is time-bound, while the intended outcomes of CCA could take much longer than the planning horizon. Loosely, CCA planning and actions can be considered as preparedness, as often used in disaster risk reduction (DRR) terminology, for anticipated impacts in the future. The effectiveness of CCA can be tested only after the exposure to anticipated impacts or disasters, as there is no certainty about when and how they will unfold. In most instance, the impacts will be incremental and exacerbating. A multiplicity of concepts and divergent understandings of CCA are hampering the development of uniform insights and standard responses. Determining the operational implications of CCA by advancing a conceptual understanding is far from adequate. Without efforts to marry the adaptation concept with real-world practices, CCA concept and practice risk continued treatment in separate silos (Biagini et al. 2014). A more pragmatic approach is required for communicating the process and outcomes of CCA over time.

The Global Goal on Adaptation (GGA) under Article 7 of the Paris Agreement on climate change could be considered one step ahead in clarifying the scope of CCA because it is more specific on the outcomes after implementing CCA actions. Although broad in scope, the GGA asks for three criteria to be examined to assess progress on CCA actions: enhancing of adaptive capacity, strengthening of resilience, and reducing vulnerability (UNFCCC 2015). The GGA is relatively practical and measurable in those outcomes of any programs or actions, whether identified as CCA or any other developmental actions, which could be evaluated by contrasting the relative contribution toward these three criteria. Though still broad in scope, these criteria offer a way forward for progressing CCA from conceptual realm into action-oriented pursuits.

The effective communication of the three GGA criteria (adaptive capacity, resilience, and vulnerability) to a wider audience is, therefore, of the utmost importance for advancing future efforts on CCA and achievement of the goals of the Paris Agreement. However, tracking and communicating CCA concerns, needs, priorities, actions, progress, and achievements is a thorny issue across local, national, regional, and international levels. CCA involves a complex set of qualitative and quantitative indicators. Measuring and aggregating adaptation outcomes or contributions is inherently challenging when compared with the mitigation, which deals with the quantification of major greenhouse gases (UNEP 2017). Projects and programs that are branded as CCA often have mixed results because of overlapping and incremental contributions, which cannot be easily segregated from the whole result (Prabhakar et al. 2015). The approach of communication varies depending on the scope and targets of CCA projects or programs. What and how to communicate CCA is by far unclear due to methodological and procedural issues.

The notion of "adaptation communication" has received significant attention since the adoption of the Paris Agreement. The agreement's Article 7 asks that "each Party should, as appropriate, submit and update periodically an adaptation communication, which may include its priorities, implementation and support needs, plans and actions, without creating any additional burden for developing country Parties." The article outlines the scope of adaptation communication with respect to priorities, needs and plans and actions. The intention is not only adding a new layer of monitoring and reporting burden on countries but also to institute a complementary process to facilitate CCA actions on the ground. How can a communication channel be established to highlight and share the CCA priorities, needs, and plans, and actions from local, sub-national to national and international levels as well as across these levels? Content, methods, and process of communication have to be figured out, tested, and implemented.

For addressing this important concern with regards to adaptation communication, this chapter considers indigenous and local knowledge (ILK) systems and practices as potential contributor to CCA, with a focus on the Hindu Kush Himalaya (HKH) region. Further, it highlights the role of community radio as a potential vehicle of adaptation communication not only across the local levels (horizontally) but also vertically to sub-national and national levels. The chapter presents a novel strategy for adaptation communication of ILK by involving media, especially, the use of community radio. It discusses the merits of ILK for CCA and challenges for their promotion in the HKH; highlights the potential of community radio for recognizing and disseminating ILK practices for CCA; and proposes a framework incorporating community radio into formal adaptation communication.

6.2 Communication of Indigenous and Local Knowledge (ILK) on Climate Change Adaptation

Indigenous knowledge refers to the knowledge, know-how, methods, and practices developed by a group of people from an intimate understanding of their local environment. ILK has formed, accumulated, renewed, and evolves over numerous generations of association with a particular environment, and guides human societies in their innumerable interactions with their surrounding environment (Shaw et al. 2008; Nakashima et al. 2012). Indigenous and local knowledge (ILK) systems also refer to the understanding, skills, and philosophies developed by societies with long histories of interaction with their natural surroundings (UNESCO 2020). For many, ILK informs decision-making about fundamental aspects of day-to-day life, including responses to climate change impacts.

ILK has been repeatedly highlighted as a potential contributor to CCA. Table 6.1 summarizes the importance of ILK for CCA as highlighted in major assessment reports, agreements, or decisions. The growing interest in the relationship between ILK and CCA in different national and international forums and major multilateral agreements offers a new window of opportunity to capitalize on its potential. A major motivation for promoting ILK is its potential for cost-effective and low-risk intervention for climate change investments. ILK involves a minimal learning curve when compared with exogenous interventions which, in most instances, have to be implemented from scratch and whose effectiveness may be thwarted by their lack of suitability and cost-effectiveness, and acceptance by the intended beneficiaries.

Since ILK stems from generations of on-the-ground climate observations and interactions with the environment, it enables a better understanding of the impacts at a finer spatial scale and a greater temporal depth (UNFCCC 2018). Further, ILK practices are grounded to the local level where most CCA actions are needed. Given that ILK systems could be the only coping measure available across diverse local contexts, their potential incorporation into planned CCA in future is critical for the overall effectiveness of efforts and investments in CCA. Focusing on ILK for CCA ensures sustainability of investments on CCA as the focus will be on continuity of already existing practices. Meanwhile, focus on ILK also helps to identify barriers for implementing CCA at the local or community level.

Notwithstanding the crucial role of ILK systems and practices for CCA, promoting ILK for CCA involves a number of preparatory steps for filling knowledge gaps and overcoming challenges. The robustness of ILK systems and practices to withstand climate change is yet to be examined in many instances and it is not yet known which internal and external factors could contribute to strengthen or weaken their effectiveness for CCA in future. Nevertheless, the salience of ILK could fade away over time unless it is given due consideration in national- and local-level adaptation policymaking, strategies, and action plans.

The pertinent questions with regards to the application of ILK for CCA are how to recognize ILK's contributions to CCA, how to attribute its merits and drawbacks, and how to systematically document both tangible and intangible knowledge systems

Table 6.1 Importance of ILK for CCA in major assessment reports and decisions

Importance of ILK for CCA	Sources
ILK systems and practices, including indigenous peoples' holistic view of community and environment, are a major resource for CCA, but these have not been used consistently in existing adaptation efforts. Integrating such forms of knowledge with existing practices increases the effectiveness of adaptation	IPCC AR5 (Pachauri et al. 2014)
A wide range of adaptation options, including ILK, are available to reduce the risks to natural and managed ecosystems. Education, information, and community approaches, including those that are informed by ILK, can accelerate the wide-scale behavior changes consistent with adapting to and limiting global warming to 1.5 °C	IPCC SR 1.5 °C (IPCC 2018)
The shrinking cryosphere in the Arctic and high-mountain areas has led to predominantly negative impacts on food security, water resources, water quality, livelihoods, health and well-being, infrastructure, transportation, tourism, and recreation, as well as culture of human societies, particularly for Indigenous peoples. While adaptation efforts have benefited from the inclusion of ILK	IPCC SR Oceans and Cryosphere (IPCC 2019)
Focusing on ILK is important for mountain communities. ILK forms the basis of community coping practices, builds up resilience to disasters, and plays an important role in DRR. Combining ILK with external expertise is vital for resilience. There is, however, a need for generating evidence to establish that such knowledge systems are equally relevant when it comes to dealing with the uncertainty and "surprises" likely to arise from future climate change and its impacts	HIMAP (Wester et al. 2019)
The application of appropriate technological innovation and promotion of ILK systems lead to increased local ownership and engagement, overcoming some of the governance deficits, enable conservation and utilization of biodiversity and nature's contribution to people, support sustainable development, and adapting to the impacts of climate change	IPBES (IPBES 2018)

(continued)

Table 6.1 (continued)

Importance of ILK for CCA	Sources
ILK operates at a much finer spatial and temporal scale than science and includes understandings of how to cope with and adapt to environmental variability and trends. ILK thus makes an important contribution to climate change policy, and Sustainable Development Goal on climate action (#13) by observing changing climates, adapting to impacts, and contributing to global mitigation efforts	UNESCO (UNESCO 2020)
Adaptation action should follow a country-driven, gender-responsive, participatory, and fully transparent approach, taking into consideration vulnerable groups, communities, and ecosystems, and should be based on and guided by the best available science and, as appropriate, traditional knowledge and ILK systems, with a view to integrating adaptation into relevant socioeconomic and environmental policies and actions, where appropriate (Article 7.5)	The Paris Agreement (UNFCCC 2015)
There is a need to strengthen knowledge, technologies, practices, and efforts of local communities and indigenous peoples related to addressing and responding to climate change and the parties thus establishes the Local Communities and Indigenous Peoples Platform (LCIPP) for the exchange of experiences and sharing of best practices on mitigation and adaptation in a holistic and integrated manner	UNFCCC (UNFCCC 2020)
It is important to ensure the use of ILK and practices, as appropriate at the national and local levels, to complement scientific knowledge in disaster risk assessment and the development and implementation of policies, strategies, plans, and programmes of specific sectors, with a cross-sectoral approach, which should be tailored to localities and to the context. Further, indigenous peoples, through their experience and traditional knowledge, provide an important contribution to the development and implementation of plans and mechanisms, including early warning	Sendai Framework on DRR (UNISDR 2015)

or practices. This is where mainstreaming ILK into formal adaptation communication becomes critical. The diversity, distributed nature, varied languages, dialects, culture, and belief systems associated with ILK make it extremely challenging to bring potential ILK on CCA to the forefront of discussion. Similarly, a number of exogenous and endogenous factors impacting continuity of potential ILK have to be identified.

Since there is no existing mechanism for identifying ILK at different localities, an appropriate system has to be devised. It should have a wide reach, operational, and be easily accessible. Before diving into the modality of such a system, it may be helpful to examine opportunities and challenges for the promotion of ILK with reference to a real context. The following section thus introduces the biophysically and socio-culturally diverse Hindu Kush Himalaya (HKH) region where ILK has played an important role in day-to-day lifestyle decisions and socio-cultural development for centuries.

6.3 Promoting ILK for CCA in the Hindu Kush Himalaya (HKH) Region

The HKH region encompasses a geographical area of over 4.2 million km^2 and the origin of 10 major river basins including all of Nepal and Bhutan and the mountainous parts of Afghanistan, Bangladesh, China, India, Myanmar, and Pakistan (Fig. 6.1) (Singh et al. 2011; Wester et al. 2019). The extensive and diverse settings of the HKH represent a complex mosaic of topography and landforms, micro-climatic zones,

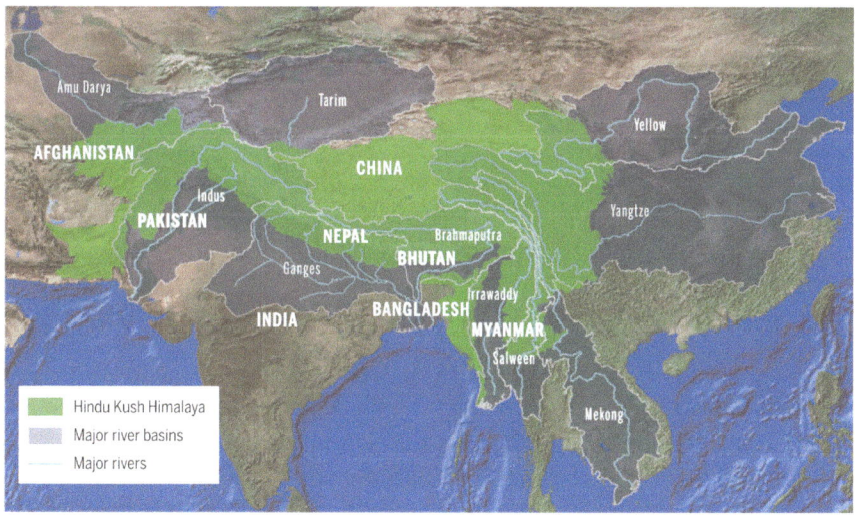

Fig. 6.1 The Hindu Kush Himalaya region (Wester et al. 2019)

biodiversity, and natural resources, and livelihood characterized by unique social and cultural settings and strong upstream–downstream linkages. Its fragile environment and the high dependency of its human inhabitants on climate-sensitive resources such as snow and glaciers, water, forest and biodiversity, and agriculture, make it a hotspot in terms of climate impact. Glacier retreat, loss of ice masses, and snow cover changes have already contributed to localized declines in agricultural yields in the region (IPCC 2019). Further, changing precipitation patterns threaten the water supply and hence hydropower, drinking water, ecosystems, and agriculture. Climate change impacts will intensify the scale and frequency of slow and fast-onset hydro-climatic disasters such as floods, landslides, and droughts. Given the dire poverty in the area, a weak asset base, and high vulnerability, the mountain communities are ill-prepared to cope with new forms of stresses resulting from the climate change impacts.

For centuries, people living in the HKH region have developed their own adaptive mechanism in response to the biophysical specificities and occasional upheavals in the local environment and weather. The region's rich ILK systems are the result of continuous interaction, experimentation, adoption, reinvention, and adaptation with the bio-physical environment. Natural resources are controlled, appropriated, and managed through norms and institutions of ILK (Ojha et al. 2019). A variety of community-based natural resource management systems evolved under traditional norms and indigenous institutions, therefore, are the foundation supporting day-to-day decision-making and development and sustenance of livelihood support systems.

The coping strategies built on the basis of ILK has been key to building the resilience of HKH mountain communities, most of whom are living under poverty and are highly vulnerable to climate change impact. ILK can help these mountain communities to cope with climate impacts and facilitate the building of resilience more easily but at the same time necessitate measures to reinforce their effectiveness (Shaw and Nibanupudi 2015; Wester et al. 2019). Most importantly, improved connectivity and exposure to technological innovations have markedly affected people's ways of life in the HKH, especially ILK sociocultural practices, enabled through the development of a range of opportunities in remote mountain areas (Wester et al. 2019). Sustaining the essence and value system inherent to ILK along with the modern changes and expected intensification of climate impacts poses a real challenge. But successful integration of ILK with the technology and innovations could in fact help to strengthen, modernize, and make them more resilient to climate change impacts.

Current research and actions on CCA in the HKH region largely ignore the instrumental role of ILK for CCA. Meanwhile documented scientific knowledge is scattered and scarce (Pachauri et al. 2014; Ojha et al. 2019; Wester et al. 2019). The blending of ILK with scientific knowledge and technological innovation can be used to capitalize the strengths of ILK for CCA. Further, integration of ILK with information and communication technology in a partnership of stakeholders, including youth, media, women, civil society, government, and development partners, along with local and indigenous communities can trigger dialogue, bridge the knowledge gap, and innovate solutions. Similarly, enhanced cooperation within and across HKH countries is critical for sharing data and information on ILK and for overcoming barriers for their application for CCA.

6.4 Potential Role of Media in Bridging the Knowledge Gaps on ILK and CCA

Compared to the efforts spent on understanding climate change and its impacts, very little attention has been paid to communicating and educating the general public about it. With increasing demand for climate change information from the general public, private sectors and business, and other sectors, there is increasing realization of the role of the media in communicating and raising public awareness on climate change. Mass media outlets such as The Guardian, BBC, NHK, and many other national and international agencies are increasingly featuring climate change and associated impacts such as weather-induced disasters. The BBC, for example, has initiated the "Our Planet Matters" project, a year-long series of special programming and coverage on climate change.[1] Asia Pacific Broadcasting Union (ABU), which is the biggest broadcasting union in the world with 270 members in over 70 countries on four continents, regularly organizes "Media Summit on Climate Action and Disaster Preparedness." The ABU Media Summit is the result of the realization of media's potential to be on the frontline of climate change adaptation and as the most efficient and cost-effective way of making climate action and disaster preparedness everybody's business.[2]

Increased media reporting is certainly beneficial for raising public awareness on issues surrounding climate change. The media's potential can be further harnessed as a partner in CCA design, implementation, and timely dissemination of outcomes. In fact, climate change communication has emerged as a field of research after years of practice—out of the need for increasing public engagement—without a solid foundation of research (Tsamopoulos et al. 2019). The bigger issue in this context is how media can become a true partner with relevant government agencies, scientists and experts, and local people. The key question is related to enhancing media capacity to understand climate change, which is a complex topic involving models, analysis, interpretation, and uncertainty. At the same time, with high public demand for information, and with established means of communicating that information, the media can customize and present it more effectively and efficiently than researchers or scientists. It becomes quite relevant to explore various ways to exploit the potential of media for the communication of CCA information. It is also contextual to explore new services, in addition to broadcasting information, the media can provide to support CCA efforts on the ground.

---

[1] https://www.bbc.com/news/world-51104776.
[2] https://cadp.abu.org.my/?page_id=434.

In the case of promoting ILK on CCA, the media can become an interface to link local priorities and concerns with the science-policy community. The media could serve as an interactive platform and a reliable interface, as opposed to a predominantly one-way broadcasting role, to establish communication with many of the local and indigenous communities located in hard-to-reach areas of the HKH region. In that respect, not all media could be equally effective and their operation modality too needs to be considered.

In the case of ILK, reliance on certain mass media such as television and newspaper could be less effective despite their wider spatial reach and audience. For instance, television can be less effective for establishing a two-way communication between media and local/indigenous people as it requires a strong network of television reporters across different communities. Similarly, the local people may not be in a position to watch television all the time. The same applies to the print media. Additionally, the print media involves logistics constraints for delivering the newspaper to each household on time.

In order to overcome the constraints of the mass media, media choice for ILK communication needs to fulfill certain requirements. The media should be convenient to access and be portable. It has to be inclusive and interactive so that two-way exchange of information becomes a principle mode of operation among the audience. Similarly, the scale of communication (i.e., coverage area or population) has to be manageable. It should be neither too big nor too small such that the broadcast contents could be grounded to the local reality (including language and ethnicity), and community's needs. It should be less costly (i.e., financially viable) and less technically challenging for operation, which could be a real issue for many communities. Additionally, the media should be compatible with recent innovations in information and communication technologies (ICT) such as the use of social media, web-radios, web-pages, viral videos, etc.

6.5   Community Radio as a Potential Medium for Communicating ILK on CCA in the HKH Region

To make a case for the role of community radios in the promotion of ILK, it is relevant to review the strengths of local community broadcasting that make it a highly desirable agency. Community radio has a rich history as a medium of information and communication that stays and operates in close proximity to the people it serves. It is based on the idea of ordinary people, often forgotten and ignored by the mainstream media, having their own means of expressing ideas, opinions, discontentment, or curiosity. The seed of such a medium was sowed during the First World War when citizens' groups took over military radios in Europe to speak out, albeit for a brief period of time. In the late 1940s, simple forms of radio broadcasting were set up by miners and workers in Colombia (1947) and Bolivia (1949). In 1949, the KPFA[3] became the first community-supported radio station in the USA.

Among the several commonalities in the HKH region, one is the spread and coverage of community radio stations. This region has a rich heritage of community broadcasting, especially in terms of the sheer numbers of radio stations present. The advent of Radio Sagarmatha[4] in Nepal in 1997 began the era of non-state broadcasting in South Asia, to be followed by hundreds of commercial and community radios across the sub-region. Today, Nepal alone has over 700 local FM radio stations, out of which approximately 400 operate on a not-for-profit basis. Similarly, there are 18 community radios in operation in Bangladesh (community radios Sagor Giri and Naf are in operation in the Chittagong Hill Tracts of Bangladesh) and an estimated 310 in India (approximately 19 local radio stations are in operation in the northeastern states of India). There are at least 30 community and local radio stations across Afghanistan. Local communities in Bhutan are served by seven community and campus radio stations, while online radio stations serve specific interest-based communities in China. A movement for community broadcasting is gathering steam in Myanmar as well, and the number of stations is expected to grow in the near future. There is one local FM station in operation already while at least five other groups are actively podcasting. Pakistan has not yet opened up to community broadcasting but there are a number of local radio stations serving local populations.

Local radio stations were established with the objectives of serving local communication and information needs, upholding freedom of expression and human rights, in general, and promoting local development, especially for people at the lowest socio-economic strata of the society. As they are rooted in local communities, the content of community radio stations is primarily targeted at those communities. Their proximity to those communities allows community radio to address relevant concerns and issues in a factual and timely manner, which a public mass media or a commercial broadcaster can seldom claim to do. Community radios also have the best grasp of local issues, as they are run by people from the local communities, who know what matters to those communities in terms of their problems, worries, likes, and disagreements. These broadcasters interact closely with community members on-air and off-air, giving them an acute understanding of the community's concerns and information needs. Community radios often carry out off-line activities such as hosting community meetings, public hearings, training programs, entertainment such as musical performances, theatre, sports, and so on that help in maintaining a close relationship between the radio station and members of the community. The fact that community radios broadcast in local dialects and languages is an important aspect of community broadcasting. Collectively, these virtues render community radios as the most accessible and best understood among all available media for a community.

Inclusivity, diversity of ownership and plurality are the pillars of any community radio station. A community radio studio is a microcosm of the linguistic, cultural,

[3]https://kpfa.org/about/.
[4]https://radiosagarmatha.org.np/about/.

social, political, and geographical diversity of a community. One of the most high-lighted features of any community radio is that it is instrumental in promoting and preserving languages, knowledge, and ideas that would otherwise be lost in time. Oral history presentation and testimonials are some of the common formats used, which are effective for the promotion and preservation of local knowledge. The fact that the broadcasting hours are best suited to the local communities is yet another seemingly ordinary but a vital strength of community broadcasting. Many rural community members do not have the benefit of accessing podcasts or downloading audio files. Hence broadcasting hours must match the daily routine of community members.

Community radio, coupled with ICT, could be an effective medium to fulfill the needs and requirements for the communication of ILK on CCA across the HKH. Improved access to mobile networks and the availability of inexpensive personal communication devices (such as mobile phones or smartphones) have greatly eased and transformed the system of communication in remote and geograph-ically isolated locations. The multi-functionality of personal communication devices, such as listening radio broadcasts or accessing Internet, has empowered the commu-nity's reach to a variety of information. Meanwhile, with the integration of ICT, the scope of community radio is not just limited to listening but also reading (social media or web-pages) and viewing (e.g., viral videos) via the Internet. Besides, ICT can help expand the scope beyond the community such as the network of community radios.

6.6   The Case of Farmer-Focused Community Radio in Nepal

A quick assessment of a community radio station in Dhunibashi Municipality in Dhading District of Nepal was conducted to explore its potential for adaptation communication of ILK during September 2019–January 2020 (Fig. 6.2). Interviews were conducted with the staff of the station as well as selected audiences to deter-mine its structure, function, and services. A trial radio program was broadcasted, discussing weather-related impacts on farming. The program was led by the station manager and facilitated by the corresponding author of this chapter, when necessary, to clarify general and technical queries related to climate change. The recording of the broadcast was attended by local agriculture experts (from government agencies, NGOs), the mayor of Dhunibashi Municipality, representatives of the Association of Community Radio Broadcasters'(ACORAB) Nepal, local farmers, agriculture traders, and operators of other community radios operating in the same district.

The community radio is Krishi Radio 101.5 megahertz[5] which was established in 2008. It is the first and only community radio devoted to agriculture in Nepal. The service area of the Krishi Radio is one of the pockets of commercial vegetable farming in Nepal. The station has proven very successful and is popular with local farmers. The

---

[5]https://www.krishiradio.org.np/.

Fig. 6.2 Interaction with staff and audience of community agriculture radio (Krishi Radio 101.5 megahertz) on climate change impacts on agriculture

operational fund is provided through donations or shareholding from local people and farmers, advertisers, or their collaborators (e.g., government projects, NGOs, INGOs). Although its main function is to broadcast news and information related to agriculture and other affairs of local interest, the activities and services of the community radio and approach of engagement with its audience are broad.

Krishi Radio broadcasts agriculture information such as regular updating of the price of agriculture commodities before the opening of the wholesale market every day. It also helps disseminate common and new issues faced by farmers such as pest attacks. The radio is a platform to discuss solutions, either by inviting experts or senior farmers with knowledge of traditional farming methods or to discuss issues among farmers. Apart from regular broadcasting, the radio staff are active in the field. They help to connect farmers with new or unfamiliar farming technology and methods, such as organic farming, and collaborate with agencies or organizations that support farmers. They also conduct field visits to assess conditions on the ground such as the health of crops, pest attacks, and crop damages, with experts and as per demand from farmers. The radio helps farmers to connect with the right person or agency who has a solution. They furthermore facilitate communication with higher government authorities or important decision-makers such as the mayor or agricultural staff from central or provincial government. They also advertise available agriculture products such as fertilizers, seeds, or veterinary medicines for livestock. These functions resemble the agriculture extension function of government agencies and private agriculture service providers.

Besides agricultural information, the community radio broadcasts a range of other programs including national and international news, music, and other entertainment, etc. It helps to connect the farmers and local people with the outside world.

Aside from being useful to local needs, building trust among the local community and network of people, they are connected directly or via radio program offers immense potential for reaching to target audience (farmers and local community) with the utmost rapidity. Unlike large-scale broadcasters such as television or national newspapers, the community radio is more convenient and useful to local farmers as the contents they provide are highly targeted to the local needs. Because of the widespread use of mobile phones, the radio can be assessed by framers while working in the field. A dedicated website and social media page further help to promote upcoming as well as completed broadcasts, including uploaded as YouTube videos.

As a member of ACORAB-Nepal, Krishi Radio may re-broadcast relevant programs aired by other community radios in Nepal. Similarly, their own program are broadcasted by a network of community radios across the country. It helps to enhance their connectivity and nationwide reach.

To assess the potential involvement of the community radio model for adaptation communication, the trial interactive radio program ("Climate change and It's Impacts on Agriculture") discussed three broad issues: recent impacts on farming due to abnormal weather; understanding climate change and impacts on agriculture; and the role of community radio to disseminate information, in particular related to ILK and CCA in the agricultural sector.

Since this was the first program on climate change by Krishi Radio, participants found it a useful opportunity to share new kinds of weather-related problems (such as water shortages, drying of water sprouts, pest attacks, lower productivity) and discuss their potential link to climate change. More importantly, there was interest in differentiating between "what is climate change and what is not." Some participants mistakenly related air pollution from local brick kilns and plastic pollution as contributing to observed weather-related impacts. The program also demonstrated the potential to use the medium of community radio to share ILK. One participant, for example, referred to a ritual at the beginning of spring when cows' milk is sprinkled onto the soil before it is first tilled. The participant said that the milk's nutrients activate certain bacteria in soil, which are dormant during cold long winter. If shared broadly, such information could support reinvigoration of organic farming and potential improvement of soil quality, which is essential for climate-resilient farming. Similarly, options related to the use of traditional seeds and the introduction of new varieties of tropical fruit tree species to tap warming environment came up as an opportunity. However, with it came questions regarding the need to connect with appropriate technologies and research findings, opportunities for climate funding, and the capacity of the community radio broadcasters. Overall, the discussion was fruitful and demonstrates potential for adaptation communication in future.

6.7   Framework for the Incorporation of Community Radio in Formal Communication of ILK for CCA

Community radio stations, coupled with ICT, are well placed to strike an optimum balance between modern knowledge and ILK. They have already been successfully put to use for improving disaster resilience of rural communities across the Asia–Pacific region and beyond. As tools of disaster risk reduction and early warning mechanisms, community radio stations save millions of lives globally. In certain instances, community radio is also used as a medium for climate change communication among communities (Srinivasan Mannar 2014; Bisht and Ahluwalia 2014), while a need for more interactive radio programs on the subject is also gaining attention (Tume et al. 2018).

Given the aforementioned background on agricultural community radio in Nepal, a framework of adaptation communication is proposed for systematic identification, documentation, and dissemination of ILK on CCA (Fig. 6.3). This framework envisions the central role of community radio stations and their distributed networks. Community radio can play three important roles. First, community radio can help to identify distributed ILK and bring them to community attention as a solution to deal with CCA challenges. Where appropriate, they can also take leadership in preparing broadcasts on ILK with the potential to promote CCA. Second, community radio can broadcast dedicated programs on ILK for CCA, either through its own station

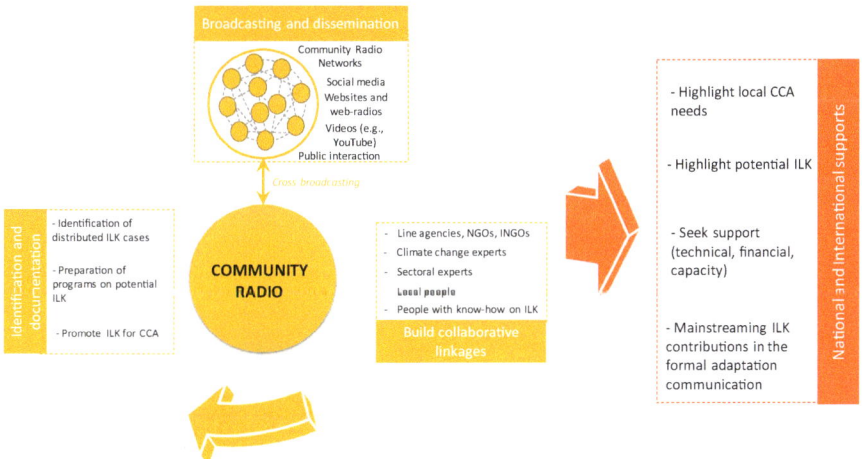

Fig. 6.3 Framework for adaptation communication of ILK through community radio networks

or through broadcasting across a countrywide network of community radios or the HKH region, after translation into local languages as necessary. Web-radios, video recording (such as YouTube), or other appropriate technologies could be utilized to enhance content or to connect with a wider audience. Similarly, dissemination of ILK could happen through social media or web portals of community radios or network such as ACORAB-Nepal. Cross-broadcasting is vital for quick identification and dissemination of ILK across a larger area but a mechanism has to be established for that. The third, and the most important, role of community radio would be to build collaborative networks with agencies, experts, and local people. The agencies (government or non-governmental) can provide administrative, financial, or technical support in the process of documenting ILK, such as agreeing on the format of documenting and broadcasting and connecting with relevant experts and resources. Climate change and sectoral experts (such as agriculture, disaster management) can provide input to prepare radio programs that are technically sound and full of necessary information on CCA. The involvement of local ILK knowledge holders will ensure that the proposed programs address local needs.

Beyond the local level, community radio and its networks can be instrumental in spreading potential ILK at the national and international level. This could be extremely effective in communicating the community needs to the government or other international support mechanisms for CCA or ILK. Further, when backed with proper documentation based on an agreed framework, the community radios and their networks can help mainstreaming the identified ILK contributions into formal channels of adaptation communication. Although realizing this kind of ideal setup might take time and faces enormous institutional challenges at different levels, it has to progress in a step-wise manner based on the lessons such as how more and more community radios got involved and successfully demonstrate their contribution in identification, promotion, and dissemination of potential ILK for CCA. For instance, community radio can help to build communication channels through appropriate agencies submitting the contribution of ILK for CCA as well as support needed to strengthen ILK. The technical experts as well as relevant agencies can help to record and document ILK and support in reporting, which will be key for national and international recognition of local efforts. The overall process can be useful in boosting the capacity of community radio in CCA and thus establish them as one of the key stakeholders in formal adaptation communication.

6.8   Conclusion and Way Forward

The need to improve communication on climate change and its impacts on the wider public is growing rapidly. Mass media is increasingly involved in broadcasting news on climate change relevant information. However, the role of media can be broadened beyond mere dissemination of information. Media can be more proactive by actually becoming a key facilitator in promoting CCA action, most of which is needed at the local level. From the discussion, it is evident that community radio can play a major role in the communication of ILK for CCA in the HKH region. Existing community radio stations can help identify and document ILK and their contribution to CCA; and connect local-level CCA efforts with national and international climate change-related processes. We propose such a framework of adaptation communication of ILK involving the community radio at the core. However, some preparation is required for this to be successfully adopted.

First, it is important to standardize the communication approach and ensure the reliability/usefulness of the information on ILK and CCA provided by the community radio. A common understanding of the definition of ILK practices and an acceptable methodology for extracting and documenting such knowledge needs to be established across the board, with an acceptable degree of flexibility to suit the diversity of different communities.

Second, uses of ICT can be a leverage for not only producing high-quality content in a cost-effective manner but also their rapid dissemination through the internet (web-radio, social website, viral videos). The convergence of modern ICT and old media technologies are important steps in developing resilient and robust media ecosystems at the local levels. This is critical if local broadcasters are to serve as an effective means of preserving ILK.

Third, enabling policy is key to the sustainability of effective community broad-casting, participation for CCA, ownership, and continuity of ILK for the advantage of the communities in the HKH region, and quite possibly far beyond. Overcoming institutional barriers between media and concerned government agencies (as well as other stakeholders) is essential for building a strong partnership. Despite the proven effectiveness of community radio, especially for the sharing of new ideas and promoting action, some countries in the HKH region are yet to open up to this medium or have done so only partially. While agencies at the local level are yet to understand the potential of community radio on communicating and promoting ILK for CCA, efforts are needed to build an environment of trust for media to play an active role in supporting government efforts on CCA such as seeking media help in disseminating CCA plans and action to communities or identifying local-level climate impacts and CCA needs.

The final and the most important aspect is the capacity building of community radio broadcasters not only to produce appropriate programs on ILK and CCA for the locals but also to highlight the ILK to the national, regional, and global audience. Community broadcasters as well as community members stand to benefit from any additional skills and capacity that can be inculcated for transforming ILKs derived from local communities into interesting radio programs so that such knowl-edge becomes a common heritage and is preserved in popular memory as well. Through capacity building, as well as policy support, community radio, and their network, could be an effective vehicle to highlight potential ILK that might need policy attention, additional supports, or be threatened by external factors such as globalization.[6]

---

[6]https://en.unesco.org/courier/2019-1/radio-lifeline-indigenous-peoples.

Acknowledgements Andre Mader, Director, NRE Area, IGES, for the suggestions and useful edits. Sarjo Paudel, Station Manager, Krishi Radio 101.5 megaherz, Dhunibashi, Dharke, Dhading Nepal and his team for sharing information and helping to organize the trial program on climate change adaptation. IGES Strategy Fund and APN CAPaBLE project (CBA2020-02MY-Mizuno) for financial support.

References

Biagini B, Bierbaum R, Stults M, Dobardzic S, McNeeley SM (2014) A typology of adaptation actions: a global look at climate adaptation actions financed through the global environment facility. Global Environ Chang 25(March):97–108. https://doi.org/10.1016/j.gloenvcha.2014.01.003

Bisht H, Ahluwalia N (2014) Community radios and climate change communication: mapping grassroots experiences of the 'Shubh Kal' project in Bundelkhand, Central India. https://cdkn.org/wp-content/uploads/2012/11/Manuscript-Community-radios-and-climate-change-commun ication-Mapping-grassroots-experiences.pdf

IPBES (2018) The IPBES regional assessment report on biodiversity and ecosystem services for Asia and the Pacific. Edited by Karki M, Senaratna Sellamuttu S, Okayasu S, Suzuki W. Bonn, Germany. https://ipbes.net/sites/default/files/2018_asia_pacific_full_report_book_v3_pages.pdf

IPCC (2014) Annex II: glossary. In: Mach KJ, Planton S, von Stechow C (eds) (Contributi) Climate change 2014: synthesis report. IPCC, Geneva, Switzerland

IPCC (2018) Summary for policymakers. In: Masson-Delmotte V, Zhai P, Pörtner H-O, Roberts D, Skea J, Shukla PR, Pirani A et al (eds) Global warming of 1.5°C. An IPCC special report on the impacts of global warming of 1.5°C above pre-industrial levels and related global greenhouse gas emission pathways, in the context of strengthening the global response to the threat of climate change. World Meteorological Organization, Geneva, Switzerland

IPCC (2019) Summary for policymakers. In: Pörtner HO, Roberts DC, Masson-Delmotte V, Zhai P, Tignor M, Poloczanska E, Mintenbeck K et al (eds) IPCC special report on the ocean and cryosphere in a changing climate

Nakashima DJ, Galloway McLean K, Thulstrup HD, Ramos Castillo A, Rubis JT (2012) Weathering uncertainty: traditional knowledge for climate change assessment and adaptation. Paris and Darwin

Ojha HR, Ghate R, Dorji L, Shrestha A, Paudel D, Nightingale A, Shrestha K, Watto MA, Kotru R (2019) Governance: key for environmental sustainability in the Hindu Kush Himalaya. In: Wester P, Mishra A, Mukherji A, Shrestha AB (eds) The Hindu Kush Himalaya assessment. Springer International Publishing, Cham, pp 545–78. https://doi.org/10.1007/978-3-319-92288-1_16.

Pachauri RK, Allen MR, Barros VR, Broome J, Cramer W, Christ R, Church JA et al (2014) Climate change 2014: synthesis report. Contribution of Working Groups I, II and III to the fifth assessment report of the intergovernmental panel on climate change. IPCC

Prabhakar SVRK, Ofei-Manu P, Solomon D, Shivakoti BR (2015) Evidence for climate change adaptation and disaster risk reduction synergies of interventions: an inductive approach. Hayama, Japan. https://doi.org/10.13140/RG.2.1.5099.2723.

Shaw R, Nibanupudi HK (2015) Overview of mountain hazards issues, pp 1–11. https://doi.org/10.1007/978-4-431-55242-0_1.

Shaw R, Uy N, Baumwoll J (2008) Indigenous knowledge for disaster risk reduction: good practices and lessons learned from experiences in the Asia-Pacific Region. Bangkok, Thailand

Singh SP, Bassignana-Khadka I, Singh Karky B, Sharma E (2011) Climate change in the Hindu Kush-Himalayas: the state of current knowledge. Kathmandu

Srinivasan Mannar I (2014) Communicating climate change using community radios. J Biodiv Bioprospect Dev 01(01). https://doi.org/10.4172/2376-0214.1000114.

Tsamopoulos K, Marini K, Skanavis C (2019) Media based education and motivation through phrasing: can they affect climate change willingness? In: Leal Filho W, McGhie H, Lackner B (eds) Addressing the challenges in communicating climate change across various audiences, pp 357–374. https://doi.org/10.1007/978-3-319-98294-6_22.

Tume SJP, Jumbam MS, Nsoseka NA, Nyarka ND, Yenla LJ, Njodzeka NG (2018) Role of the media in climate change communication in the northwest region of Cameroon, pp 47–60. https://doi.org/10.1007/978-3-319-70066-3_4.

UNEP (2017) The adaptation gap report 2017. Nairobi, Kenya

UNESCO (2020) Local and Indigenous Knowledge Systems (LINKS) (2020) https://en.unesco.org/links

UNFCCC (2015) The Paris agreement. https://unfccc.int/process-and-meetings/the-paris-agreement/the-paris-agreement

UNFCCC (2018) Report of the multi-stakeholder workshop: implementing the functions of the local communities and indigenous peoples platform. https://unfccc.int/topics/local-communities-and-indigenous-peoples-platform/events-meetings-and-workshops/multi-stakeholder-workshop-of-the-local-communities-and-indigenous-peoples-platform

UNFCCC (2020) Introduction to the local communities and indigenous peoples platform (LCIPP) (2020) https://unfccc.int/LCIPP

UNISDR (2015) Sendai framework for disaster risk reduction 2015--2030. In: Proceedings of the 3rd United Nations world conference on DRR, Sendai, Japan, pp 14–18

Wester P, Mishra A, Mukherji A, Shrestha AB (eds) (2019) The Hindu Kush Himalaya assessment. Springer International Publishing, Cham. https://doi.org/10.1007/978-3-319-92288-1

Chapter 7
Challenges and Lessons: Reporting from Ground Zero—Diaries of Journalists Covering Disasters in the Asia Pacific

Suvendrini Kakuchi

Abstract This chapter offers the diverse reporting experience of Asian journalists when covering major disasters in their countries for leading domestic and international media. Through their voices—as quoted in their personal contributions for this book—the reader has access to a special insider look into the intricacies of media reporting. In addition, this chapter opens a window into the varied topics covered by journalists before, during and after the disaster. A critical aspect of this section is the compilation of their recommendations based on their experience. We hope the information will contribute to the ongoing development of disaster communication practices and media research.

Keyword Journalist field reports · Foreign correspondent reports · Personal reporting versus objective reporting · Gender in disaster reporting

7.1 Introduction and Need for Journalist's Diary

Often the reporters' coverage is an important source of independent communication from disaster sites to readers. Story content is a combination of official information and reporter's interviews. Journalists reply on government sources to provide statistics and data of the disaster including official activities responding to the tragedy. Field stories and analysis are captured through the eyes of the reporter—onsite interviews—and reflect the guidance of their editors (Alexander 2002).

Journalists' reports are often reliable sources for private-sector humanitarian aid and assistance to the disaster sites. Their stories provide information on humanitarian issues such as the lack of goods, assistance and financial help and the impact on survivors. Given the wide public appeal of disaster reporting, especially during a massive tragedy, news organizations view the topic as both a social commitment and an important financial source. As the media expands with expanding private cable television channels and new online media outlets spawning the Internet, competition

S. Kakuchi (✉)
Tokyo Correspondent, University World News, Tokyo, Japan
e-mail: suven@kdp.biglobe.ne.jp

© Springer Nature Singapore Pte Ltd. 2021
R. Shaw et al. (eds.), *Media and Disaster Risk Reduction*, Disaster Risk Reduction,
https://doi.org/10.1007/978-981-16-0285-6_7

between media has grown intense. With news companies relying on advertising for financial stability, viewer rates become imperative for survival. This backdrop has affected the media coverage of disasters. Large-scale destruction provides unusual news coverage, dramatic photos and stories representing trauma and adventure. The coverage evokes massive emotional appeal to the public-making disaster stories some of the most read, watched and listened. Ref Media Capacity Building and Disaster Risk Reduction: Building Resilience and Protecting Socio Economic Development Gains in Southeast Asia. International Development. Australia Broadcasting Corporation.

Against this context, the media invests heavily in human resources and technology to gain readership and thrive for successful coverage. The focus of disaster reporting is then on the visibility of the disasters—shocking images of suffering is an example of the high priority to produce emotive reporting (Pantti 2018).

International news on disasters is dependent on geo dominated by the bigger and richer media companies. Journalists in these companies have access to vast funds and technology, such as employing drones, that give them an edge over smaller companies. Bigger companies can dispatch their journalists to foreign disaster sites. Better access to a network of researchers, contacts in the foreign governments and the private sector also contribute to more coverage and visually attractive production of stories. Their perspectives shape public opinion in foreign audiences (Pantti 2018).

Journalist reports can also convey misleading information, which can be conspicuous in news filed by reporters from large mainstream companies who are not familiar with the local settings. A potent example cited by researchers is in reference to the 2004 massive Asian tsunami when western media emphasized victim helplessness by covering displaced children when the reality was that orphans were taken care of by the community and were rarely placed in orphanages (Sterling 2009).

With the growth of social media, information sharing has become a two-way flow. New technologies—laptops, cell phones digital cameras—have changed the way news is gathered and disseminated. Online access to disaster news is immediate and covers large populations. Social media tools such as Twitter and blogs have become key news sources. The growth of the popularity of social media has changed the way mainstream media organizations cover the news—journalists covering disasters are required to upload short social media messages on their I-phones from disaster sites. Longer stories are disseminated later. Social media has also pushed the framework of transparency and accountability. As more ordinary citizens, referred to as First Informers, use the technology to send messages based on real experiences, their messages can counter official information leading to holding people and organizations responsible. In addition, the social media has fostered the importance of participatory journalism in news organizations. More disaster reporting is based on multimedia format. The dependence on photos and videos sent by the people from the disaster sites are now viewed as vital resources in news reporting (Haddow and Haddow 2014).

Blogs Message Board, Hotlines, Message boards provide critical information about missing persons, shelter locations, support organizations and other important information necessary for the survivors and other stakeholders. Bill Gannon, owner of

Yahoo, a major online provider, is quoted as saying referring to the Katrina hurricane in august 2005, "what we realized is that user's wanted not just to read the information but they wanted to be empowered. They wanted to be personally involved either through a message board or simply through a donation" (Haddow and Haddow 2014). Research has also indicated the social media provides pinpoint information that is first accessed during disaster—Twitter messages on lifeline information were most read during the March 11, 2011 triple disaster. Television news was most popular 1 week after the disaster (NHK 2013).

7.2   Diaries of Journalists

Freelance reporter and photographer for almost three decades. Indonesia. Disaster: July 2. 2013. Disaster:Ache earthquake. Indonesia

It was the day when an earthquake with tremor 6.1 on the Richter scale jolted Aceh province. The epicenter was in the districts of Central Aceh and BenerMeriah. Thirty-nine people died and 420 were injured. In one area, the land was split up into two, creating a huge and long hole. Three villages were shattered and 3000 houses were destroyed.

I went to the site the next day with a photographer, when the aftershocks were still occurring. The National Disaster Management Body has set up an emergency office close to the offices of national and international voluntary, humanitarian organizations. As I worked busily to gather information from the site and these offices I realized that covering a big disaster by one or two journalists would not result in reliable information. The best approach is when news organizations employ at least three people. A team of four or five people dispatched to the site for disaster reporting can contribute to stable story coverage.

Why: because any disaster is a huge occurrence, involving many people, organizations, institutions that require information that covers a wide area. In disaster, everybody and concerned parties want to say things, want to be heard, want to get your attention.

Victims would say that they have not to get food, clothes and other relief items. Social organizations would say that they are conducting many activities that have helped victims. Corporations would report that they have donated money and other relief items, and the government officials will try to convince the journalist that everything is under control.

Amid these mass of information I am faced with a limitation of time because the situation demands that I should verify most of what I am being told. This is imperative because during this disaster every victim I interviewed conveyed the same story: they had not got assistance; or they did not get enough. Even unaffected people said to me that they lost many things with the purpose that they can now apply for international and national assistance.

The other reason why I recommend journalists to be work in teams is to be better able to meet the pressure to attend as many daily briefings by officials in the field. These events are important to gather official statistics and statements. But very often these press conferences go on till late night. Therefore, I missed the first-hand information about the refugee camps and from the voluntary organizations.

Working alone forced me to make a difficult selection for my coverage, including among my news sources. When it came to gathering information about the condition of victims, I chose to interview the refugee's leader, or village heads. While the information was mostly true and reliable, as a journalist I faced the obstacle of not being able to listen to diverse sectors of people who would be able to convey diverse viewpoints.

On the site, my reporting pattern was to talk to government disaster management organizations and local administration officials to gather information on disaster management. For my reports on the importance of prediction of the aftershocks or other quakes, I talked to climate, meteorology and geophysics organizations.

Given the fact that Indonesia is one of the most disaster-prone countries in the world, disasters are of important news value in the media. The sad fact, however, is that disasters make news only when it happens.

Former News editor Sunday Times, Sri Lanka; 2004 Asian tsunami disaster tragedy in a war zone

I am sharing with you my experience working for a foreign news company covering the massive Asian tsunami that devastated one-third of Sri Lanka's coasts on December 26 2004. Six days after the disaster, we crossed into less reported area in the northeast of Sri Lanka, an area that was facing a civil war. As we got closer to the town, we noticed a stench emanating from the town. The strong odor was unbearable and was from the corpses of victims that were still lying around. It was a disaster of unparalleled proportions, as almost the entire town had been wiped out. Everyone had been taken unawares by the tsunami. But the focus of our report was about the animals because we were told they had fled before the disaster. We saw hundreds of dogs running around the town because they were lost and looking for food. The story of animals escaping the tsunami is well known in Sri Lanka. When the earth rumbled from the massive earthquake that shook Indonesia, there were experts who reported the animals escaped to safety. Now they were back. The dogs were looking for their masters, who were all dead. This situation was one of our disaster stories, which was filed from the site.

The foreign media crew set up operations on the beach and by evening they were ready to transmit via satellite the coverage to the USA. The correspondent reported news on an hourly basis. We had to shut down power completely between broadcasts because we needed to conserve energy. Apart from the technology issues, the challenge of reporting a disaster for an international audience is that the viewer is sitting in a living room thousands of miles away. We have to reach an audience removed from the reality we faced. The basic rule was that people far away will not be able to understand the full extent of the tragedy. Therefore, sometimes a point needs to be overemphasized, and iconic examples were used, to depict a situation.

One such example was when a stray dog walked towards the foreign crew that was broadcasting live to the camera. The dog rubbed against the television anchor and he bent down to pet the animal and told his viewers the story of how these dogs had lost their masters. The dog was the commonality shared with the foreign audience and was a potent symbol to portray the tragedy of the tsunami.

Effective disaster reporting is to make people understand is to be able to relate the story through emotional content while also balancing the objectivity. Yet, it is also true that as the reporter becomes deeply embedded into the tragic surrounding, his own subjectivity makes him become deeply involved in the story.

Newsrooms have to understand these perspectives and need to give reporters on the ground, a chance to vent their emotions by allowing them a place in the story. In many cases, media, both domestic and foreign, have started a segment on their news, which gives space to the reporter to talk about what he felt about the situation and how he connected the story to his personal feelings. The assignment produces beautiful stories that are popular with the viewers.

I will add that when reporting a disaster, journalists have to make the rules. Yet at the same time journalists are aware that their reporting must be ethical—our reports have to contain facts and be balanced. Our goal is to capture a situation as it is and makes it relevant to the reader or viewer.

Former Tokyo Correspondent. Taiwan TV; March 11.2011. Great East Japan

The March 11, 2011 disaster emerged as a sudden shock. I was not prepared. The ordinary public can escape to save their lives. But journalists cannot do that. So my big lesson from the March 11, 2011 Great East Japan disaster is that journalists must be prepared better to act faster and be ready to minimize the stress they face during a disaster. To make this happen, the first step is that news organizations must be prepared by making plans to provide immediate food and transport for journalists who must report from the disaster sites, and part from providing physical support to them the news organizations but also prepare their journalists with the correct knowledge of that particular disaster. During the Fukushima nuclear plant disaster, the big lesson for me was that I was not prepared to report because I lacked in-depth nuclear information. We need access to science information before so we can write good reports.

At that time of the disaster, my office sent helmets, radiation check monitors, gasoline to the media team—2 Taiwanese journalists and a cameraman. But this was not enough. This disaster raised the risk of radiation contamination so going to the site means we face a dangerous situation. The bottom line is news media organizations are not prepared ahead for natural disasters.

During the triple disaster, my editors decided to follow the Fukushima nuclear plant meltdown. This is because Taiwanese readers who also depend on nuclear energy and reports from Japan will cater to this need. Overall the stories I filed from the disaster focused on the data and predictions on safety from the radiation contamination and also included reports to show our readers the response from the Japanese public to the dangerous situation. I took care to tell readers that the Japanese survivors were careful and serious and were following orders from disaster experts.

For my 1-year anniversary recovery story, I focused on environment protection as an important disaster mitigation measure. I quoted data compiled by experts to show the loss of the natural tree barricade in the area caused the tsunami to enter the area faster resulting in wider destruction. Huge amounts of aid and assistance were dispatched from Taiwan to the Japanese victims. Therefore monitoring the aid story is important for Taiwanese reporters. My stories on the way Taiwanese aid was spent by the affected people were popular. My story about Taiwanese assistance sent the message that Taiwan was returning generosity extended to us by Japanese public during disasters in our country.

Senior reporter. Daily Star, Bangladesh on major Fire in Dhaka

The deadliest disaster I covered was on February 21 2019. The fire occurred in the crowded Chawkbazar, the older part of the city, and killed 71 people. It was a national holiday. I got the news at night and rushed to the site around 12:30 am. But I could not reach close to the fire area because the firefighters blocked the road and stopped the reporters.

I saw the fire had turned the whole sky reddish. In my haste to tell the news I remembered a very important aspect for journalists reporting disaster. In a training program for the media organized by Japanese NGO, SEEDS Asia, we discussed the issue of safety of journalists that must always be the first priority for the reporter. Most often we are overwhelmed to report the facts of the disaster quickly to satisfy the reader and our stories have to be available as quickly. Updates are essential and must be sent repeatedly. At the same time, the journalist must take precautions to save his own life and this means that journalists too must be knowledgeable about disasters and how to protect themselves.

How I covered the fire: I first took a number of photos from the spot and sent it to the office through WhatsApp so that the office can update on its website. I sent reports about people screaming for help and also the firefighters working hard to provide a stable water supply. As the disaster site was located in a narrow area, there was a shortage of water supply. I saw a number of people came forward to provide water to help to stop the fire. They opened their water pumps to supply water. I took some pictures and dropped the story in our office.

Old Dhaka is also known as a hub for stocking counterfeit perfume products, including scent and deodorant that is inflammable. Numerous warehouses have been set up to store counterfeit products. Storehouses are built in some almost unreachable and undetectable rooms and buildings, meaning these are inaccessible to firefighters. The area became slippery due to the tons of water and I struggled to walk safely in the area. I had to find my way among the huge crowd of hundreds of reporters and photographer sas all pushed alongside each other to cover the event.

I reported the firefighters had become tired of spraying water over so many hours— the fire came under control at 4:30 am. The firefighters were exhausted. They just lay down on the floor, unbuttoning their uniforms and taking off their boots. They were asking for water and food. I reported it was a terrible situation. When the fire came under control, I went to the disaster site and found there was nothing but ashes and some plastic waste. I saw some bodies but the authorities were finding it difficult to identify them. I was exhausted myself but it now time to file the longer stories. These were the scenes I witnessed and communicated in my disaster reporting.

Contributor, Dawn Newspaper, Pakistan on Kashmir earthquake

The October 8, 2005 earthquake was one of Pakistan's biggest disasters. The epicenter of the 7.6 earthquake that struck the Himalayan region of northern Pakistan and Kashmir was located approximately 9 km northeast of the city of Muzaffarabad, capital city of the Pakistani-administered Kashmir also known as Azad Jammu Kashmir (AJK). The official death toll as of November 2005 stood at 87,350, an approximately 38,000 were injured and over 3.5 million were rendered homeless.

Since I could not visit the disaster site immediately I collected information from sources in Karachi. I also talked on the phone to people on the site and involved in rescue operations. The purpose of my disaster reporting was to give the tragedy a human face. For a journalist, the human story can be cathartic as it is my contribution to make the world understand the situation. I also pledged that part of the money I earned from my reporting will be donated to the needy.

The earthquake happened at the time when private channels had just started their broadcast with almost all major media houses and newspaper owners establishing their own TV stations. With competition heating, this was also the first time that Pakistani journalists learnt about the ethics of humanitarian reporting. A major lesson was that we should refrain from capturing on screen the shots of people grieving over their loss, the dead and also those in physical pain due to bad injuries.

A month later, I visited the devastated area, this time focusing on the humanitarian side of recovery. I had to walk in the cold and face the regular tremors and rats while sleeping in tents. I reported about the necessities not available for the survivors. I also reported in 2009. At that time, the media was banned because the Pakistan army launched an operation to seed out the militants belonging to the Tehrik-e-Taliban Pakistan (TTP). I covered the topics of displacement focusing on the impact on women who were also badly affected by the military conflict. My contacts in the military and among the militants were very valuable for my reporting.

Reporter on March 11, 2011 Great East Japan Disaster—3-month anniversary story

I focused on gender issues in disaster for my 3-month anniversary story to mark the massive March 11, 2011 triple disaster—earthquake, tsunami and nuclear plant blast—that ravaged the north east parts of Japan. The theme was unique among the many anniversary stories filed by the male-dominated Japanese media. I wanted to take a different angle by highlighting the efforts and courage of female survivors, a sector that faces marginalization and stereo-typing in mainstream. The gender subject is also relatively new in disaster management and is a focus point in ongoing research. Turning the spotlight on their stories in Tohoku conservative society was about flushing out new angles and new thoughts from the affected women. Breaking new ground is a key goal in journalism. An anniversary story that focuses on recovery is aimed at readers who are looking for hope after the shock and sadness that was caused by the tragedy. Readers are eager to help and the journalist's job, in this context, is to cater to these needs by providing interesting stories.

My gender story highlighted the traumas caused by the disaster impact on women—how they coped with physical destruction and deaths in their families. But it did not stop there. By spending many weeks with large groups of survivors, I also reported about their activities that contributed to the recovery of their homes and neighborhoods. Their role as grandmothers, mothers, single women and widows placed them in the position of caring for their families, especially young children and the elderly. They cooked and cleaned in the evacuation centers and organized themselves into groups to make sure the work was shared to ease the burden on women. At the same time, they had got together to lobby the authorities to pay attention to the specific needs of women survivors such as providing privacy in shelters and access to goods that catered to their personal needs. In one story, I followed a woman who was appointed as a public spokesperson, a major feat in Tohoku where social norms accept that men speak on behalf of their community. In Fukushima, which was ravaged by the nuclear plant explosion, I focused on women who emerged as leaders in the new anti-nuclear energy movement that was rocking the country. My stories conveyed that disaster recovery cannot be achieved without listening to the voices of women and making them partners at the national and local disaster management authorities.

7.3 Postscripts

The importance of the local media gained attention in the reporting experience during of the Great East Japan March 11, 2011 triple disaster—earthquake, tsunami and the Fukushima nuclear plant meltdown. The lives of hundreds of thousands of people's living in the disaster sites and beyond were disrupted. Research indicates while big media such as Nippon HosoKyokai and major newspapers had larger staff and carried wider coverage, the mainstream news sided with official information released from government and Tokyo Electric Power Company that operated the damaged nuclear power plant. In comparison, local media, radio and newspapers gained popularity as a source of information for the community because the information was aimed at the local post-disaster needs and recovery efforts.

Referred to the "Age of the Extreme Weather," the topic of disasters has become an important beat in mainstream reporting. But research also indicates that natural disaster reporting is linked to extreme weather stories that are in turn reported under the topic of global warming. The trend has raised its profile in the news mostly related to the international spotlight on Climate Change with its focus on the impact on national and local economic development. Disaster coverage topics, when not during a major tragedy, are therefore heavily based on the release of new scientific data, binding regulations and other newsworthy information. Reporting specifically on the impact of hazards is restricted to its short-term impact describing a media situation where the implementation of capacity building measure remains crucial (DRRAJ 2016).

References

Alexander D (2002) Principles of emergency planning and management. Oxford University Press, UK, 340 pages
DRRAJ (2016) Media Capacity building and disaster risk reduction: building resilience and protecting socio-economic development gains in southeast Asia. International Development Australian Broadcasting Corporation, Australia, 33 pages
Haddow G, Haddow K (2014) Disaster communication in a changing media world. Elsevier publication, Netherland, 282 pages
NHK (2013) Public opinion survey on "Disaster Prevention and Energy" conducted three years after the Great East Japan Earthquake. https://www.nhk.or.jp/bunken/english/reports/summary/201404/01.html. Accessed 14 July 2020
Pantii M (2018) Crisis and disaster coverage. https://onlinelibrary.wiley.com/doi/full/https://doi.org/10.1002/9781118841570.iejs0202. Accessed 13 July 2020
Sterling C (2009) Encyclopedia of journalism. Sage publishing, UK, 3136 pages

Chapter 8
Re-instating Sustainability of Community Radio Operations in Disaster Management—Lessons from Indonesia and Haiti

Vibhas Sukhwani, Adnan Fabyandi, Sri Purwanti, and Rajib Shaw

Abstract Being governed and managed by the local people, community radios effectively serve for addressing local concerns in local language and cultural context. However, their sustainable operations during disaster situations are often interrupted due to technical issues like power blackouts, limited frequency range, etc. While contemporary research is focused on overcoming the social, financial and institutional challenges to community radio operations, this chapter mainly deliberates on overcoming the technological challenges. In that regard, digital technologies like mobile phones and internet are presenting newer means of information sharing that complement the community radio operations, helping cover a wider audience from within and beyond their geographical frequency range. The chapter discusses two selected case study examples of Jalin Merapi (Indonesia) and Signal FM (Haiti) based on literature review. Notably, the community radio operations in both cases were restrained during disaster situations, however, the integration of digital technologies enhanced their effectiveness in disaster communication. The study derives key lessons from the selected cases and suggests feasible strategies for integrating digital technologies with community radio operations. To enhance the sustainability of community radio operations in long term, the study emphasizes on enhancing community engagement and raising digital awareness.

Keywords Community radio operations · Digital technologies · Disaster management · Disaster communication · Information sharing

8.1 Introduction

Natural disasters are unpreventable events that are increasingly posing grave threats to human societies (Tipson 2013). Their growing frequency and intensity in recent years have raised serious concerns at global level, particularly for those living in high-risk areas (CRED 2015). In reference to Mathbor (2007), communities with

V. Sukhwani (✉) · A. Fabyandi · S. Purwanti · R. Shaw
Graduate School of Media and Governance, Keio University, Fujisawa, Japan
e-mail: vibhas@sfc.keio.ac.jp

© Springer Nature Singapore Pte Ltd. 2021   125
R. Shaw et al. (eds.), *Media and Disaster Risk Reduction*, Disaster Risk Reduction,
https://doi.org/10.1007/978-981-16-0285-6_8

limited resources like those in rural areas suffer the worst effects of disasters. The timely flow of accurate information (verbal, non-verbal or written) therefore plays a fundamental role in suitably responding to emergent disasters at local level. Several studies (Tanesia 2007; PAHO 2009; Wall and Robinson 2012; Tasic and Amir 2016) have pointed out that 'communication' aspect plays a fundamental role in disaster management. In that context, broadcasting media like radio, television, newspapers, electronic media, etc. play a channelling role between key actors like disaster victims, local governments, humanitarian organizations, donors, etc. (Dave 2001).

Different forms of media-based communications educate and empower people to take precautionary measures against natural hazards (Cate 1994). Of the various forms, there are 'Traditional media' (like radio and television) and 'Digital media' (like the Internet and social media). Reilly and Atanasova (2016) defined traditional media as those forms that were introduced before the advent of internet. On the other hand, digital media are referred to those forms that are encoded in a machine-readable format and can be created, viewed, distributed, modified and preserved on computers. According to Beena and Mathur (2012), 'digital technologies' refer to all the electronic tools, systems, devices and resources that generate store or process data. They include social media, mobile devices, online games and applications, programming tools, etc. In reference to the above definitions, the authors have used the term 'digital technologies' in this chapter to relate to all forms of digital media and technologies.

In disaster situations, information is often shared through a wide range of sources that serve different interests and needs. Among all other forms, radio as a traditional mass media is highly recognized for its immediacy and its wide outreach to community and national audiences, including the poor and illiterate population (Howley 2005; PAHO 2009; Tucker 2013). The news and information provided through radio broadcasting could be heard by large audiences, however, it has been found that the mainstream media does not always provide locally relevant information (Gultom 2016; Guo 2017). Resultantly, community radios are preferred by local communities as a reliable and trustworthy source of information. According to UNESCO (2015), community radios represent a third form of radio broadcasting in addition to commercial and public broadcasting. It is controlled by a geographic community or a community of identity or interest. Being governed and managed by local communities, community radios effectively serve for community empowerment at local level. However, their sustainable operations are often challenged by legal, financial, technical and human resource-related factors (Mendel 2013, cited in UNESCO 2015).

While sustainability of community radio operations is increasingly becoming a challenge, digital technologies have recently opened new spaces and possibilities of radio programming that go beyond the geographical boundaries to embrace translocal and diasporic communities (Buckley 2011; Chiumbu 2014). Radio stations today are increasingly using mobile phones and internet to connect with their audiences from local to global level (PAHO 2009). However, the existing research on community radio operations is mostly based on defined territories and geographical frequency range. Chiumbu (2014) underlined that the contemporary research on integrating digital technologies with radio operations is focussed on commercial and public broadcasting, and limited research is done on community level broadcasting. Also, the current research lays more emphasis on social, financial and institutional challenges to community radio operations and limited work has been done on technical issues like limited frequency range, hefty equipment, power blackouts, etc.

To bridge the identified research gaps, this chapter draws insights from two selected case study examples of Jalin Merapi, Indonesia and Signal FM, Haiti. Both the cases were selected based on three key considerations: (1) Employed in a disaster situation, (2) Had pre-existing mass audiences who trusted their content, (3) Integrated their operations with digital technologies. It is important to note that unlike the case of Jalin Merapi in Indonesia, Signal FM (Haiti) is not directly related to community radio operations. However, it is based on a disaster situation wherein all the community radio operations were knocked off. Both the case study examples showcase how radio operations combined with digital technologies helped in enhanced information sharing. The authors acknowledge that several other community radio stations around the world have employed digital technologies in disaster situations. However, to the author's knowledge, they were mostly established after the disaster had occurred. That said, this research mainly intends to assess how these established radio stations addressed the information sharing during a disaster situation by utilizing the digital technologies and to identify the key shortcomings. It is also important to highlight at the outset that the two selected cases are completely different, and the community contexts are also varying. Thus, the lessons learnt from both the cases individually may or may not be applicable to other cases.

The remaining part of the chapter is structured as follows: Sect. 8.2 explains the key aspects of 'community radios' and their historical development. It emphasizes on rethinking the 'community' aspect beyond the geographic boundaries. Section 8.3 explains the different roles of community radios in disaster management followed by the key sustainability challenges to their continued operations in Sect. 8.4. Section 8.5 presents a methodical overview of two case study examples from Indonesia and Haiti, with the objective of extracting key lessons about integrating digital technologies with community radio operations. Section 8.6 then discusses the key findings from the chapter and Sect. 8.7 provides some conclusions about enhancing the sustainability of the community radio operations in the digital era. The key limitations and directions for future research are discussed at the end.

8.2 Understanding 'Community Radios' and the 'Community'

Radio broadcasting is generally referred to as the unidirectional wireless transmission over radio waves that are intended to reach a wide audience (Deitz 2018). However, the idea of community radio is primarily intended for disseminating information to a narrow audience which relates with the term 'narrowcasting'. Narrowcasting applies to the spread of information to a limited audience which is by nature geographically limited (Goncalves et al. 2013). Hibino and Shaw (2014a) explained that a community radio station generally has a low output frequency and they cover a relatively small area. Typically, their frequency range is limited to 10–15 km, which varies in different countries (CRFC 2018). Further, majority of the community radio stations broadcast on FM (frequency modulation) transmitters as compared to AM (amplitude modulation), due to their multi-faceted benefits like less power requirement, better signal quality, cost-effectiveness and smaller associated hardware (Hallett and Hintz 2010; Ideta et al. 2012).

To date, several studies have investigated about the historical development of community radios (da Costa 2012; Ideta et al. 2012; Hibino and Shaw 2014a; Khan et al. 2017; Shahzalal and Hassan 2019). Together these studies pointed that community radios first emerged in 1947, when two community radio stations were established in Latin America in the backdrop of poverty and social injustice. Since then, the number of community radio stations has increased to thousands throughout the world. Ideta et al. (2012) summarized that community radios have historically been recognized with different names in different countries like Popular or Educational radio (Latin America), Rural or Bush radio (Africa), Public radio (Australia), low-power FM (United States), community FM (Japan), Free or Association Radio (Europe), etc. However, 'Community Radio' is the common term used by International Institutions like UNESCO, the United Nations Development Program, the World Bank, and the International Telecommunications Union.

The World Association of Community Radio Broadcasters 'AMARC', started in 1983, now covers more than 3,000 community radios, federations and media stakeholders in more than 110 countries (AMARC 2007). AMARC defines a community radio station under the three following conditions: (1) is a non-profit organization, (2) is owned and managed by the community, and (3) is independent of politics and commercialism (Hibino and Shaw 2014a). Its central tenet is to encourage the local communities to own, control and manage their own means of media to disseminate information in consideration to different community groups such as ethnic or minority groups (Berrigan 1979). Shahzalal and Hassan (2019) underlined that community radios mainly serve the rural, disadvantaged, vulnerable and hard to reach populations in their local languages and cultural context, by mainstreaming local problems and concerns.

While commercial radio is driven by the need to generate profits, community radios have a mission to serve geographic communities and communities of interest on a non-profit basis (UNESCO 2015). In relation to 'community radio', the word 'community' has usually been referred to geographical communities (people living in defined geographical area like hamlet, village, etc.) or communities of interests (people with common interests not necessarily living in defined geographical area) (Ideta et al. 2012; Khan et al. 2017). Wellman (2001) pointed that the latter being groups of people with common interests, the understanding of word 'community' becomes very complexed. Guo (2017) also theorized that there could be three types of local and translocal communities based on geography, interest and identity. With the growing body of literature on community radios, the study finds that more emphasis is now been placed on redefining the meaning of communities, so as to engage a wider audience including the community members, volunteers, diaspora community member, etc. in contributing the content and viewpoints for community development.

8.3 Role of Community Radio in Disaster Management

Referring to Waxman (1973), it is evident that the radio stations and broadcasting in disaster management have for long been in practice. Over the years, community radio has become a vital communication platform for local communities in every phase of a disaster management namely mitigation, preparedness, response, recovery and rehabilitation (Hibino and Shaw 2014a). A number of authors (Birowo 2010; Kanayama 2012; Ewart and Dekker 2013) have reported that community radios provide detailed and timely information that assist in disaster management at local level. Shaw et al. (2012) summarized four key goals of community radios in disaster management as: (1) circulate important information during disaster situations, (2) provide relief and support related information of local governments and NGOs, (3) provide recovery-related information and promote the exchange of residents' opinions, and (4) contribute to mental and physical health of disaster victims. To achieve these goals, community radio stations play specified roles through on-air and off-air modes. The on-air activities of community radio correspond with the broadcast programs like for providing information or healing mental trauma while the off–air activities entail mutual support events, workshops and recovery activities for disaster victims.

   Hibino (Personal communication, July 7, 2018) theorized that, in today's context, digital technologies have enhanced the role of community radios to on-line activities as well. Mobile phones and internet have expanded the outreach of community radios and have transformed the nature of audience engagement in disaster situations. The potential of digital technologies in community radio operations has been realized in several occasions like during Tohoku Earthquake in Japan (Kanayama 2012; Umihara and Nishikitani 2013), Haiti Earthquake (Nelson et al. 2011) and Merapi Eruption in Indonesia (Gultom 2015). Accordingly, the three specified 'On's': On-Air, On-Land (Off-Air) and On-Line need to be coordinated simultaneously in order to effectively harness the potential of community radios in disaster management. The key functions of community radio in reference to the three 'On's' are discussed below:

1. On-Air Activities: The On-air activities of community radios entail circulating educational information, disaster-related news, entertainment programs etc. for the local communities. The on-air programs broadcasted by community radio majorly aim for: (1) Providing locally relevant information, (2) Community participation, (3) Healing mental trauma and (4) Monitoring activities (Hibino and Shaw 2014b). During disaster situations, the community radio broadcasts necessary information like early warning, evacuation advisory, recovery status etc. The on-air activities of community radio provide a communication medium

to the affected communities wherein disaster victims are encouraged to express their feelings through the radio. In that way, it helps the disaster victims to connect with each other and ensure collective recovery.

2. On-Land or Off-Air Activities: Community radio stations also play a significant role off the air by connecting community members within and outside of the broadcasting area. In the post-disaster phase, they serve as a channel for enhancing community awareness by means of workshops and training programs. As Zane Ibrahim (founder of Bush Radio), known as the father of South African community radio underlined that 'community radio is made up of 90 percent community, 10 percent radio', that is the community radio uses the radio for community creation (Hollon 2006). The community radio stations also have the function of encouraging disaster victims to engage in community-based activities wherein they hold memorial events, discussion meetings for recovery events etc.

3. On-line Activities: The on-line activities of community radio relate to the utilization of digital technologies for information sharing. Digital technologies like mobile and internet facilitate for the faster flow of information during emergency situations compared to other traditional means like newspaper or television. Platforms like social media, mobile applications or even internet radio broadcasting have demonstrated extreme potential in disseminating information faster and with a wider coverage. With increasing penetration of technology in human societies, social media platforms like Facebook and Twitter have become an integral part of human societies. The global outreach and instant processing of real-time information in these platforms are giving additional lead time to the affected communities for necessary response actions. Many community radios today are coordinating with the local communities through websites and social media groups. Digital technologies have also enhanced the abilities of community radio stations in terms of information exchange, networking, joint reporting etc. (Chiumbu and Ligaga 2013; Hashimoto and Ohama 2014; Shah and Nawaz 2015).

8.4 Sustainability Challenges to Community Radio Operations

Siemering and Fairbairn (2007) explained that 'sustainability' of community radio refers to the ability of any radio station to maintain good quality broadcasting service over a period of time. It could also be understood as the capacity of radio station to manage available resources (like ideas, skills, labour, donations etc.) to sustain its service without compromising its key principles (Fairbairn 2000, cited in Tavhiso 2009). Based on the existing scientific literature (Lush and Urgoiti 2012; Farren et al. 2014; Arora et al. 2015), sustainability of community radio operations could broadly be discussed under three dimensions that were first defined by Gumucio Dagron (2001) as below:

1. Social Sustainability: It refers to the community ownership of community radio stations, and their active participation in the production and airing of programmes at both decision-making and operational levels.
2. Institutional Sustainability: It refers to the ways in which broadcaster's function; station policies, democratic processes, management styles, internal relationships and practices, and partnerships with external agencies.
3. Financial Sustainability: It is mainly related to the broadcaster's finances, its income-generating potential, and how money is used and accounted for.

A number of researchers (Sullivan 2007; Gondwe and Mavindidze 2014) have pointed that community radios are also faced with wide-ranging technical challenges for their sustainable operations. Technical issues like poor backup systems, inadequately trained staff, power black outs, equipment failure etc. often cause the community radio stations to go off-air for long periods of time. However, the study finds that they are not well recognized in the definition of sustainability. AMARC (2007) highlighted that 'financial and technological' sustainability continues to be a pertinent challenge that restricts the improvement in radio broadcasting, community engagement and appropriate programming. Gondwe and Mavindidze (2014) further underlined that emerging digital technologies are outpacing the transmission capacities of community radios and there is negative implication on listenership among communities. In view of that, the authors theorize that 'Technological sustainability' has today become an important factor in community radio operations. The numerous media platforms, the need for real-time and two-way coordination in disaster situations, the lack of training, limited coverage etc. are some of the key factors concerning the sustainability of community radio operations. Figure 8.1 highlights various challenges in all four dimensions of sustainability as discussed.

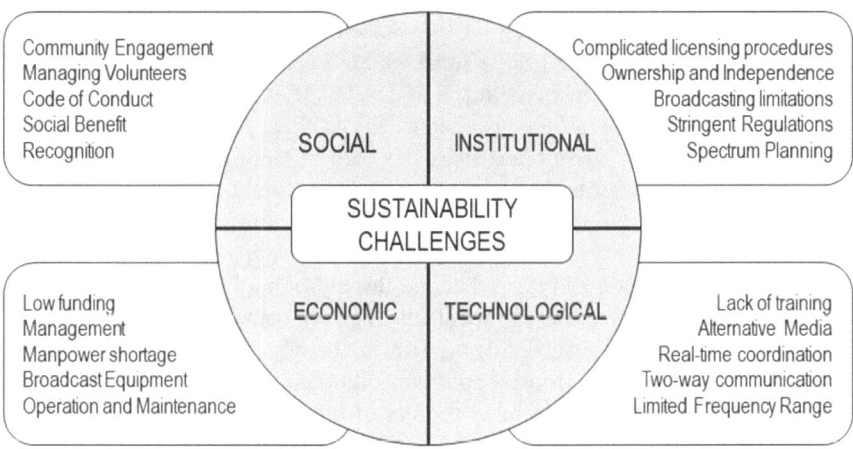

Fig. 8.1 Sustainability challenges for community radio operations (*Image Source* Author)

8.4.1   Impact of Digital Technologies on Radio Operations

In recent years, several studies have discussed the changing nature of community radio operations (Chiumbu and Ligaga 2013; Chiumbu 2014; Hibino and Shaw 2014b). It is evident that digital technologies like mobile phones, computers etc. are gradually transforming the traditional form of radio operations (Shah and Nawaz 2015). More and more community radios are now using Internet and social media platforms to distribute their content and interact with the audience (Myers 2011; Chiumbu and Ligaga 2013). While the limited frequency range of community radios has for long confined their audiences to a specified territory, digital technologies by means of internet are helping them to easily connect with wider audiences beyond their frequency range and also ensure greater listener participation from remote places. EBU (2011) stressed that increasing number of people are listening to radio on their computers and mobile phones. Subsequently, radio broadcasters today are increasingly streaming content over the internet and experimenting with newer formats of information communication such as podcasts and video (Freeman et al. 2012; Cookson 2013). Internet is also helping radio stations to connect with diasporic communities and keeping cultural traditions alive while raising support for development projects back in the home community (Chiumbu 2014). Through the Internet, it has become possible for people outside the disaster-hit areas to access community radio programs and get to know detailed information that the mainstream media cannot provide (Hibino and Shaw 2014b).

8.5   Case Study Examples

This section presents an overview of two selected case study examples of Jalin Merapi (Indonesia) and Signal FM (Haiti) wherein the digital technologies played a strategic role in enhancing the outreach of community radio operations in disaster situations. While the case of Indonesia represents an excellent case of media convergence with community radio operations, the case of Haiti underlines the tactical role played by digital technologies at the time when majority of the community radios was knocked off during a disaster event. It is important to note that all the community radio stations in Haiti had gone off air during the disaster situation, however, the information sharing was done through innovative solutions utilizing digital technologies. The study, without making any comparison, explicates how the selected case study examples demonstrated the effective utilization of digital technologies for enhancing disaster communication at grassroot level. The authors methodically discuss the vulnerability profiles of Indonesia and Haiti, the impact of concerned disasters on local communities and the response of selected radio stations in conjunction with digital technologies. Towards the end, the key shortcomings in both cases have been underlined. Table 8.1 below highlights the key features of both the selected case study examples.

Table 8.1 Key features of two selected case study examples (Compiled by Author)

Case study	Jalin Merapi (Indonesia)	Signal FM (Haiti)
Disaster context	Merapi volcano eruption, 2010	7.3 magnitude earthquake, 2010
Key characteristics	Cross-platform strategy to share information and community-based information network	Nationwide operationalization of numerous digital technologies
Digital technologies used	Radio, Website, telephone, SMS, Closed Circuit Television, Facebook, Twitter, Blackberry Messenger, Yahoo Messenger, E-mail, shout box, Google docs and Google maps	Radio, SMS, Interactive online maps, radio-cell phone hybrids, Blogs, Twitter, Facebook, web-based tools like Ushaidi, Open Street Map etc.
Key points	(a) Coordinated network of radio stations (b) Strong volunteer network (c) Cross-validation of information	(a) Application of crowdsourcing technique (b) Strong connect at international level (c) Enhanced disaster reporting
Key concerns	(a) Fake Information (b) Technical and financial constraints (c) Long-term community engagement	(a) Validating crowdsourced information (b) Collapsed communication infrastructure (c) Limited community radio stations

8.5.1 Case of Jalin Merapi, Indonesia

8.5.1.1 Disaster Profile of Indonesia and Impact of Merapi Volcano, 2010

Indonesia is highly prone to natural disasters due to its location in a tropical region along the Pacific Ring of Fire, sandwiched between three continental plates. It is vulnerable to a variety of disasters including earthquakes, tsunamis, volcanic eruptions, floods, landslides, droughts and cyclones (Birowo 2010). The 2010 Merapi volcano eruption was one of the biggest natural disasters in Indonesia that caused 353 casualties and affected around 1,335,885 residents (Mei et al. 2011). Although Mount Merapi, located in the north of Jogjakarta Special Region, is an active volcano, the 2010 eruption was the largest since the 1870s (Sumaryono 2011). It posed serious threat to residents of 42 villages in 9 sub-districts along the slopes of volcano (Hibino and Shaw 2014a).

8.5.1.2   Jalin Merapi Network 'JMN' and Its Role During 2010 Merapi Eruption

JMN (Jaringan Informasi Lingkar Merapi), a community-based information network, was established in the Merapi circle following the Bantul earthquake in 2006 that killed around 5,000 people and also caused Merapi eruption. JMN was primarily initiated by three community radio stations that were located around the volcano namely Lintas Merapi FM Community Radio, Radio MMC FM and Radio K FM, two community radio networks, and four local NGOs (Saputro 2014, 2016; Tasic and Amir 2016). Since the 2010 earthquake was bigger than the previous ones, two other radio stations namely Gema Merapi FM and Lahara FM were engaged in JMN to connect the districts around the volcano and ensure a circular coordination (Gultom and Joyce 2014).

   To enhance the restricted coverage of community radio stations around the volcano, JMN developed a cross-platform strategy to produce and disseminate information during the 2010 Merapi eruption (Gultom 2015). After the 2006 eruption, JMN had been using communication tools such as radio, website, Yahoo Messenger, Shoutbox, live audio streaming and SMS gateway. However, it expanded its outreach in 2010 by engaging social media platforms, like Facebook and Twitter, to cover a wider audience. Thus, it became a media convergence that utilized a combination of around 14 traditional and newer digital technologies. The main intention behind using so many communication tools was to accommodate the varying media preferences of the target community. COMBINE Resource Institution (COMBINE), a local NGO in Jogjakarta, developed a community-based information system through which it could write down all the information received through walkie-talkies and other means, and then later post it on the website of Jalin Merapi. Additionally, JMN opened a specific channel for aid distribution, through which donors could access the verified information about the evacuees. Hibino and Shaw (2014a) pointed that cross-posting was performed to provide necessary information to communities through all forms of media. By employing digital technologies for information dissemination, JMN provided fast and accurate information to a wider group of local communities and enhanced the disaster response.

   While the mainstream media and the local government were unable to function effectively during the 2010 eruption (Wall and Robinson 2012; OCHA 2013), the success of JMN was mainly due to the media convergence and a well-organized participation of volunteers. Birowo (2012) underlined that during the emergency response phase in November 2010, JMN coordinated with more than 3,000 volunteers, which were primarily from affected areas (Saputro 2014). The integrated model of information sharing by JMN was also supported by government agencies like Badan Meteorologi dan Geofisika/BMKG that is responsible for meteorology, climatology and geophysics in Indonesia. Moreover, JMN helped to connect various factors including disaster victims, donors, government, mainstream media and volunteers, and enabled the effective distribution of aid from donors to disaster victims (Birowo 2010; Tanesia and Habibi 2011; Tasic and Amir 2016).

8.5.1.3 Key Challenges

(a) Fake information: JMN applied a methodical way to validate fake information through different means including public verification, through volunteers and through professional editors, although the process took a long time. Therefore, it has been pointed that the information published (especially for aid distribution) on Jalin Merapi website may not have represented the real-time situation (Gultom and Joyce 2014; Gultom 2015).

(b) Technical and financial constraints: JMN experienced technical and financial challenges pertaining to receiving international amount transfers and information sharing through numerous platforms (Tasic and Amir 2016).

(c) Community engagement in long term: The number of volunteers gradually reduced after the situation became normal and the financial support was limited (Saputro 2014).

8.5.2 Case of Signal FM, Haiti

8.5.2.1 Disaster Profile of Haiti and Impact of Haiti Earthquake, 2010

Haiti is one of the most vulnerable countries in the world that is prone to hurricanes, floods, earthquakes, landslides and droughts (GFDRR 2019). The country has been repeatedly flattened with major earthquakes causing extreme damage to life and property. The violent 7.3 magnitude earthquake that struck the impoverished country of Haiti on January 12, 2010 caused nearly 8 billion dollar worth of damage (Bailey 2014) and 230,000 deaths (Heinzelman and Waters 2010).

Radio has invariably been the most dominant medium of information dissemination in Haiti due to its low cost, its penetration potential and emphasis on spoken language (Gomes and de Castro Oliveira 2015). At the time of 2010 earthquake, Haiti had around 375 radio stations, which were dominated by commercial and public media. It included 40 community radio stations (Infoasaid 2012) with low production standards, limited funding, and high volunteer-staff turnover (Regan 2008). Several studies (Nelson et al. 2011; Regan 2014) pointed that most of these radio stations were knocked off by the 2010 earthquake.

8.5.2.2 Signal FM and Its Role During 2010 Haiti Earthquake

Signal FM is a popular Haitian radio station located in the Port-au-Prince, which provides news updates and other information. While the massive 2010 earthquake disrupted the communication infrastructure around the country, Signal FM was the only radio station that managed to continue broadcasting to an audience of around 3 million around Port-au-Prince. While other radio stations struggled due to the collapsed infrastructure and power blackouts, signal FM turned into a community bulletin board. It helped in ensuring effective disaster response that included locating missing people, search and rescue operations, spreading news like for food, water and hospital information to Haitians across Port-au-Prince. It also helped in connecting to the diaspora population due to its global outreach through the internet (Philips 2010; Burnett 2010; Nelson et al. 2011). Surveys following the earthquake found that radio was the most effective source of information for the affected population (University of Michigan and Small Arms Survey 2010). Due to their broadcasting in native language, the radio stations played a vital communication role for rural population, wherein 80% of the homes are said to contain radios (Coz 2010; Waits 2010).

Nelson et al. (2011) emphasized that the coverage of radio operations was scaled up to a wider audience as it complemented other of forms of digital media such as text messaging and social networking. While most of the radio stations were down, Haiti's cell phone networks were quick to recover (Large 2010). Mobile phones thereafter became a direct means of communication as they were accessible to around 85% of Haitian households during the earthquake (Heinzelman and Waters 2010). Mobile phones amplified the radio operations as SMS text alerts were used for directing the injured disaster victims to hospitals and for search and rescue operations. Apart from receiving critical news and information, Haitians were also able to send free text messages into the system (Myers 2011). The aftermath of Haitan Earthquake therefore witnessed a stream of on-ground information that helped aid groups in providing emergency assistance to the affected communities.

The 2010 Haiti Earthquake marked the emergence of new approaches to connect disaster victims and relief workers such as crowdsourcing, that combined the abilities of mobile phones and radio operations. Many different web-based tools (like Ushaihidi, CrisisMappers and Open Street Map) were applied to generate information from the ground via text messages, emails and other social media platforms like blogs, Twitter and Facebook (Rencoret et al. 2010; Nelson et al. 2011). Ushaihidi, an open-source crisis-mapping platform, encouraged new forms of collaboration, wherein the diaspora population and other volunteers from around the world contributed in mapping, translating, and processing work (Heinzelman and Waters 2010; Wall 2011). The crowdsourced information from the affected population was displayed on web-based interactive map of Ushaihidi, which significantly helped the humanitarian agencies to access information about the damage, needs, locations, and road and security conditions.

8.5.2.3 Key Challenges

(a) *Validating information*: Verifying the accuracy of crowdsourced information on ground was a huge challenge during the 2010 Haiti earthquake. Heinzelman and Waters (2010) pointed that only 202 of more than 3500 messages published on Ushahidi-Haiti crisis map were verified.

(b) *Collapsed Communication Infrastructure*: Majority of the radio stations were knocked off air for a long time and the internet service was widely disrupted (Nelson et al. 2011).

(c) *Commercially Dominated Radio Stations*: Although radio is the fundamental means of information in Haiti, the number of community radio stations is highly limited (Infoasaid 2012; Gomes and de Castro Oliveira 2015; Koenig et al. 2015).

8.6 Integrating Digital Technologies with Community Radio Operations

The importance of integrating digital technologies with community radio operations has been highlighted through both the selected case study examples of Indonesia and Haiti. The case studies revealed how digital technologies unleash innovative platforms that enable new forms of communication between the community radio stations, disaster victims and also donor organizations. Digital technologies also enable the community radio stations to connect with volunteers and diaspora community members, opening new doors for addressing the issues of manpower shortage and limited frequency. In case of Haiti, the innovative usage of digital technologies enhanced the coverage of radio operations to global level, as International volunteers and humanitarian agencies were able to engage via Internet. On the other hand, the media convergence in Indonesia helped in directly connecting the donor organizations with disaster victims. In both cases, digital technologies served for improved local communication and helped in scaling up the radio coverage at regional, national and international levels.

Through this study, it has been realized that community radios continue to serve for effective disaster communication at local level. This is mainly because it provides locally relevant information in consideration with the local languages and cultural context. However, the sustainability of community radio operations in disaster situations has become a huge challenge, as they are faced with financial, technical and human resource-related issues. Against the growing frequency and intensity of natural disasters, it has also become highly important to gain external support and mobilize funds for disaster recovery and rehabilitation (conceptual explanation shown in Fig. 8.2), especially in disaster-prone countries like Indonesia and Haiti. In that regard, digital technologies are helping to revolutionize the community radio operations by enhancing both horizontal and vertical communication with a range of actors including the diaspora communities, donor organizations, volunteers, local governments, disaster victims, humanitarian organizations, etc. While community radio operations are presently focused on serving the geographic communities, digital technologies are helping to accommodate the concerns of diaspora communities of identity or interest.

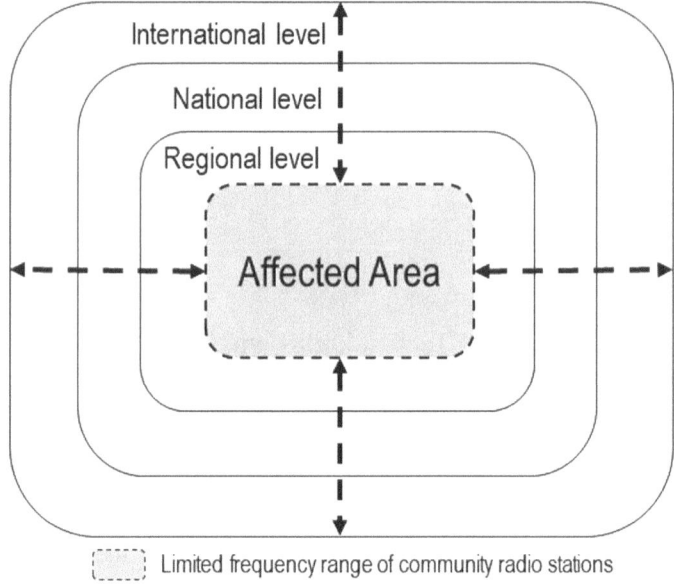

Fig. 8.2 Highlighting the limited outreach of community radios in disaster situations

In case of Jalin Merapi (Indonesia) and Signal FM (Haiti), the radio operations were successfully integrated with digital technologies. However, they were also faced with a variety of case-specific challenges as discussed in Sect. 8.5. Drawing on the lessons learnt from the two case study examples as well as literature review, the chapter recommends three key strategies that need to be considered for easing the technology integration with community radio operations, particularly for enhancing disaster management.

8.6.1 Connecting Traditional and Digital Media

Myers (2011) pointed that digital media will continue to pose a critical threat to sustainable operations of traditional media, like community radio, unless they find a way to converge with it. Based on the two case study examples of Indonesia and Haiti, it has been realized that disaster communication with actors beyond the geographical boundaries of community is equally important to that of local communication. Therefore, to enhance the sustainability of community radio operations in long term, digital technologies need to be feasibly integrated with the functioning of community radio stations. In this manner, the community radios can continue to address local concerns in local language and cultural context, while connecting with concerned people across the world through digital technologies.

The study acknowledges that there are significant challenges in connecting the traditional and digital media. First, it is important to understand that the modern society comprises of both old and newer generations, as also pointed Hashimoto and Ohama (2014). The technology usage accordingly varies between different user groups, as newer generations are more familiar with emerging technologies, while older generations are still not acquainted with the internet environment. At the same time, there are also widespread infrastructure development gaps at spatial level between urban and rural areas. While many of the rural areas have limited access to internet, the current outreach of digital technologies is limited only to certain groups of society. Further, community radios mainly serve the rural, disadvantaged, vulnerable and hard to reach populations, which may not necessarily be able to afford new digital technologies like mobile phones and internet.

Nonetheless, more and more community radio stations are using Internet and social media platforms today to distribute their content and interact with a wider audience. To achieve last mile connectivity and enhance disaster communication, the study emphasizes on On-Line mode of information sharing, in addition to the On-Air and On-Land modes. However, emphasis should be put on overcoming the identified challenges of limited technology outreach and varied user groups.

8.6.2   Cross-Validating Information Through Local Community Engagement

Digital technologies bring in a huge amount of information and its timely validation is a huge challenge in disaster management, as highlighted from the cases of Indonesia and Haiti. The fabricated information threatens the 'trust factor' of community radios and therefore it is highly important to validate any dubious information before it has been broadcasted. As highlighted from the case of Haiti, necessary information during disaster events could be crowdsourced through different means. However, the key purpose of information sharing will not be achieved until the information is deemed to be accurate and trustworthy. Accordingly, there is need for further research on key aspects of data verification and filtering in a swift manner.

Learning from the case of Jalin Merapi (Indonesia), the study advocates for an integrated operation of digital technologies and community radios with a strong volunteer network. The information received through digital platforms like website, telephone and social media groups will undeniably enhance the transparency and outreach. However, the uncertain news needs to be essentially verified through local volunteers and public verification, before it has been broadcasted (conceptual explanation shown in Fig. 8.3). This will not only prevent misinformation to spread during the critical disaster situations among the local communities but also ensure idealistic integration of digital technologies with community radio operations, while maintaining its credibility and trustworthiness at local level. Referring to the case of

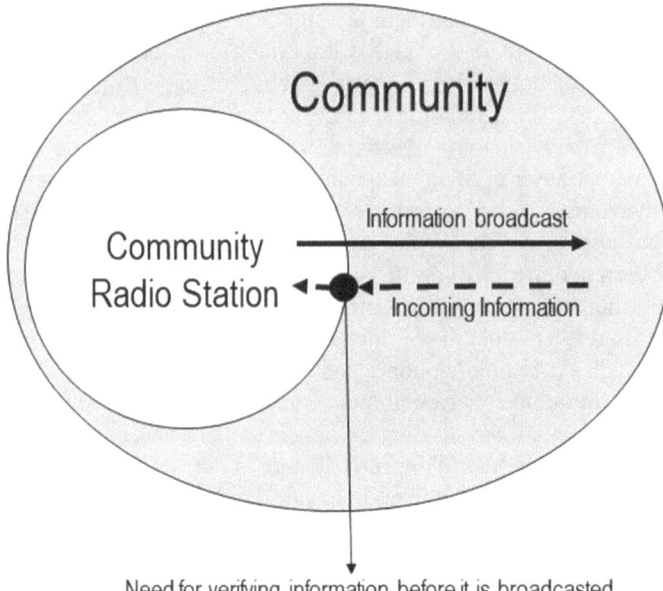

Fig. 8.3 Need for maintaining the credibility of community radios in disaster management

Indonesia and Haiti, it has been learnt that the timely validation of information is highly important for ensuring effective disaster response.

8.6.3 Enhancing Digital Awareness

Community radios primarily build on the local community involvement. Thus, for the healthy integration of digital technologies in community radio operations, the community members need to be acquainted with advanced technologies like mobile phones, social media and internet. Since the access to digital technologies is presently limited only to certain groups of society, the key role of volunteers in disaster communication has gained high prominence. Notably, community volunteers (both local and international) played an important role for information sharing in both the case study examples of Indonesia and Haiti. It has been realized that the local volunteers have an advantage of being the frontline reporters of the grounded problems on field, while the International volunteers are restricted to software tools and online support. Acknowledging the need for improved disaster communication at local level, there is need for capacity building to ensure active engagement of local volunteers during disaster situations. Emphasis should be put on strengthening the local volunteer networks as long-term community engagement is recognized to be one of the key issues in sustainability of community radio operations.

While communication infrastructure gets disrupted during the disaster situations, the continued information sharing is highly essential to timely respond to the disaster impacts. In that regard, the local communities have an important role in disaster reporting as the mainstream media may not be able to cover issues at local level. As highlighted in this study, digital technologies have today made it possible for communities to aggregate information from affected areas and share it to the community radio stations. To empower community members, the community radio stations should regularly organize training workshops while building an information network so that the local communities are familiar with digital technologies and can also contribute as information volunteer, when required.

8.7   Conclusion

Digital technologies have today become an integral part of modern society. Their growing prominence in disaster situations has also raised concerns for the firmness of community radios operations in long term. However, based on the overview of two selected case study examples, the study emphasizes that digital technologies should be seen more as an opportunity rather than a challenge for the sustainability of community radio operations. While digital technologies provide wide-ranging benefits, community radios effectively serve for information sharing at local level. Despite the many limitations, community radios continue to be relevant at local level as they address local concerns in local language unlike the mainstream media. In view of the extreme potential of digital technologies, the study stresses that they should certainly be integrated with community radio operations. However, it will be important to ensure that they do not replace the existence of community radio itself. The selected cases of Jalin Merapi (Indonesia) and Signal FM (Haiti) serve as an important learning experience for global media organizations, community media practitioners, donor organizations, local governments and other local actors in enhancing the sustainability of community radio operations.

The authors acknowledge that this research has certain limitations in its scope and methodology. It discusses the two selected case study examples only based on the available literature, however, there is a need for further field research on the effectiveness of digital technologies. The findings from the individual cases may also not be generalizable to other countries, but the notion of integrating digital technologies with community radio operations is of universal concern. Future research should consider rethinking community radio operations in the increasingly globalized and network world. Further research could also be done in the areas of validating fake information and enhancing digital awareness.

Acknowledgements   The first author (V.S.) is thankful to the Ministry of Education, Culture, Sports, Science and Technology (MEXT), Japan for the scholarship. The second (A.F.) and third (S.P.) authors are thankful to the Pusbindiklatren Bappenas, Republic of Indonesia for the scholarship. The authors also acknowledge the support received from the 'Disaster Resilience and Sustainable

Development' Program of Graduate School of Media and Governance, Keio University, Japan in conducting this study.

References

AMARC (2007) Community radio, social impact assessment. Removing barriers, increasing effectiveness. World Association of Community Radio Broadcasters (AMARC)

Arora V, Ramakrishnan N, Fernandez L (2015) Community radio and sustainability—a participatory research initiative, Ideosync MEDIA COMBINE, CEMCA and UNESCO. https://unesdoc.une sco.org/images/0023/002330/233084E.pdf. Accessed 30 Nov 2019

Bailey S (2014) Humanitarian crises, emergency preparedness and response: the role of business and the private sector—a strategy and options analysis of Haiti. Overseas Development Institute. https://www.odi.org/sites/odi.org.uk/files/odi-assets/publications-opinion-files/8788.pdf. Accessed 30 Nov 2019

Beena, Mathur M (2012) Role of ICT education for women empowerment. Int J Ecol Res 3(3):164–172

Berrigan FJ (1979) Community communications: the role of community media in development. UNESCO Press. ISBN: 92-3-101771-3. https://unesdoc.unesco.org/images/0004/000440/044035eo.pdf. Accessed 30 Nov 2019

Birowo MA (2010) The use of community radio in managing natural disaster in Indonesia. Bull Am Soc Inf Sci Technol 36:18–21. https://doi.org/10.1002/bult.2010.1720360506

Birowo MA (2012) Community media and civic action in response to volcanic hazards. In: Crisis information management: communication and technologies, pp 139–153. https://doi.org/10.1016/B978-1-84334-647-0.50008-4

Buckley S (2011) Community media: a good practice handbook. United Nations Educational, Scientific and Cultural Organization (UNESCO), France. https://unesdoc.unesco.org/images/0021/002150/215097e.pdf. Accessed 30 Nov 2019

Burnett J (2010) Haitians find lifeline in local radio station. In: Haiti quake: ruin and recovery, special series. https://www.npr.org/templates/story/story.php?storyId=122948825. Accessed 30 Nov 2019

Cate FH (1994) The role of the media in disaster mitigation: roundtable on the media, scientific information and disasters. In: International disaster communications: harnessing the power of communications to avert disasters and save live. https://www.annenberg.northwestern.edu/pubs/disas/disas32.htm

Chiumbu SH (2014) The world is our community: Rethinking community radio in the digital age. J Afr Media Stud 6(3):249–264. https://doi.org/10.1386/jams.6.3.249_1

Chiumbu SH, Ligaga D (2013) Communities of strangerhoods?": internet, mobile phones and the changing nature of radio cultures in South Africa. Telemat Inform 30(3):242–251. https://doi.org/10.1016/j.tele.2012.02.004

Cookson R (2013) Radio broadcasters face challenge from tech heavyweights. Financial Times, 28 Oct 2013. https://www.ft.com/content/12b76dd8-3675-11e3-8ae3-00144feab7de. Accessed 30 Nov 2019

Coz CL (2010) Local radio keeps Haiti earthquake survivors connected. In: MediaShift. https://mediashift.org/2010/01/local-radio-keeps-haiti-earthquake-survivors-connected026/. Accessed 30 Nov 2019

CRED (2015) The human cost of natural disasters 2015—a global perspective. Centre for Research on the Epidemiology of Disasters. https://reliefweb.int/report/world/human-cost-natural-disasters-2015-global-perspective. Accessed 1 Dec 2019

CRFC (2018) Availability of frequency range remains an issue. Community Radio Facilitation Centre, Ministry of Information and Broadcasting, Government of India. https://crfc.in/availabil ity-of-frequency-range-remains-an-issue/

da Costa P (2012) The growing pains of community radio in Africa—emerging lessons towards sustainability. Nord Rev 33(Special Issue):135–148. https://doi.org/10.2478/nor-2013-0031

Dave R (2001) Role of media in disaster management. Academia.edu. https://www.academia.edu/7402446/Role_of_Media_in_Disaster_management-Dr_Dave-2. Accessed 1 Dec 2019

Deitz C (2018) How technology is redefining radio broadcasting. In: Lifewire. https://www.lifewire.com/the-changing-way-we-define-radio-2843702. Accessed 1 Dec 2019

EBU (2011) The future of terrestrial broadcasting. Technical Report 013, Version 1.1., Geneva. https://tech.ebu.ch/docs/techreports/tr013.pdf. Accessed 1 Dec 2019

Ewart J, Dekker S (2013) Radio, someone still loves you! Talkback radio and community emergence during disasters. Contin: J Media Cult Stud 27(3):365–381. https://doi.org/10.1080/10304312.2013.772106

Fairbairn J (2000) Community Participation and sustainability in community radio. Paper presented at a workshop on gender and sustainability in community radio. GAP: Open Society Foundation, South Africa

Farren N, Murray C, Murphy K (2014) Community radio development and public funding for programme production: options for policy. Ir Commun Rev 14(1):Article 7. https://doi.org/10.21427/D7DT53

Freeman BC, Klapczynski J, Wood E (2012) The relationship between broadcast and social media software in the US, Germany, and Singapore. First Monday Open J Syst 17(4). https://doi.org/10.5210/fm.v17i4.3768

GFDRR (2019) Haiti-GFDRR. Global facility for disaster reduction and recovery. https://www.gfdrr.org/en/haiti. Accessed 30 Nov 2019

Gomes RM, de Castro Oliveira V (2015) International cooperation Brazil-Cuba-Haiti: the role of community radios in strengthening social mobilization in the public health context in Haiti. CienSaude Colet 20(1):199–208. https://doi.org/10.1590/1413-81232014201.20512013

Goncalves J, Kostakos V, Venkatanathan, J (2013) Narrowcasting in social media: effects and perceptions. In: 2013 IEEE/ACM international conference on advances in social networks analysis and mining (ASONAM), Canada, Aug 2013. https://doi.org/10.1145/2492517.2492570

Gondwe T, Mavindidze ZN (2014) An exploration into the operations and sustainability of Community radio stations in South Africa. Sustain Community Broadcast Sect 1(1). https://www.fxi.org.za/documents/Sustainability_in_the_community_broadcasting_sector.pdf. Accessed 30 Nov 2019

Gultom DI (2015) Re-thinking disaster communication: community radio as an act of participatory disaster communication. Australian and New Zealand Communication Association Inc. (ANZCA) conference papers

Gultom DI (2016) Community-based disaster communication: how does it become trustworthy? Disaster Prev Manag 25(4):478–491. https://doi.org/10.1108/DPM-02-2016-0026

Gultom DI, Joyce Z (2014) Crisis communication capacity for disaster resilience: community participation of information providing and verifying in Indonesian volcanic eruption. Paper presented to ANZTSR 2014 conference, Christchurch, Nov 2014. Available via Analysis and Policy Observatory. https://apo.org.au/node/53138. Accessed 30 Nov 2019

Gumucio Dagron A (2001) Art of aerialists: sustainability of community media. The Rockefeller Foundation, New York

Guo L (2017) Exploring the link between community radio and the community: a study of audience participation in alternative media practices. Commun Cult Crit 10(1):112–130. https://doi.org/10.1111/cccr.12141

Hallett L, Hintz A (2010) Digital broadcasting—challenges and opportunities for European community radio broadcasters. Telemat Inform 27(2):151–161. https://doi.org/10.1016/j.tele.2009.06.005

Hashimoto Y, Ohama A (2014) The role of social media in emergency response: the case of the great East Japan earthquake. NIDS J Def Secur 16(2):99–126

Heinzelman J, Waters C (2010) Crowdsourcing crisis information in disaster-affected Haiti, Special Report 252. United States Institute of Peace (USIP). https://www.preparecenter.org/sites/default/files/crowdsourcing_crisis_information_in_disaster-affected_haiti.pdf. Accessed 30 Nov 2019

Hibino J, Shaw R (2014a) Role of community radio in post disaster recovery: comparative analysis of Japan and Indonesia, Chapter 20. In: Shaw R (ed) Disaster recovery: used or misused development opportunity. Disaster risk reduction. Springer Japan, pp 385–410. https://doi.org/10.1007/978-4-431-54255-1_20

Hibino J, Shaw R (2014b) Roles of community radio in disaster management: reflections from Japan, Chapter 7. In: Shaw R (ed) Community practices for disaster risk reduction in Japan. Disaster risk reduction. Springer Japan, pp 121–132. https://doi.org/10.1007/978-4-431-54246-9_7

Hollon L (2006) Community radio is 90% about community. In: Global citizenship, media & culture. https://www.larryhollon.com/blog/2006/06/18/community-radio-is-90-about-community/. Accessed 1 Dec 2019

Howley K (2005) Community media: people, places, and communication technologies. Cambridge University Press, Cambridge. https://doi.org/10.1017/CBO9780511489020

Ideta A, Shaw R, Takeuchi Y (2012) Post disaster communication and role of FM radio: case of Natori, Chapter 5. In: Shaw R (ed) East Japan earthquake and tsunami: evacuation, communication, education and volunteerism

Infoasaid (2012) Media and telecoms landscape guide—Haiti. In: Internews https://internews.org/sites/default/files/resources/haiti_media_guide_final_211012_with_retyped_index_19.12.12.pdf. Accessed 1 Dec 2019

Kanayama T (2012) Community radio and the tōhoku earthquake. Int J Jpn Sociol 21(1):30–36. https://doi.org/10.1111/j.1475-6781.2012.01157.x

Khan MAA, Khan MMR, Hassan M, Ahmed F, Haque SMR (2017) Role of community radio for community development in Bangladesh. Int Technol Manag Rev 6(3):94–102. https://doi.org/10.2991/itmr.2017.6.3.3

Koenig M, Widdershein N, Janini N (2015) Media, human rights and development communications in Haiti: an assessment of the media, with particular attention to the human rights and development communications aspect. United States Agency for International Development or the United States Government (USAID)

Large T (2010) Cell phones and radios help save lives after Haiti earthquake. In: World news. https://www.reuters.com/article/us-haiti-telecoms/cell-phones-and-radios-help-save-lives-after-haiti-earthquake-idUSTRE60O07M20100125. Accessed 30 Nov 2019

Lush D, Urgoiti G (2012) Participation pays—the sustainability of community broadcasting in perspective. Friedrich-Ebert-Stiftung (FES), fesmedia Africa. https://library.fes.de/pdf-files/bueros/africa-media/08865.pdf. Accessed 30 Nov 2019

Mathbor GM (2007) Enhancement of community preparedness for natural disasters: the role of social work in building social capital for sustainable disaster relief and management. Int Soc Work 50(3):357–369. https://doi.org/10.1177/0020872807076049

Mei ETW, Lavigne F, Picquout A, Grancher D (2011) Crisis management during the 2010 eruption of Merapi Volcano. In: Regional geographic conference. International Geographical Union, Santiago, Chile

Mendel T (2013) Tuning into development. International comparative survey of community broadcasting regulation. UNESCO, Paris. https://unesdoc.unesco.org/images/0022/002246/224662e.pdf. Accessed 30 Nov 2019

Myers M (2011) Voices from villages-community radio in the developing world. A Report to the Center for International Media Assistance. CIMA Research Report. https://www.cima.ned.org/publication/voices-from-villages-community-radio-in-the-developing-world/. Accessed 30 Nov 2019

Nelson A, Sigal I, Zambrono D (2011) Media, information systems and communities: lessons from Haiti. https://reliefweb.int/report/world/media-information-systems-and-communities-lessons-haiti. Accessed 30 Nov 2019

OCHA (2013) Humanitarianism in the network age: including world humanitarian data and trends 2012. OCHA policy and studies series. United Nations Office for the Coordination of Humanitarian Affairs (OCHA). https://www.unocha.org/sites/unocha/files/HINA_0.pdf. Accessed 30 Nov 2019

PAHO (2009) Information management and communication in emergencies and disasters: Manual for disaster response teams. Pan American Health Organization, Area on Emergency Preparedness and Disaster Relief, Washington, D.C.

Philips R (2010) Haitian radio station becomes post-quake lifeline. In: Haiti earthquake. https://edition.cnn.com/2010/WORLD/americas/01/24/haiti.earthquake.radio/index.html. Accessed 30 Nov 2019

Regan J (2008) Baboukèt la tonbe—the muzzle has fallen! Media Dev 2:12–17. https://www.academia.edu/32672281/Babouket_la_tonbe. Accessed 30 Nov 2019

Regan J (2014) Watchdogging Haiti's reconstruction from the grassroots. Paper presented at the global investigative journalism conference, Rio De Janeiro, Oct 2013. https://ijec.org/2014/01/28/watchdogging-haitis-reconstruction-from-the-grassroots/. Accessed 30 Nov 2019

Reilly P, Atanasova D (2016) A report on the role of the media in the information flows that emerge during crisis situations. CascEff Deliverable D3.3. https://library.college.police.uk/docs/role-of-media-crisis-situations-2017.pdf. Accessed 30 Nov 2019

Rencoret N, Stoddard A, Haver K, Taylor G, Harvey P (2010) Haiti earthquake response-context analysis, ALNAP. https://citeseerx.ist.psu.edu/viewdoc/download?doi=10.1.1.176.2823&rep=rep1&type=pdf

Saputro K (2014) Engaged audiences in the mediated disaster of Mount Merapi in Indonesia 2010. Unpublished PhD thesis, Sheffield Hallam University, Sheffield

Saputro K (2016) Information volunteers' strategies in crisis communication—the case of Mt. Merapi eruption in Indonesia 2010. Int J Disaster Resil Built Environ 7(1):63–72. https://doi.org/10.1108/IJDRBE-07-2013-0027

Siemering B, Fairbairn J (2007) Community radio: guidebook on sustainability: developing radio partners

Shah A, Nawaz A (2015) Impacts of globalization and digital technologies on access to radio: a survey of teachers in Gomal and Qurtuba universities, Dikhan, KP Pakistan. Glob J Hum Soc Sci: F Polit Sci 15(1)

Shahzalal M, Hassan A (2019) Communicating sustainability: using community media to influence rural people's intention to adopt sustainable behaviour. Sustainability 11(2):812. https://doi.org/10.3390/su11030812

Shaw R, Hibino J, Matsuura S (2012) The role of community radio in disaster. Church World. https://www.preventionweb.net/files/29931_29931radioalllowres1.pdf. Accessed 30 Nov 2019

Sullivan MH (2007) Community radio: its impact and challenges to its development. Center for International Media Assistance (CIMA) Working Group Report. https://www.cima.ned.org/wp-content/uploads/2015/02/CIMA-Community_Radio-Working_Group_Report_0.pdf. Accessed 30 Nov 2019

Sumaryono A (2011) Managing the Mount Merapi sediments, CRBOM small publication series no. 37

Tanesia A (2007) Woman, community radio, and post-disaster recovery process. Community Indep Media 2:69–76

Tanesia A and Habibi Z (2011) Jalin Merapi community information system in response to Mount Merapi's 2010 eruption 5362:2–10

Tasic J, Amir S (2016) Informational capital and disaster resilience: the case of Jalin Merapi. Disaster Prev Manag 25(3):395–411. https://doi.org/10.1108/DPM-07-2015-0163

Tavhiso M (2009) Sustainability challenges facing community radio: a comparative study of three community radio stations in Limpopo Province. Master thesis, Faculty of Humanities, University of Limpopo. https://hdl.handle.net/10386/231. Accessed 30 Nov 2019

Tipson FS (2013) Natural disasters as threats to peace, special report. United States Institute of Peace (USIP). https://www.usip.org/publications/2013/02/natural-disasters-threats-peace. Accessed 30 Nov 2019

Tucker E (2013) Community radio in political theory and development practice. J Dev Commun Stud 2(2/3):392–420

Umihara J, Nishikitani M (2013) Emergent use of twitter in the 2011 Tohoku earthquake. Prehosp Disaster Med 28(5):434–440. https://doi.org/10.1017/S1049023X13008704

UNESCO (2015) Background Paper—community radio sustainability—policies and funding. In: Community media sustainability: strengthening policies and funding, international seminar. The United Nations Educational, Scientific and Cultural Organization (UNESCO), pp 1–20

University of Michigan and Small Arms Survey (2010) Assessing needs after the quake: reviewing security and basic services in Haiti. Assessment commissioned by UNDP and the Canadian International Development Research Centre (IDRC), Mar 2010

Waits J (2010) Community radio's challenges after the Haitian quake. In: Community radio, emergencies, international, localism. https://www.radiosurvivor.com/2010/02/04/community-radios-challenges-after-the-haitian-quake/. Accessed 30 Nov 2019

Wall I (2011) Citizen initiatives in Haiti. In: Forced migration review (FMR): the technology issue. https://www.fmreview.org/technology/wall. Accessed 30 Nov 2019

Wall I, Robinson L (2012) Still left in the dark? How people in emergencies use communication to survive—and how humanitarian agencies can help. Policy Briefing No. 6. BBC Media Action, London, UK

Waxman JJ (1973) Local broadcast gatekeeping during natural disasters. Journal Q 50(4):751–758. https://doi.org/10.1177/107769907305000419

Wellman B (2001) Physical place and cyberplace: the rise of personalised networking. Int J Urban Reg Res 25:227–252. https://doi.org/10.1111/1468-2427.00309

Chapter 9
Creating an Enabling Environment for Urban Disaster Reporting

Suvendrini Kakuchi and Rajib Shaw

Abstract This chapter examines the measures taken toward enabling media to report urban disasters with depth and accuracy. Bangladesh, a highly populated and disaster-prone country, has developed good response systems, especially focusing on coastal disasters where regular typhoons have led to widespread human and environmental destruction. But the emergence of deadly urban disasters with higher losses experienced in the country's cities has raised the urgent need to adopt and implement measures to strengthen urban resilience. The media case study presented here highlights that specific support is necessary for journalists to deepen their knowledge about urban disasters and there is a pressing need to strengthen their Disaster Risk Reduction (DRR) reporting capacity that is a key to educating the public. Dhaka, the capital city with a 15 million population is highly vulnerable to fires, urban floods and air pollution. Journalists participating in the training program focused on disasters in North Dhaka and were introduced to Japan's advanced reporting experience under the platform of learning from each other. Another prominent aspect of this study is the development of collaborative activities between journalists and communities toward build disaster resilience in Dhaka. This network worked smoothly and facilitated the journalists to highlight DRR topics in their reporting (Urban Disaster Resilience of Dhaka North City Corporation 2017).

Keywords Urban disasters · Media and community collaboration · Disaster communication · Disaster media fellowships · Japan media disaster reporting

9.1 Methodology

The 3-year project targeted more than 30 journalists employed in mainstream and social media in Bangladesh. Activities were aimed at addressing local disasters in the

S. Kakuchi (✉)
Tokyo Correspondent, University World News. UK, Tokyo, Japan
e-mail: suven@kdp.biglobe.ne.jp

R. Shaw
Graduate School of Media and Governance, Keio University, Fujisawa, Japan

© Springer Nature Singapore Pte Ltd. 2021
R. Shaw et al. (eds.), *Media and Disaster Risk Reduction*, Disaster Risk Reduction,
https://doi.org/10.1007/978-981-16-0285-6_9

media and discussing the challenges faced by journalist when covering the events. A key goal in the media training was raising the profile of DRR themes in news reporting. Dhaka grapples with regular fires, urban flooding, and dangerous levels of air pollution linked to heavy traffic congestion. The city is located on a major fault line facing the serious threat of earthquake. With a large population living in poverty and employed in hazardous livelihoods, the city faces the threat of disaster that can be widespread resulting in mass losses.

Yet the media does not cover crucial mitigation topics regularly. Editorial policies place priority on disaster reporting during the tragedy and publish stories soon after the aftermath, a trend that showcases a short-term approach. Discussions held during the training raised the issue of the lack of interest in DRR topics in news organizations and identified measures to overcome the challenges. Workshop agendas included sharing and learning from the experiences of the Japanese media organizations that have incorporated policies that promote working closely with disaster management authorities. Japanese journalists play a primary role in the communication of disaster news (SEEDS Asia 2017).

The training program also emphasized the merits of collaborating with stakeholders to enable better disaster and DRR reporting. Participants in the selected workshops comprised of journalists, urban authorities and local communities. Sitting in round table settings, they exchanged views on their disaster experience leading to discussions on enhancing cooperation to strengthen resilience in the city. Under the collaboration model, the training offered journalist DRR fellowships and photo exhibitions that featured their learning experience so they could learn from each other. The other important aspect of the training was the physical presence of a Japanese editor and experts in Dhaka. They shared their experience in disaster reporting covering Japanese earthquakes and tsunami. They spoke about the concept of creating new partnerships to enable better DRR reporting as this network was a source for journalists searching new topics for investigation. The project training concluded with a media round table attended by news editors representing mainstream media who debated the challenges in disaster reporting. The participants acknowledged that disaster mitigation topics were usually buried in environmental news rather than assigned as a specific topic. The editors later recommended new guidelines to strengthen in-house disaster reporting systems such as creating a disaster beat on the news desk and adopting regular training programs for young journalists. Concrete strategies that were implemented during the training were visits by journalists to communities for gathering information on the new DRR activities in the area. This experience led to television and radio broadcasts from the field and the publication of news features. In the wrap-up sessions, participating journalists reported that they were motivated by the opportunities, they were given to investigate the positive stories from disasters. They learned from the community organizations about the steps they had taken to improve disaster preparedness in the local areas. Communities that participated in the training program echoed the same sentiment pointing out that media attention fostered their motivation to continue and expand DRR activities (Table 9.1) (SEEDS Asia 2018).

Table 9.1 Participating media and community organizations

Media	Community
Bangladesh Sangbad Sangstha (BSS)	Mohakhali East Ja Block Society
The Daily Star	Aeon Buddies Youth Club
The Financial Express	Paikpara anirban kallyan somity
Dhaka Tribune	Rupnagar Tinshed Barir malik Kallyan Somity
Daily Jugantor	Kallyapur Communitry Policing Samaj Kallyan Parishad
Daily Samakal	Monipuripara kallyan Somity
Daily Kaler Kantha	Purbo Tejturi Bazar Kalyan somity
Bangladesh Television (BTV)	Moinarbag Unnoyon Porishad
ATN News	Dhaka University
SATV	Dhaka North City Council
	Ward Councillors

9.2 Background

Bangladesh is highly vulnerable to earthquakes given its location close to a tectonic plate and in addition to with five active faults within the country—active faults are geological faults that are likely to become the source for earthquakes sometime in the future. The area was hit by a great earthquake (8.1 magnitudes) in Assam, India in 1897. However, there have been no major earthquakes that have occurred around Bangladesh since then. According to experts, earthquakes occur over a 100-year interval in this region.

Surveys indicate that one of the reasons for the huge extent of damage projected from an earthquake is the vulnerability of many buildings in Dhaka and in the country. Poorly constructed buildings are not stable during disasters that occur from natural and man-made causes. In April 2013, the collapse of Rana Plaza building in the suburb area of Dhaka city became the worst accident in the garment industry. The tragedy is linked to illegal construction that avoided legal monitoring of building codes. Many private buildings built in the recent past did not follow the Bangladesh National Building Code (BNBC) enacted in 1993, and many have not undergoing building checks for quality management. Hence, it was not possible to verify if construction of many constructions in Dhaka city followed the BNBC.

Disaster surveys indicate that most roads could be blocked from buildings collapses that can occur simultaneously. In such cases, emergency rescue by public organizations, such as fire departments, cannot respond in a timely manner. Moreover, without preparedness, panic during evacuations can become a serious issue. The sober picture was that an earthquake poses a serious threat to the current construction system, a situation is not likely to change in a short span of time. The most important mitigation measure in this context is focusing on capacity building in communities to face the risk and enhances coordination capacities among DRR stakeholders to assist people to cope with the disaster (SEEDS Asia 2017).

According to the CDRI study, floods have occurred annually inundating riverside areas in North Dhaka. Severe urban flooding spilling into main roads caused regular heavy roadblocks and inundated housing during the rainy season. These urban disasters were exacerbated due to poor drainage facilities and garbage not appropriately processed. Discarded trash that was thrown by people into drains blocked the drain pipes contributing to floods. The number of fires has been increasing every year. Dhaka saw a total of was 15,185 cases of fire in 2011 and 17,192 cases in 2013. Many fire cases occurred in urban areas, and Dhaka North city was not an exception. Many fire cases were caused by electrical failures resulting in fires in kitchens, irresponsible discarding of cigarette buts, poorly ventilated factories, gas cylinder accidents, and old piping in the city causing leaks (Daily Star newspaper 2019).

9.3   Training and Capacity Enhancement

The training agenda was conducted over the 3-year timeline and was comprised of three main activities.

9.3.1   Activity 1: Introduction to Responsible Disaster Reporting

Workshops and discussion-led seminars were conducted to learn the scientific causes and the social aspects of disasters. Program content was divided into disaster themes—mitigation, relief activities during postdisaster, and long-term disaster recovery. The journalists shared their challenges in writing their reports. The key issues presented were the lack of support from news editors, that news organizations placed priority on political and economic themes over environment and disaster news. They also revealed that the lack of financial resources for journalists to visit the disaster sites and access to disaster experts were major barriers to better disaster reporting. The training was also an opportunity to broaden their knowledge of disasters and gain story ideas.

Identifying DRR Story themes for journalists:

1.   Measures taken by stakeholders to establish safe cities

Objective of the reporting: To educate the public about the importance of implementing DRR activities in their communities.

Effective DRR news reporting should quote reliable sources to explain disaster risks in Dhaka city. An important DRR subject is coverage of National Building Codes to empower people to understand construction regulations and standards and the importance of reinforcement of the current weak city infrastructure. Reporting on the topic includes solutions such as state-of-the art technology and also showcases alternative preparedness solutions from experts promoting reliable and economically affordable construction methods. Other interesting subjects can feature initiatives taken by diverse sectors—authorities, individual and local communities—with the collective aim to strengthen city's earthquake resilience. Another topic taken up in DRR reporting is featuring the successful lessons undertaken internationally by the communities in different countries to boost personal safety.

2.   Seasonal disasters in Dhaka

Urban flood, fire, heat wave or building collapse are common urban disaster. City preparedness relies heavily on promoting science-based community actions. The DRR story can feature some steps taken in this practice such as the importance of investing in fire extinguishers in buildings or exposing the risks posed from unauthorized encroachment that has contributed to the disaster vulnerability of the community.

3.   The importance of community-based disaster preparedness

Objective of the report: To promote community networking and sharing information.

Points of the story: What was the challenge/response to the disaster from the affected community to the disaster and how did they cope with the tragedy on the immediate, mid-term and long-term. The story can showcase how can DRR reduced the losses by quoting examples of a community that has invested in boosting its resilience.

4.   How can the media reduce the disaster risk?

Objective: DRR reports can save lives by sharing relevant information with the public. Publishing lessons from past disasters are particularly effective as the examples are from the ground and can connect with people living in similar environments.

Points of the report: The key point of the story is to investigate the actions of a person or community that has helped minimize loss or fatalities during a disaster. The story interviews the survivors to strengthen this point. The story content features simple steps that were taken to help others during the tragedy—a popular theme is that photos in newspapers helped families to locate their lost relatives. The media can also stop rumors that cause panic by disseminating facts in radio broadcasts or social media. News reports on the impact of the disaster on the journalist—the emotional and physical toll on journalists in the disaster zone—are important stories that can be shared with the public.

5.   Memorial Day

Objective of the story: To promote remembrance of the tragedy by recognizing the courage of the survivors. Anniversary day stories contribute to reducing mental stress of the survivor by giving them a voice in public.

Story points: Coverage of a Memorial Day event must illustrate the progress made in disaster preparedness after the fateful event and also focuses on individual courage to implement behavioral changes after the disaster.

6.   DRR themes to reduce economic loss or health risks during disasters

Objective: To educate and prepare the public to save lives, protect from sicknesses such as dysentery, delivery of food during a disaster.

Story points: The economic damage caused in the city covers infrastructure loss, shops, banks, schools and hospitals.

7.   Mental stress and gender stories in urban disaster

Objective: To educate the public to create deeper understanding of the disaster impact on vulnerable populations.

Story points: Disaster impacts women and children differently due to their economic and social vulnerable status. The story explains the different experiences of their male counterparts. The story must also include how women can be empowered to take leadership to save their communities. Quotes from women and children are crucial to make a good story.

8.   Culture. Arts/Religion

Objective: To analyze the role of this sector in DRR, postdisaster recovery, and remembrance. An example is the role of the mosque to provide emotional support and as a place for evacuation. Museums and cultural shows in street theater that promote DRR knowledge are important story themes.

Story points: Visit local and national museums established for recording disasters. Journalists can interview the curator and report on the disaster and the role played by the museum to raise awareness. The importance of religious organization in providing disaster relief and working for resilience building can be highlighted.

9.   DRR and volunteers

Objective: News reports can highlight the crucial role played by volunteers promoting DRR and also disaster recovery.

Story points: Interviews volunteers who helped the affected people during a disaster.

10. Schools and DRR

Objective: To introduce the role of a school in DRR and during a disaster.

Story points: The school in DRR is a place for children to learn and be empowered to save themselves during a disaster. The school is also an evacuation site. Teachers must be prepared to save students. Schools are venues for emergency drills and collaboration with local communities.

11. Indigenous DRR Knowledge

Objective: Learning from our elders and ancestors about traditional practices practiced by ancestors to protect people from disasters.

Story points: DRR practices conducted by our grandparents or ancestors that demonstrate their preparedness and mitigation skills. Learning from historical disasters.

9.3.2 Activity 2: A Media Manual Was Prepared for the Journalists

What is a disaster:

Disasters follow natural hazards that include earthquakes, cyclones and flood. Its impact reflects the scale of the loss and damage on the affected society. Disasters could be human-induced—dependent on decisions and activities implemented by people.

Major global disasters are earthquakes, tsunami, Typhoons, Hurricanes, Cyclone, Flood, Urban flood, Heat Wave, Cold Wave, heavy Fog, Fire, Tornados, Landslide and Drought.

The role of the media in DRR:

The media can generate and disseminate information to strengthen public DRR knowledge to minimize human and property loss during a disaster. This role has become crucial against the increase of global calamities now linked to climate change-related weather changes and rapid urbanization.

News reports and broadcasts provide the public with:

- Crucial early warning information and disaster risk reduction knowledge that can help people to be prepared.
- Disseminate important DRR research and scientific data.
- The documentation of the tragic consequences of disasters—such as earthquake, flood or typhoon—on a society and nation. By traveling to devastated areas journalists record testimony of survivors and investigate the destruction of human life, environment and infrastructure.

- The documenting of relief operations during the aftermath. By disseminating important information on relief operations, the journalist can contribute to effect and equal aid distribution and speed recovery.
- The disaster beat is also about healing and bringing hope. Reporting testimony from survivors on the ground are important articles on the lessons learned from the aftermath. Journalists examine the factual causes of the disaster and steps that are necessary for the future to prevent a similar tragedy.
- Media stories can be News, Features, Radio and Television broadcasts, Podcasts, Photojournalism, Blog, Multimedia.

9.3.3 Activity 3: Capacity Building DRR Fellowships for Journalists

Fellowships were extended to 12 journalists who applied to develop in-depth knowledge and writing skills to improve their disaster reporting. The successful journalists published stories in their publications that featured disaster risk management practices and trends in their country. The fellowship budget provided journalists access to travel and research. Mentoring was also provided by DRR experts.

The jury panel was comprised of a combination of working and retired journalists and disaster experts. The selected journalists represented television, radio and print news. They reported two stories each on a disaster topic of their choice. Comments from the recipients illustrate the purpose of their decision to apply:

- An opportunity to gain new and in-depth knowledge about disasters.
- Develop their writing skills.
- To pursue an in-depth story that needs time and financial support.
- An opportunity to build a new network with experts, academia and local community.
- A career step.

DRR Themes reported by the media fellowship:

- **Local development incorporating safety measures**: examples: retrofitting of buildings and infrastructure, policies on environment protection and implementation of DRR measures.
- **Health**: stories covering DRR preparedness in hospitals and local clinics, trauma counseling, medical relief operations,
- **Gender, Disability and Minorities**: reports focusing on experience of disaster on women, children, the handicapped and minority populations including foreigners who do not have access to local language disaster prevention information.
- **Environment**: reports on environment degradation linked to disasters and eco-friendly policies and activities.
- **Science and Technology**: new technology to implement disaster resilience and factual understanding of natural hazards and disasters.

- **Economy and Business**: economic loss during disasters and building business reliance to disasters.
- **Safe Schools**: schools as evacuation sites and centers for DRR education.
- **Religion**: the role of religious leaders to spread DRR education and knowledge.
- **Indigenous knowledge**: traditional and local DRR knowledge to prevent disasters.

9.3.4 Activity 4: Planning the DRR Story

- **First 2 weeks**: Emergency stories focus on lifeline capacity, national and local government decisions, rescue, medical help, evacuation centers, recovery, damage and loss.
- **One month later**: Recovery stories focus on domestic and international aid, economic and social loss on affected populations, infrastructure and rebuilding, capacity building and reports on where to donate, volunteers, economic and environmental loss of affected areas.
- **Six months later**: Recovery/rehabilitation, resilience of survivors, actions of government and civil society.
- **One year later**: Anniversary story focuses on recovery achievements, lessons learned—before and after stories.
- **Five years later**: Anniversary. Lessons learned from the survivors. Recovery process and updates from the disaster site.

9.3.5 The North Dhaka City Newsletter

The key activity in the media project was the publication of a bi-annual newsletter with the North Dhaka City Council with the mission of sharing safety information with the residents. The goal was to raise public awareness of the risks facing the city and the diverse tasks undertaken by authorities and experts to safeguard the local population. Apart from official information, the newsletter also raised the profile of community-based work toward empowerment. Stories of people acting to strengthen their neighborhoods such as launching new cleaning programs and study programs to facilitate the use of fire extinguishers were published (Nogoria 2018).

9.4 Key Findings

The above case study has promoted the importance of building a network of diverse stakeholders—the academia, non-governmental organizations and communities—to enable effective disaster reporting. Activities implemented under the model proved that the collaborative actions were satisfactory to the participating groups despite their busy schedules and diverse targets. Closer communication was observed in the three main stakeholders linked to stronger trust based on sharing information between each other.

Other key findings include:

- The DRR story can be reported as mainstream news by linking to political, economic and development issues.
- Collaborative approach to disaster reporting is crucial for in-depth reporting.
- Disaster reporting can cover experiences in other countries to share lessons and stimulate action in the public.
- Urban disasters are an important topic and treated separately in natural disaster reporting.
- The memorial story is an important theme to support recovery in postdisaster environment.
- Media training in disaster reporting is essential for the media in developing countries

References

Daily Star (2019) Daily Star newspaper. https://www.thedailystar.net/backpage/news/cigarette-butts-cause-1355pc-fire-incidents-1646275. Accessed 27 July 2020

Nogoria (2018) Official newsletter by North Dhaka City Council. North Dhaka City Council Publication, Dhaka, Bangladesh, 16 pp

SEEDS Asia (2017) Urban disaster resilience of Dhaka North City Corporation. SEEDS Asia Publication, Kobe, Japan, 68 pp

SEEDS Asia (2018) Tell us your story. SEEDS Asia Publication, Kobe, Japan, 50 pp

Chapter 10
New Paradigms of Natural Disaster Reporting and Its Risk Communication in China in the New Media Age

Tianhai Jiang and Rajib Shaw

Abstract China is one of the countries most affected by natural disasters. Disaster reporting and risk communication have played critical roles in face of the unexpected and catastrophic natural disasters in China, and even more so in the digital age. The innovative development of social media and new media technologies brings enormous potentials for exploring new paradigms of effective communication and reaching the public proactively and effectively. It serves as a catalyst for not only disaster professionals, but also media and science communication practitioners, even the lay population to engage in the communication. This chapter first introduces the diversified active players involved in the arena in the new media age. It then discusses the new media approaches and advanced technologies applied in practice. To further understand the tendencies, we summarize some of the new dynamics of risk communication in China. The chapter closes with discussions on how to contribute to effective risk communication with sufficient qualified professionals and quality contents.

Keywords Natural disasters · Risk communication · Disaster reporting · New media · Social media

10.1 Introduction

China is one of the countries most affected by natural disasters in the world. Earthquake, typhoon, landslide, flood and drought, fire and snow disaster, among other natural hazards, are widely distributed throughout the country, affecting more than 100 million people and causing billions of dollars of economic loss each year (Wang and Jiang 2019). Statistics show that the total count of people affected by natural disasters in China reached 130 million in 2019, among which 909 were dead or

T. Jiang (✉)
Institute of Mountain Hazards and Environment, Chinese Academy of Sciences, Chengdu, China
e-mail: jth880228@gmail.com

R. Shaw
Graduate School of Media and Governance, Keio University, Fujisawa, Japan

© Springer Nature Singapore Pte Ltd. 2021
R. Shaw et al. (eds.), *Media and Disaster Risk Reduction*, Disaster Risk Reduction,
https://doi.org/10.1007/978-981-16-0285-6_10

missing. 126,000 houses had collapsed and 19.26 million hectares of croplands were affected. Direct economic loss was 327 billion RMB (Ministry of Emergency Management of the People's Republic of China 2020).

Media has always played an important part in the whole gamut of disaster risk reduction. Its role in disaster reporting and risk communication has evolved significantly when embracing the new media age with joys and pains. The new media age has transformed people's ways of information uptake and developed a better-educated lay population capable of accessing rich information by themselves. It also witnessed the increasing demands for quality risk information and qualified risk communication professionals.

Traditional authoritative information sources such as the government, public agencies, and science organizations are exploring effective ways of risk communication through social media, directly interacting with the public as the sources, producers, and disseminators themselves. With the establishment of the Ministry of Emergency Management of China in 2018, multi-hazard, cross-sectoral efforts are further integrated as a more effective and collaborative emergency management system at various levels. This institutional development of disaster risk reduction in China has started a new wave of innovations and applications in disaster reporting and risk communication.

The multi-directional communications on social media, the convergence between mass media and social media, and the rise of citizen journalism and content aggregators further diversify the communication. Information sources, disseminators, and receivers are switching roles constantly at different stages when facing the unexpected, creating an interactive, adaptive, and dynamic risk communication environment.

However, there are still issues that remained to be explored in future studies and practices, such as the further exploration of media's systematic roles in early warning and emergency response, the abilities to identify rumors and take effective countermeasures in crisis, and the enormous demands for well-trained professionals to produce quality information content.

Disaster reporting and risk communication is a vital part of disaster risk reduction, even more so in the Digital Age. It is through multi-disciplinary, multi-stakeholder, and cross-sectoral efforts that the most effective approaches can be found.

10.2   New Trends and New Paradigms

The growth of social media in China brings enormous potentials for new paradigms of disaster reporting and risk communication, as well as opportunities to reach the public proactively and effectively.

WeChat, the most influential social network provider in China, has 1.15 billion monthly active users (MAU) in 2019 according to its annual report. Analysis for WeChat public subscription accounts in 2019 (news media or public affairs official accounts were not considered) shows that 983,000 articles were published by the Top

500 most viewed WeChat public accounts in 2019, with 38.1 billion views and 380 million likes. Education and Science related public accounts were highly popular. Guokr, a science communication account, is among the top 20 with over 180 million views for its 1,095 articles published in 2019.

In a time of information fragmentation, microblog flourishes. Weibo, the biggest multi-media microblog platform in China, has around 130 million and 120 million daily posts of texts and pictures in 2018, respectively, along with over 1.5 million video clips and live streams. Celebrity bloggers and opinion leaders on Weibo exceeded 47,000 in 2018, who generated 6.5 million original contents monthly on average with 1.6 trillion reads, and acquired 4.7 billion new followers on average every month, according to its V Influence Summit of 2018.

Social media permeates into every corner of the society, changing ways of information production, dissemination, and consumption. Disaster reporting and risk communication is no longer the sole responsibility for traditional media players, but a prioritized agenda for the government and public agencies, science organizations, citizen journalists, and science communication practitioners. Mass media, social media, institutional players, and academics are working more collaboratively in the field, and misinformation becomes an essential responsibility for them all. Disaster reporting and risk communication in China has taken advantages of the Digital Age and vitalities of different stakeholders, and it has shown the following features.

10.2.1 Diversified Active Players in the Arena

When analyzing risk communication in the traditional communication system (Shannon 1948), information sources are normally the governments, public agencies, science organizations, or affected people interviewed in the disaster areas. News production and dissemination are mainly achieved through the mass media, which take a certain amount of time for the downward communications, and even longer for further updates. That is not the case in the new media age.

The new media age has created an ideal environment for instant risk communication, which requires fast sharing to a wider public, to be simple and complete, to be credible and accurate, and to have constant interaction and adaptation.

The shifting balance of power between journalism and its publics, the rise of a more self-conscious and better-educated audience as both the information producers and consumers, the disintermediated institutional players addressing a wider audience directly have indelibly altered the landscape of risk communication (Bardoel and Deuze 2001).

10.2.1.1 Disintermediated Institutional Engagement

It is fairly advantageous for government, public agencies, scientists to directly engage in emergency and risk information dissemination, because trustable and authoritative information can facilitate the risk perception and lead to effective actions.

Institutional players used to be only the information source for emergency and risk communication. With the advantages of social media, institutional players are geared up into social networks such as Weibo, WeChat, and news apps, and directly act as broadcasters and communicators with the public at all times. These constant efforts have managed to amplify the delivered messages and established an effective and reliable way of multi-directional risk communication.

The public accounts of Ministry of Emergency Management on WeChat, Weibo, and news apps have attracted 5.49 million followers eight months after its establishment in April 2019. Investigated on January 27, 2020, @China Fire and Rescue owns around 5 million followers on Weibo, which posted 6,608 microblogs in 2018 with 1.6 billion total reads. @China Earthquake Networks Delivery has 9.4 million followers on Weibo and @China Meteorological Administration has 4.2 million followers with over 1 million reads every day. These are ranked among the top of public affairs official accounts in Weibo. Various types of emergency and risk information are posted constantly, such as early warning, disaster events, and updates at home and abroad, rescue and relief, reconstruction and memorial, risk knowledge, etc.

In the 2013 Ya'an Earthquake of Sichuan Province, the first microblog was posted by the Institute of Care-Life of Chengdu on its Weibo 53 s after the earthquake happened (Zhang et al. 2016). Another example is the Beijing Earthquake Agency, which has been trying to integrate its communication channels in mass media with social media. When the earthquake happened on February 12, 2018 in Langfang, a city to the southeast of Beijing, it has also raised the tension among Beijing citizens. The Beijing Earthquake Agency has soon posted a dozen of information updates on Weibo, its website, and through mass media, to clear the air while introducing some risk knowledge on earthquake. The posts have attained 3.5 million reads (Gu 2019).

Weibo is considered as part of the new media communication matrix of the national emergency management system, which also consists of WeChat public account, news app, informational website, the newspaper *China Emergency Management News*, several related journals, along with other mass media channels. Since the establishment of the Ministry of Emergency Management in China, emergency and risk information can be fast gathered and integrated, and quickly disseminated to the public through multi-media approaches, including early warning information for extreme weather events, flood and drought, earthquake, geohazard, and fire disaster, information for emergency response, rescue and relief, and reconstruction, etc. (Wang and Jiang 2019).

The China Emergency Information website (www.emerinfo.cn), established by the Ministry in April 2019, is an informative platform for non-stop emergency and risk information updates. The multi-media platform has utilized video clips, maps, cartoons, photo illustrations in its seven major columns. The emergency response column mainly consists of disaster updates, volunteer applications, skill contests, and evaluations for rescue and relief. Case studies, lessons to be learnt, academic output, and expert opinions categorized by different disaster types at home and abroad are widely presented. Risk communication column has information about emergency signals, self-rescue and support, evacuation routes, family plans, safe venues, food and resources, and digital seismological science museum. There are also columns about live on rescue and relief, monitoring and early warning system, international disaster events and relief actions, etc.

10.2.1.2   Citizen Journalist

With the universal access to mobile terminals and the Internet, more and more citizens are engaged in news production. These eye witness contents are generated from the citizen culture and can be widely recognized and fast shared through social media platforms. These can be valuable sources or materials for news production by media professionals (Hu 2017).

These decentralized and geographically dispersed citizen journalists are "eyes and ears" for the unexpected, and the fresh blood to bring new dynamics into the risk communication. They have proven to be actively engaged as information producers and disseminators on social network, contributing their findings and expertise and diversifying the agenda setting (Xu and Liu 2013).

When disaster just happens, the first several hours is the best timing for rescue and relief. But it is also a difficult time for disaster reporting, when traffic, electricity, or communications are down, reporters haven't arrived on site yet, or cannot gather enough information to satisfy the public's curiosity and ease the anxiety. Microblog with instant production and dissemination ability serves in place, where people in the affected area can provide valuable text and visual information or updates for government agencies and the media (Liu 2011).

The visual information of the disaster event documented by citizens can also help emergency responders and scientists to gain a better understanding of the disaster. Real-time videos of a disaster can be hardly found because of its random occurrence, hindering researchers from observing and analyzing the whole process of a disaster event. Most researches are done by laboratory experiments, which have limitations due to scale effects and cannot appropriately reflect the dynamic features of a disaster event. For the Daanshan landslide that happened in Fangshan District of Beijing on August 11, 2018, real-time videos were taken by local residents, which documented the whole process of the landslide (access on https://www.iqiyi.com/w_19s9349w4p. html). Those videos were not only widely distributed by the media platforms, but also provided valuable real-life data for researchers to reconstruct and study the propagation process of the landslide (Zhou et al. 2020).

10.2.1.3 Science Blogger and Science Content Aggregator

Guokr and China Science Communication are flagships in science communication in China. Some of them started as science bloggers and soon grew into science content aggregators, integrating academics, communication practitioners, and media partners into the same platform. The convergence has produced thousands of original and quality science contents for communication and education. Among which risk communication is a very popular topic.

China Science Communication (kepuchina.cn), one of the biggest science communication platforms in China supported by the China Association for Science and Technology (CAST), is in collaboration with science media, public agencies, academic organizations, and other science communication partners. Disaster risk reduction related topics such as earthquake, typhoon, fire disaster, landslide, urban inland inundation, early warning, emergency response, and reconstruction, are presented in texts, videos, cartoons, photo illustrations, and disseminated widely on its multimedia platforms. It has 3.5 million followers on Weibo, with 31,384 microblogs published in total, and 1 million daily views, according to the data investigated on January 28, 2020.

Guokr.com is a multi-media science communication aggregator dedicated to making science interesting. Its Chinese name originated from nutshell as in *Hamlet* and *The Universe in a Nutshell*. It is especially popular among the young generation. Its WeChat account is among the top 20 most viewed WeChat public subscription account. Its famous column, Rumor Shredder, cleared the air of the "earthquake cloud" which was claimed to be the forewarning of an earthquake that happened in World Heritage Jiuzhaigou Valley (M_s 7.0) on August 8, 2017. This practice was widely recognized as an effective approach to convey accurate and actionable knowledge during difficult times of disasters.

Institute of Planet, with evocative and neat storytelling and beautiful photos of the natural landscape collected from thousands of photographers and geographers, is an emerging science communication practitioner in WeChat. It worked with institutions of the Chinese Academy of Sciences (CAS), and published several risk-related articles, such as *Disaster and human civilization* with CAS Institute of Mountain Hazards and Environment which received over 160,000 reads (https://mp.weixin. qq.com/s/7OAQypD3485WpjSC_EKx9w). Its photos on the theme of disaster and human civilization were exhibited in the 2019 International Conference on Silk-road Disaster Risk Reduction and Sustainable Development on the memorial day of the devastating Wenchuan Earthquake that happened in 2008.

The scale-up efforts in risk communication have attracted more attention from the lay population. People with varied demands can easily access different education materials that fit their needs. The aggregated education materials also attained more interests from the new media players, who are craving for huge amount of knowledge contents to attract more traffic to their platforms in the knowledge-driven economy.

The emerging paradigms also attract a crowd of academics and well-educated practitioners to write as opinion leaders on the platforms. Science blogging starts to become a popular leisure-time activity for scientists who are willing to contribute their expertise to the public, and for media professionals in need of transitions. The quality original contents are disseminated widely on multi-media platforms such as WeChat or Weibo, and many are reproduced by the mass media.

10.2.1.4   Mass Media and Media Convergence

With the fundamental changes in media technologies and information dissemination channels, the advantages of traditional mass media have worn off (Xiong 2017). However, with lessons learnt from the past catastrophic disaster events and the trends of media convergence, mass media in China starts to reposition itself with better strategies in risk communication. They have not only taken advantage of their own multi-media platforms such as websites and news portals, but also work very closely with the social media in disaster reporting and risk communication.

Mass media utilizes Weibo and WeChat to broadcast their news in a simpler and more interesting way. A news portal is another way of quick dissemination to the audience. In 2008, the Xinhua News Agency news portal updated information about Wenchuan Earthquake 18 min after it struck. Five years later in 2013, the Sohu news portal started live streaming 17 min after the Ya'an Earthquake (Zhang et al. 2016).

Social media has advantages such as fast sharing, where everyone can produce information. But people tend to spend more time in processing and verifying the information if they want to make the right decision and get prepared during the critical moment. While information provided by TV, radio, newspaper, and other mass media tend to be more authoritative, complete, and evident-based with which people can make quick decisions and take actions accordingly (Liu et al. 2016).

One successful entry point for mass media is to debunk rumors and deliver the right information. Active disinformation is very problematic in risk communication. Seeking the Truth column of people.com.cn is a mass media column to rebuttal the rumors with evident-based reporting. This type of news story can also serve as a good opportunity to stimulate and fulfill citizen's information demand for risk knowledge. It also helps the mass media to regain its ground and build trust with the lay population, and serves as an interesting topic to boost traffic on their social media accounts (Feng 2018).

One example is the so-called "earthquake cloud" photos that went viral on the Internet during the 2017 Jiuzhaigou Earthquake, claiming it can predict the earthquake. Several mass media soon produced articles and disseminated them on several media platforms. The meteorological and geological experts explained that there was no evidence indicating the correlation between the weather and the earthquake, neither can satellite cloud images predict earthquakes (Feng 2018). Rumors about typhoons and explosions are further explained by mass media or public agencies on social media platforms.

Li (2008) analyzed the mass media agenda setting in 2008 Wenchuan Earthquake and found it well-organized for disaster reporting as well as for rescue and relief support. The first day after the disaster event, reporting was mainly focused on the disaster situation and ease the panic for surrounding areas; on the second day, when nothing was heard back from the epicenter, Wenchuan, the reporting focus was put on the disaster relief of the seriously affected areas such as Dujiangyan and Beichuan around the epicenter; on the third day, media coverage focused on the rescue and relief work into the epicenter. On the fourth day, after the best rescue timing, media reporting turns to topics such as don't give up, leave no one behind. Stories about a truck driver saved on hour 100, a bank staff saved on hour 104, then hour 129, hour 137, hour 139, until hour 164 and 169…, miracles kept happening with people's respect for life.

Mass media has also functioned as a rescue and relief lifeline during this earthquake. They alerted the public of information such as shortage of antibiotics and tents. Many enterprises volunteered the donation and even worked overtime to produce more supplies. Media has also introduced risk knowledge along the way. They have interviewed geologists to explain the geologic structure in the affected area, and medical expert to teach first-aid knowledge. The weather forecast paid special attention to the temperature, rainfall, and landslide of the affected area. The comprehensive and thoughtful disaster reporting has experienced significant improvement during this catastrophic event (Li 2008).

Radio, with advantages of fast sharing, authoritative, flexible, and stable, as well as lower barrier for literacy, is advantageous in disaster risk reduction. Wang (2009) illustrates the role of radio as emergency media in disaster events. In the beginning of 2008, southern China had encountered a 50-year return period snow disaster, which caused traffic, electricity, and communication to break down when people were rushing on the way back to their hometowns for Spring Festival. Dozens of local radios across regions tried simulcast and continuously reported on the traffic conditions, serving as an emergency management platform during the critical time.

Worse conditions happened in the 2008 Wenchuan Earthquake with the traffic and communication. Almost all radios and TVs started to activate the emergency reporting plans right after it happened. China National Radio (CNR) and local radios had explored their roles beyond just as the information provider, but also as the emergency operation center for rescue and relief, as well as an emotional resonance and psychological crisis intervention channel.

Effective communication strategies can be useful in disaster response, not only for physical support, but also to provide emotional assistance in extremely difficult and uncertain times (Takahashi et al. 2015). At 14:55 on May 12, 2008, radio presenter Jing Sun of a Chengdu local radio stopped the live program and spoke out with the very first sentence about this earthquake: "Guess everyone was frightened, I felt the shake too… Please do not be afraid and panic. Where ever you are, please do not expose yourself into dangerous places…" Even though there was no confirmation about the earthquake at the time, the voice of the presenter comforted the audience. Later on, presenters started to convey actionable knowledge in face of the earthquake (Wang 2009).

Meanwhile, disaster reporting and risk communication in China are now trying to promote the collaboration between traditional media and new media, institutional media and citizen media, as well as professional media and comprehensive media, to share the information more effectively (Wang and Jiang 2019). In December 2018, the Ministry of Emergency Management has made an agreement with China Media Group to collaborate on disaster reporting, risk communication, professional training, national emergency broadcasting system, etc. China Media Group will organize special coverage to promote risk awareness with multi-media approaches. They will also explore emergency radio in disaster-prone regions, and gradually introduce the system into public safety and emergency management plans across the country (China Broadcasts 2019).

10.2.1.5 Academics

Chinese Academy of Sciences initiated the SELF Forum, which stands for Science, Education, Life, and Future. It is a Ted talk-style science communication forum, inviting scientists and experts to talk about climate change, disasters, tectonic activities, among other science topics. Before scientists going up to the stage, science communication professionals will help the scientists to popularize their language, making it more understandable and attractive to the lay public.

CAST, which supports kepuchina.cn as one of the biggest science communication platforms, has initiated the Scientists and Media Face-to-face Forum in 2011, and held 48 forums since then. Each time, it invited over 30 media reporters and several experts to discuss one science-related topic. The hosts were one science expert and one media expert in the idea of mutual understanding for better science communication. Several topics related to disaster risk reduction were well discussed in the forums, such as the 4th disaster medical rescue and disaster health science forum, 7th forum of interpreting extreme weather, 17th forum of scientific solutions for urban inundation and psychological crisis intervention, and the 31st forum of how to deal with meteorological hazards in medium and small towns. These discussions and explanations were further disseminated through the mass media and then social media in promoting risk awareness and understanding among different communities.

Scientists, researchers, and educators are more engaged in science communication in China. Funding agencies require more science communications to be done in research projects, and budgets are allocated to communicating the research findings to the public. Certain funds are set to encourage the creation of quality communication contents. Interesting knowledge audios and videos, exhibitions, books created by individuals or institutions can apply for funding to support the production. These are very important catalysts for the development of the science communication industry in China, which has been trying very hard to find ways in turning knowledge into profit. And these also ignite more collaboration interests among the science community, the media, and visual content producers.

Laihua, a visual content producer, specializes in producing knowledge cartoons, animations, and infographics to explain complex and dry knowledge in fun ways. And these companies have witnessed the market growing with enormous demands for visual knowledge communication. Their collaborations are not just with the scientists and educators, but also with the mass media to tell the dry findings or hard data in a more interesting and attractive way. The company now has started to provide platforms and training courses for media professionals and institutions to produce visual illustrations in a simpler and faster way.

10.2.2 Fun New Media Approaches and Advanced Technological Applications

10.2.2.1 Visualization of Risk Communication

Given the sheer abundance of information on the Internet and visualization and fragmentation of information uptake, risk communication can maximize its impact with short video clip, microfilm, audiobook, live broadcast chatroom, etc.

Although the industrial development of mobile Internet slowed down during the past two years, short video apps are rising up and taking more user time. The daily average use time for Chinese short video apps has gone from less than 100 million hours to 600 million hours from April 2017 to April 2019. Douyin App, the top one in this industry, announced its daily average users exceeded 300 million in mid-2019, only 3 years after its launching.

A picture is worth a thousand words, and now a video clip is worth a thousand pictures. That is especially true in risk communication with the evocative power of video illustrations. And that is one of the major strategies government agencies, science organizations, and risk communication practitioners are exploring with the social media.

What should we do when there is an earthquake? How to use electricity safely during rainy days? What are the potential risks that we often fail to pay attention to? On May 12, 2019, the memorial day of the 2008 Wenchuan Earthquake and 11th National Disaster Prevention and Mitigation Day, Ministry of Emergency Management of China and China Meteorological Administration started the theme, #Disaster Risk Reduction, on Douyin to promote risk awareness and emergency preparedness among the public. Related short video clips generated by fire-fighters, earthquake departments, experts, and bloggers as real-life cases, drills, animations, and infographics, attracted 700 million views within 3 days. The view counts reached 1.2 billion at the end of 2019.

A national early warning information release center has announced its collaboration with Douyin app and Toutiao.com on May 10, 2019, to invite its over 2,000 agencies at national, provincial, city, and county levels to join these social media platforms and fast share authoritative early warning information.

It was also announced that Douyin will develop a technique to automatically convert early warning information collected from agencies into 15 s of short video clips, and auto-match them to the target region's account in Douyin, aiming to realize automatic information production and accurate dissemination to target regions. It will only take around 1 min from information release, video conversion, to reach the public (https://news.cyol.com/content/2019-05/10/content_18014119.htm).

Miaodong Baike, a knowledge short video producer and aggregator of the Chinese search engine company Baidu, has managed to aggregate knowledge videos of 1–3 min and attach them to the related entries in Baidu Baike (Baidupedia). This active exploration matches perfectly with how people prefer to consume information, and started to transform the Baidupedia from text and image-based to the multi-faceted Baike 2.0. Many animation producers have seen the opportunity and started their collaborations in producing knowledge animations. This is also a great opportunity for risk communication professionals to reach the public in their everyday search.

Take the entry "earthquake" as an example, if you search Earthquake in Chinese in Baidu.com, the entry in Baidupedia will come on the first page (https://baike.baidu.com/item/%E5%9C%B0%E9%9C%87/40588?fr=aladdin). When you enter into this entry, 74 related knowledge video clips will show on the top, such as learning earthquake in 2 min with 1.4 million views, how to survive from earthquakes with over 416,000 views (as of January 28, 2020). All information you need to know about earthquakes are aggregated into one entry by multi-media approaches, catering different information demands and consumption habits.

Audio sharing platforms have also proven to be applicable for risk communication, especially at a time when people are craving for knowledge in multiple ways. Himalaya Audiobook platform in China serves as a radio accompany for people during commute or bedtime, or when they are tired of staring at screens for information access. Its user number reached 600 million in September of 2019, with 170 min daily average use for active users. In search of risk communication materials, several related audiobooks and introduction of worldwide best practices can be found with adequate subscribers. One example of the audiobook *What should we do in disasters?* has 97 episodes of 3 min audios introducing all types of disasters and coping strategies.

Experiential projects can also facilitate communication. At the science fair in Shanghai, the fire department set up an activity to experience the use of fire distinguishers in person. Learning by doing. Interested participants have lined up to explore the practice (Qiu 2017).

10.2.2.2 Advanced Technologies Spice up the Communication

Qiu (2017) suggests that risk communication, like all the other scientific communications, needs interaction, enjoyment, popularization for different age groups with different educational backgrounds. Games, experiments, cultural products such as movies or videos, can facilitate effective communications.

BabyBus, an early childhood education brand based on mobile Internet, produced a number of interesting child games on its app for disaster knowledge, among others. Children can follow the game instructions on cellphone or tablets to, for example, guide the Panda for safe escape during an earthquake, hiding in solid corners and covering heads and noses, or to close even tape the window before typhoon comes, etc. Young children can gain a better understanding of natural disasters with interests, and practice their coping strategies in the visual games.

Advanced technologies can also be attractive in the application scenario, such as artificial intelligence, unmanned aerial vehicle (UAV), virtual reality (VR). At 21:40 on August 8, 2017, China Earthquake Network Center released an information on its WeChat blog, reporting "the magnitude of 7.0 earthquake in Jiuzhaigou Valley of Sichuan." At the end of the article, marked that the 540 Chinese character content was written by the machine within 25 s automatically at 21:37:15 on August 8. The blog provided eight parts of information, such as parameters, topography of the epicenter, population, weather and historical earthquakes, etc., and four pictures. The 13 updates on the aftershocks were also produced by the machine. And about the news about the earthquake that happened the next day in Xinjiang, it took only 8 s to write the story. The production is reported to be based on the current earthquake data management and service system, through data capturing, data processing, auto writing, editing, and releasing (https://media.people.com.cn/n1/2017/0810/c14677-29462088.html).

The local media in Hunan Province utilized several new approaches to report the huge flood in 2017, which affected over 4 million people. UAVs, helicopters were deployed for panoramic images and live broadcasting, VR and cartoons used to reproduce the scene, LED screens at each highway exit, and TV screens at elevators were utilized to disseminate the disaster updates and risk communication. The local newspaper's helicopter live broadcasting of the Xiangjiang River during the disaster has over 100,000 viewers (Xiong 2017).

3D panorama was applied for emergency response and public sharing on the landslide that happened in Maoxian County of Sichuan Province on June 24, 2017, in which 83 were dead or went missing and over 103 houses were destroyed. It was constructed and widely shared on WeChat and QQ with around 465,000 views (access on https://720yun.com/t/e2y72oo58dsq3ja6sx?pano_id=SLPrtIgYAriwZ8JV). The 360° panorama informed the public who were keen to know the situation in the affected area, and updated the evacuated people with what was going on around their destructed houses. More importantly, the UAV images provided the emergency responders and researchers with the overall feature of the event, such as the location and volume of the landslide. So they were better prepared before going in for rescue and relief. And those UAV images were utilized in producing high-resolution topographic maps for overall evaluation (Ouyang et al. 2017).

A research team studies water simulation and water disaster management at Xi'an University of Technology is developing multiple visual approaches, such as on Unity 3D, to simulate urban inland inundation. Now they are trying to apply this 3D flood demonstration scheme to both the lay population to gain visual knowledge of the hydraulic characteristics and dynamic processes, and the government agencies to evaluate their flood control plans and make evident-based decisions.

10.2.3 New Dynamics of the Risk Communication in China

10.2.3.1 Multi-directional Communications with Active Stakeholders Shifting Roles at Different Stages

Risk communication used to be unilateral. The rise of social media platforms and citizen journalism, among other driven factors, have transformed the top-down communication model and broken the information monopoly by the mass media, and diversified the information flow and agenda setting.

Liu et al. (2016) have summarized the development of risk communication theories into three phases. The preliminary stage of one-way communication emphasizes on informing, persuading, guiding, and educating the public. The development stage pays attention to two-way communications, where the emphasis is on the interaction among stakeholders and diversity of communication contents, and encourages the public to do active thinking, questioning, and make suggestions even decisions. The mature stage is about the way of communications structured by social relations, which not only focuses on the information but also the social relations supporting the communication.

The social network supported by social media platforms facilitates the popularization of citizen culture. Top-down communication is more authoritative to lead proper actions, while horizontal communication allows people to fast share, verify, feedback, and reproduce new information on social media. The disseminated information can be easily gained as feedback and updated during the multi-directional communications, contributing to the disaster events evolving at a fast pace.

Citizens and institutional players, apart from the media, can shift roles as information producers, disseminators, or receivers at different stages of the same disaster event. The convenience of communication and the strong possibility of being heard stimulate citizens to contribute their finding and expertise to the communication.

When disaster first happens, citizen journalists are very important information sources and disseminators. Especially for citizens in the affected areas, their cellphones and tablets can post news so much faster than the mass media, providing first-hand information and visuals for the public and for mass media (Xu and Liu 2013). Then media professionals come into play and produce more evident-based and comprehensive news reports, while social media provides the platform to re-disseminate the news stories, gather more updates, and stimulate further news productions.

In the case of 2010 Zhouqu Catastrophic Debris Flow, Liu (2011) has taken Weibo blogger Kayne as an example for analysis. At 03:23 on August 8, Kayne posted a microblog on Weibo of the affected area, which was later recognized as the first microblog from the disaster area. Limited by Kayne's followers, the blog only received 44 comments and 67 reposts.

The first turning point was when an opinion leader with 6,000 followers, at 18:14, inquired if Kayne was really from the affected area and notified @Weibo assistant to verify and contact the source. The Weibo assistant soon verified the source and posted on its official account with the rescue information within an hour. Hence, Kayne started to attract major attention as the vital information source to connect the affected area with the public and journalists who were keen to know the situation and provide support. Kayne's Weibo soared up to 119 microblogs on August 9, constantly providing information for social media opinion leaders and mass media to produce huge amount of contents, attracting massive attention from the public (Liu 2011).

In this case, social media platforms served also as the gatekeeper for rumors. Old photos of Salvador earthquake were disseminated in Weibo as the photo of Zhouqu debris flow. During the wide dissemination, some bloggers started to question the authenticity of the photo and reported to @Weibo editors to verify the information. It only took 51 min from the first voice of questioning to when the Weibo official account clarified the rumor. From rumor dissemination, questioning, and reporting, to the process of verification, reproduction, and re-dissemination of the correct information (Liu 2011), it is a fairly effective and efficient gate-keeping mechanism in instantaneous disaster information dissemination.

10.2.3.2 The Benefit of Media Convergence

Media convergence has integrated collaborative efforts of mass media and social media, which diversified the communication process, the agenda setting, and bridged the expert culture and civic culture.

During natural disasters, social media has been recognized as the key communication channel by scholars and practitioners which complement the traditional channels. Social media accelerates the speed of emergency response and disaster reporting from hours to minutes, even seconds. It is also considered as the lifeline during disasters, which can have one-to-many, many-to-many communications, such as safety check, search and rescue, and support.

Mass media produces more balanced and evident-based disaster reports, while social media needs to obtain news topics from mass media. Such as online content aggregators which have huge information demands but have less professionals, or bloggers on social media who would like to repost and interact under the news topics. These re-disseminations further promote the risk communication into the broader public. The dissemination, interaction, and reproduction with efforts from both the mass media and the social media also bridge the gap between expert culture and citizen culture, making the communication more dynamic and effective (Xu and Liu 2013).

Mass media professionals also take the responsibility to identify, respond, and debunk disinformation before it causes undue panics. During the 2013 Ya'an Earthquake, Seeking the Truth column of people.com.cn identified the Top 10 rumors and explained the true stories, including find Xujing to go home, whether a magnet can predict earthquake, another rescue truck drove off the cliff, etc. These stories were then widely disseminated through social media.

Many started the convergence during major events. In the 2017 Jiuzhaigou Earthquake, social media flagship Toutiao worked with China National Radio and set up a platform for missing persons. Over 2,500 notices were broadcasted and around 50 people got in contact with their relatives through the platform (Xiong 2017).

The agenda setting of the mass media and the social media also complement each other during risk communication. It can be seen that the number of microblogs related to 2010 Zhouqu debris flow boosted to over 10,000 each day during August 8–12 when the disaster first happened, and then rebounded to even higher numbers on August 14–15 when the memorial events were reported by mass media. The number of microblogs related to the disaster event topped on August 15 as 335,100 microblogs (Liu 2011). After the disaster events, relief and reconstruction as well as risk communication were spearheaded by mass media, which can generate new waves of risk communication in the social media platforms.

The massive amount of information generated by social media can be exhausting and time-consuming. These noises complicate the communication and delay the actions. During chaotic times of disaster information dissemination, mass media are adjusting themselves to set their own agenda.

At 15:00 on the day of the Wenchuan Earthquake on May 12, 2008, the nearby province Guizhou has also taken a certain hit. *Guizhou Daily* newspaper received hotline calls from citizens, wanting to know what to do, and wanted the outsiders to know what happened in the affected area. The paper soon produced articles and published on the front page the second day that Guizhou was less likely to have destructive earthquake activities. Xinhua News Agency also reported that Guizhou experienced the earthquake but with no casualties, "please do not believe the rumors and carry on with your daily schedule." These mass media messages soon reassured the public and eased the panic (Rao 2018). During the flood in Hunan in 2017, the mass media opened a public service column, and explained actionable knowledge, such as how to sanitize the drinking water and home environment after the flood (Xiong 2017).

10.2.3.3   The Normalization of Risk Communication Facilitated by Social Media with More Qualified Professionals and Quality Content

Although one-time risk communication at disaster events are effective in a short time, its impact will diminish over time. This suggests that the stakeholders should normalize risk communication. No single method of message delivery is the best. Risk communication strategies that incorporate the needs of the target audiences with a multi-faceted delivery method are most effective at reaching the audience (Fitzpatrick-Lewis et al. 2010).

Risk communication is important even when the disaster risk is low, especially for decision-makers and people at risk (Wang et al. 2010). Natural hazards are hard to predict and prevent. This demands the public to understand risk and how to avoid or lessen its impact. The most effective risk communication practice is to inform the size of the risk and how to respond to it, to explain how to avoid and reduce the influence on the individuals that are exposed to the risk (Kondo et al. 2019).

Fitzpatrick-Lewis et al. (2010) suggested that factors influencing response to risk communications are impacted by personal risk perception, previous personal experience with risk, sources of information, and trust in those sources. When studying the decisions made during crisis, Janis and Mann (1977) found even when people are aware of a coming risk, and they tend to underestimate the risk impact if they cannot find effective responding solutions. People need simple and actionable knowledge to avoid or lessen the impact of the risk. Wang et al. (2010) suggested the main purpose for communication before and during disasters is to perceive risk and take effective actions. Thus, the information delivered should be precise, simple, and understandable, and the decisions made should be scientific and evident-based.

The current risk communication focuses have made significant transitions from obscure disaster mechanisms to specific response strategies, such as prevention and mitigation measures, how to avoid or escape from danger, self-rescue and rescue others, emergency response, etc.

It is through effective risk communication and risk education in advance that around 2,300 faculty and students of Sangzao middle school in Mianyang City, Sichuan, successfully evacuated to the safe zone in only 1 min 36 s in the 2008 Wenchuan Earthquake, with zero casualties. (Wang and Jiang 2019).

On the morning of August 11, 2018, a serious landslide occurred in Fangshan District of Beijing, and soon hit the Junhong Road. But because of a patroller, who was engaged in the local public participated monitoring and warning system, discovered the risk and blocked the traffic 10 min before the landslide. Hence there was no casualty during the disaster (Wang and Jiang 2019).

Li (2018) suggested that disaster risk reduction in the past focused on the physical capacity to prevent and mitigate disasters. Then the emphasis on resilience helped shift the focus to public risk awareness and risk literacy to increase individual's emergency response and adaptation ability. It can be the knowledge about local historical disasters, emergency response and self-rescue, evacuation route and safety shelter, etc. Proper risk communication can help people access the information they need, which raises situational awareness to make the right decisions and take actions.

Social media has played a significant role in raising risk awareness and supporting relief coordination. The strong possibility of being listened stimulates public participation in information production and dissemination. More and more social media content producers and aggregators lay their emphases on risk communication.

Take a Guokr article as an example, "Super Typhoon Mangkhut finally blew away, why extreme weathers become more extreme?" explained the disaster mechanism, and teased about how Mangkhut might be expelled from the typhoon name list for being too strong. It elaborated on the exacerbated situation under climate change, and presented an interesting cartoon of whether we can bomb away typhoon with nuclear weapons. The article ended with the point that we can actually do something to reduce the risk by limiting human activities that can worsen climate change. The education material is informational and popularized with good timing. The platform also has articles such as whether we can precisely predict aftershocks of earthquakes, is there a number increase for earthquakes happened in Sichuan after the Wenchuan, Ya'an, and Jiuzhaigou earthquakes, and how to evacuate when there is debris flow which was published during the rainy season.

10.2.3.4 Information is More Integrated with Thematic Focuses, with Popular Language and Diversified Angles

Disaster information is more integrated into themes on social media platforms and news portals, and diversified by new media approaches and resources such as historical information and learning materials, and experience from other countries. The thematic integration will amplify its attraction to the public, and provide neat but complete information and resources for the public.

Huge amount of disaster information in the forms of images, texts, videos, and livestreams are integrated into topics. The most viewed list on Weibo is also the place to look for abundant information during disasters. And the mass media will produce thematic articles in face of rumors. Statistics showed that at 17:00 on April 20, 2013 after Ya'an Earthquake happened earlier that day, Weibo tweets related to disaster updates, relief, and rescue reached 64 million, among which, 2.3 million is to search the missing, 10 million is for safety check (Fan 2013).

Attempts to visualize the expression of dry data or response measures are explored with the support of social media. The China Meteorological Administration personalizes itself as Xiangxiang in its Weibo microblog and uses cute animal pictures or cartoon images to interpret the hard data, such as Xiangxiang's freezing face in purple to illustrate the 10–12 °C temperature drop (colored in blue and purple) in the map. It also collects fun facts of meteorological knowledge in photos and videos around the world, and creates cartoon illustrations. Before Super Typhoon Mangkhut came, @Weather in China, Weibo account of weather.com.cn, has posted several interesting ways of how to "seal" the super typhoon, such as spiderman style with a magic spell.

Pure data sometimes means nothing to the public. Pseudo-environment (Lippmann 1922) is considered to be an evocative approach in risk communication. Luo (2012) suggested that if explaining early warning data in the pseudo-environment, such as what does 100 mm of rainfall mean to the traffic and mountain areas, people can take actions accordingly. Take the high risk that occurred in the heavy rain in Kama Reservoir of Guangxi as an example, experts integrated the meteorological, hydrological, and geographic information, and produced a high-risk early warning map for flood and presented it on TV. The evidence-based illustrations facilitate the situational awareness of the public. Analogies can also help with the understanding. A cartoon of eight secrets of cold air compares the average moving speed of cold air on land, 50 km/h, to the car drive speed on city roads.

10.2.3.5 Prioritized Agenda Setting in the Media House

Disaster reporting and risk communication have become a prioritized agenda in the media house. It is also an important criterion to measure the reporter's abilities and literacy, as well as the response and coordination capacity of a media agency.

Take a mass media reporting in 2017 Hunan flood as an example, the local news website sent out 500 reporters and produced 4,517 pieces of reports, received 170 million views in total; local TV sent out 360 reporters and its 14 columns reported with 3,200 news pieces. Articles such as 150 college graduates of National University of Defense Technology missed their graduation ceremony to fight the flood, and shovel cars were used for evacuation, provided diversified report angles during the flood.

Individuals pay more attention to their safety in the modern age, especially the unexpected, which may create undue stress among the public and maximize the desire for disaster information. Failing to provide accurate or sufficient information can easily lead to social panic. Thus, one of the main strategies of effective risk communication is to learn about the information demands of the public, and to clear or lessen the psychological impact on individuals. Li (2018) suggests that risk communication that used to be top-down. When authoritative information is absent, rumors will flourish, even induce unnecessary panic. Thus, it is fundamental to know the risk information demand.

Media practitioners also face many challenges in disaster reporting, whether with the interviews or the environment, such as traffic, electricity and communication barriers, sanitation and resource problems. How to produce quality reports during difficult times, and coordinate between the media house and the public, require professional training (Tian 2016).

With the growing demand for media to be more systematically involved in disaster reporting, media professionals in China have done a lot of retrospections and discussions on the best practices. Seminars of disaster reporting were held in 2005, 2009, 2013 in China to look at media's professionality and responsibility. Practitioners from the leading media agencies discussed about responsibilities, ethics, angle, accuracy, clarity, visualization, and data illustration, etc.

Two books, How to Report Disaster Events and Media Handbook on Disaster Reporting, were later published in 2009 and 2014, discussing principles in disaster reporting. Topics include stay calm and respect; being professional rather than sensational; how to better prepare yourself for live coverage on site and how to support coordination; distance and camera setting for an interview to minimize the harm; different disasters and coping strategies; best practices from other countries, etc.

Information dissemination problems such as information distortion and false information in disaster events are also considered as top priorities in the media house. Gao and Xue (2012) pointed out that the misinformation should not just be dealt with during emergency, but be more intervened and prevented in our everyday life. It needs the joint efforts of the media to improve information literacy, while to establish an emergency communication system and make psychological intervention and adjustment proactively.

10.3 Discussion

China has valued the risks since ancient times. The Spring and Autumn Annals, Zuo Zhuan, in 403–386 BC wrote that people should "be aware of the risks even when it's safe, this awareness will make you prepared, and preparedness can avert the perils." Mencius (372–289 BC) wrote an article titled with risk and argued that the philosophy of individuals and nations was to survive with the awareness of risk in mind, or perish in comfort and pleasure. Many legends of disasters are especially popular for children's bed stories, such as Goddess Nvwa patches the sky, Archer Houyi and the Suns, King Yu combats with the flood, etc.

There are also several eminent engineering projects against natural hazards in China. The World Heritage Dujiangyan Irrigation System (256–251 BC) was constructed in battle with flood and drought in the Chengdu Plain in western China, and successfully turned it into the land of abundance. In the case of the World Heritage Jiuzhaigou Valley Scenic and Historic Interest Area, the historical disasters and the current disaster risk reduction and mitigation measures have played an important part in the formation and protection of the heritage. These projects are well promoted with cultural and educational value.

This chapter has discussed the new paradigms of disaster reporting and risk communication in natural disasters that happened in China in the new media age. The innovative development of social media platforms and new media approaches create a dynamic and interactive risk communication environment. Disintermediated institutional players, citizens and social media, academics, science bloggers and content aggregators, engage directly in the risk communication process. They have taken full advantage of the new media approaches and advanced technologies, and benefited the risk communication, as well as emergency management and research studies.

With the active and innovative stakeholders, natural disaster reporting and risk communication in China have shown several features. The communication is multi-directional with stakeholders shifting roles at different stages. The media convergence has brought together the advantages of mass media and social media, and facilitated the communication process and the reconciliation between the expert culture and civic culture. The risk and emergency information are more integrated with thematic focuses in media platforms, and the language and angles are more diversified and popularized. Risk communication has gained more and more attention as prioritized and normalized agenda in the media house.

Although media and disaster risk reduction have proven to integrate and develop significantly during the last decades, there are still many challenging issues, such as the need for more original risk communication contents to be produced with attractive new media approaches. The contents need to raise public awareness and guide them with actionable knowledge, who are from different age groups with different educational backgrounds. There are also issues about how to normalize media's systematic roles in early warning and emergency response, how to improve people's media and risk literacy in identifying rumors and take effective countermeasures in critical times, and how to fulfil the growing demand for well-trained professionals to produce quality knowledge contents in visuals, etc.

It takes a long time and skillsets to produce an evident-based risk communication content in popularized language and angle with attractive new media approaches. Dedicated professionals with both writing skills, new media skills, and science background are one in a million (Xu 2013). The urgent need for quality content and qualified professionals suggests that there is still a huge gap for well-trained risk communication practitioners. It either needs the collaborative work of skill and expertise from different communities such as the media, scientists, and emergency management agencies, or interdisciplinary professionals with the skill sets. Either way, media and disaster risk reduction are longing for capable professionals from different stakeholders to take one step further with the joint endeavors.

References

Bardoel J, Deuze M (2001) Network journalism: converging competences of old and new media professionals. Aust Journal Rev 23(2):91–103

China Broadcasts (2019) China Media Group and Ministry of Emergency Management signed the strategic collaboration memorandum. China Broadcasts 1:22. https://doi.org/10.16694/j.cnki. zggb.2019.01.006

Fan MJ (2013) Role of new media in catastrophic disaster events. J Kaifeng Univ 27:34–36

Feng Y (2018) Analysis on the communication challenges and strategies of disaster events by mass media. The Press 16:28–29 (in Chinese)

Fitzpatrick-Lewis D, Yost J, Ciliska D, Krishnaratne S (2010) Communication about environmental health risks: a systematic review. Environ Health 9:67. https://doi.org/10.1186/1476-069X-9-67

Gao H, Xue BQ (2012) Characteristics and causes of public crisis in disaster events under the new media environment. In: 6th national doctoral symposium on journalism and communication, Beijing. Communication University of China, Beijing, pp 618–627, Dec 2012

Gu YX (2019) Build consensus, promote the development of news communication in emergency management. Disaster Reduct China 7:20 (in Chinese)

Hu N (2017) Application of eye witness contents in convergent journalism. China Radio TV Acad J 7:65–68 (in Chinese)

Janis IL, Mann L (1977) Decision making: a psychological analysis of conflict, choice, and commitment. The Free Press, New York. https://doi.org/10.5465/amr.1980.4288953

Kondo S, Hirose Y, Shiroshita H (2019) Risk communication and disaster information. In: Abe S, Ozawa M, Kawata Y (eds) Science of societal safety. Trust (interdisciplinary perspectives), vol 2. Springer, Singapore, pp 129–140

Li M (2008) Breakthrough of disaster reporting in mass media, from snow disaster to earthquake. Media Obs 7:8–9. https://doi.org/10.19480/j.cnki.cmgc.2008.07.002 (in Chinese)

Li SS (2018) Risk communication for disaster risk reduction in resilient cities. Beijing Plan Rev 2:22–26

Lippmann W (1922/1965). Public opinion. The Free Press, New York

Liu H (2011) Studies of microblog communication in disaster events, taken Zhouqu catastrophic flash flood and debris flow as an example. Mod Commun 4:89–92 (in Chinese)

Liu TZ, Han X, Li HR, Zhang HB, Li XW (2016) Risk communication practical experience of U.S.A. government and its enlightenment for China. J Inst Disaster Prev 18(02):72–79

Luo GX (2012) Promote pseudo-environment communication and facilitate disaster risk reduction. J Meteorol Res Appl 33:157–161

Ministry of Emergency Management of the People's Republic of China (2020) Natural disasters in China in 2019. https://www.mem.gov.cn. Accessed 26 Jan 2020

Ouyang CJ, Zhao W, He SM et al (2017) Numerical modeling and dynamic analysis of the 2017 Xinmo landslide in Maoxian County, China. J Mt Sci 14(9):1701–1711. https://doi.org/10.1007/s11629-017-4613-7

Qiu CL (2017) Innovate science communication and improve risk awareness. City Disaster Reduct 1:46–49

Rao XM (2018) Analysis on social responsibility of mass media in emergencies. West China Broadcast TV 13:43–44

Shannon CE (1948) A mathematical theory of communication. Bell Syst Tech J 27(3):379–423. https://doi.org/10.1002/j.1538-7305.1948.tb01338.x

Takahashi B, Tandoc EC, Carmichael C (2015) Communicating on Twitter during a disaster: an analysis of tweets during Typhoon Haiyan in the Philippines. Comp Human Behav 50:392–398. https://doi.org/10.1016/j.chb.2015.04.020

Tian YL (2016) Learning from disaster reporting of Japanese media. Abil Wisdom 30:218–219

Wang W, Du X, Shao GW, Zhou C (2010) Transmission and communication of risk information in disaster emergency network system. China Saf Sci J 9:152–157. https://doi.org/10.16265/j.cnki.issn1003-3033.2010.09.028

Wang Y (2009) Thoughts on the role of radio as an emergency media in disasters. Public Commun Sci Technol 3:29–31 (in Chinese)

Wang YY, Jiang H (2019) Promote emergency communication and education, improve disaster risk reduction. China Occup Saf Health 04:44–47 (in Chinese)

Xiong P (2017) Communication challenges and strategies for mass media during disaster event. Youth Journal 35:41–42. https://doi.org/10.15997/j.cnki.qnjz.2017.35.026 (in Chinese)

Xu ZP (2013) Four goals of disaster information communication. J News Res 8:45–46

Xu ZP, Liu LY (2013) Communication characteristics of disaster information in the new media age, taken extreme rainfall caused flash flood and debris flow in Beijing on July 21, 2012 as an example. Journal Res 5:48–53. https://doi.org/10.15897/j.cnki.cn51-1046/g2.2013.05.009 (in Chinese)

Zhang N, Huang H, Su B (2016) Comprehensive analysis of information dissemination in disasters. Phys A 462:846–857. https://doi.org/10.1016/j.physa.2016.06.043

Zhou S, Ouyang CJ, An HC, Jiang TH, Xu QS (2020) Comprehensive study of the Beijing Daanshan rockslide based on real-time videos, field investigations, and numerical modeling. Landslides, published online on 23 Jan 2020. https://doi.org/10.1007/s10346-020-01345-2

Chapter 11
Importance of Reporting Local Disasters: Lessons from Varanasi, India

Suvendrini Kakuchi and Rajib Shaw

Abstract Local disasters—usually smaller in scale in terms of fatalities and loss comparison to the major tragedies—are commonly ignored in the mainstream media. But, as a case study in Varanasi has illustrated, disasters occurring close to home have impacted local societies gravely by causing lasting destruction. Their occurrence tends to be regular and linked to seasonal changes, and local reporters reporting the disasters say that their coverage is widely disseminated in the public and respected for providing crucial information. The case study also indicates news reports that capture the reality on the field, have played a role in facilitating aid and assistance for the affected from outside. Journalists participating in the study further noted that when losses from local disasters have reached large proportions creating difficult political and economic consequences spreading beyond the area, local disaster reporting has gained the attention of the national media and central authorities.

Keywords Local journalists · Local disasters · Seasonal disasters · Word Cloud analysis · Media booklet

11.1 Introduction

The three-year Varanasi project that was concluded in 2018. It aimed to delve deeper into the theme of local disasters by examining past stories published in the media and speaking with the journalists currently reporting disasters affecting their small communities. An emerging pattern in the research was disaster media coverage in small towns clearly operated in similar patterns to the media in larger companies. The local disaster was reported frequently and printed or broadcasted as top stories in the local media. Disaster news topics also covered similar themes to the mainstream media—loss and destruction, humanitarian issues such as personal suffering

S. Kakuchi (✉)
Tokyo Correspondent, University World News. UK, Tokyo, Japan
e-mail: suven@kdp.biglobe.ne.jp

R. Shaw
Graduate School of Media and Governance, Keio University, Fujisawa, Japan

R. Shaw et al. (eds.), *Media and Disaster Risk Reduction*, Disaster Risk Reduction,
https://doi.org/10.1007/978-981-16-0285-6_11

and deaths, and, in the aftermath, the focus was on lack of preparedness among authorities and their late response to providing relief. In reporting local disasters, journalists also focused on the link between development projects and natural disasters by exposing the perennial dilemma in disaster management—the link between prioritizing infrastructure development to modernize cities and suburbs that can lead to bigger loss from disasters as a result of the destruction of the natural environment (Chatterjee et al. 2015). The removal of large swaths of greenery in Varanasi City and surrounding areas that had traditionally acted as protection against natural disasters has increased the city's vulnerability to destruction from floods, toxic air pollution, and other hazards. The findings were documented in a booklet named "Media Reporting Disasters," that also contains personal comments from journalists in Varanasi on their reporting experience (SEEDS Asia 2017). The conclusion was that reporting trends in the local media were neatly divided into floods and urban flooding issues during the rainy season, and topics on drought and heat strokes were restricted to the summer months, revealing a pattern where disasters were linked to regular seasonal beats for journalists. In the winter months, the media reported tragedies related to fires that are made by low-income populations in the city and its outskirts. It is a common practice for poor people, who cannot afford heating in their homes, to start fires to keep themselves warm. The other important discovery in the project was that stories on disaster mitigation and lessons learned from past disasters were not extensively investigated or followed by journalists. Sadly, disaster reports receded drastically after the event.

11.2   Background

Varanasi is the heritage city of India with a history of more than 2000 years. The holy Ganges River flows through the ancient Ghats that are placed in a crescent moon shape on the riverbanks. The city represents a spiritual journey for pilgrims in India and around the world. The population has grown to half a million people over the recent decades but that number expands to almost triple during festivals when pilgrims from other parts of India and around the world arrive in the city. The situation is straining the city's ancient infrastructure and environment. (Chatterjee et al. 2015).

The city faces flooding during the rainy season months when the Ganges River overflows and affects the lives of thousands of people who live close to the riverbanks, recent rapid infrastructure development to cope with the increasing population has resulted in the vast devastation of local greenery making air pollution a major disaster. High levels of Nitrogen oxide are reported in the winter months when air pollution gets worse mostly from fires lit outside by poor populations to keep warm. This practice has badly affected the health of the residents and hospitals report growing cases of patients suffering from chronic lung and respiratory diseases. Yet another local disaster—the increase of heat waves has resulted in near-fatal sunstrokes—is recorded in the summer. Seasonal changes have led to soaring temperatures reaching

Table 11.1 Newspapers and their circulations

AAJ	Dainik Jagran	Hindustan	Times of India
1,86,823 circulation in Varanasi	1,50,000 circulation in Varanasi		10,000 circulation in Varanasi

into mid-forties centigrade in the months of April and May. In July and August, during the rainy season, the heat is accompanied by high humidity, posing yet another threat to people's health.

11.3 Methodology

The media research that captures local disaster reporting trends marks the first step conducted in this topic in Varanasi City. The objective of the study was to strengthen the reporting content in the local media by sharing the research with media and development experts. The study also highlights the fact that local disasters are often overlooked by the larger mainstream media organizations. The media project was divided into three main activities.

The first step focused on the collection of past media reports on disasters that were published in three newspapers—two English and one Hindi language mainstream newspapers published in Varanasi (Table 11.1). The collected news and feature reports spanned three decades—starting from 1986 to 2016—with the final collection of 800 newspaper articles. The articles were analyzed through the Word Cloud Application that identified the most commonly covered disasters in the media. In addition, the application identified the most commonly used words by the writers to describe the disasters. The Word Cloud analysis was captured in a variety of images that represented the different disasters in Varanasi. The findings were printed in a booklet—"Media Reporting Disasters"—that was shared primarily with journalists, libraries, schools, disaster management organizations, and civil society in the city. The book identifies the five major local disasters that strike Varanasi—Flood and Urban flood, Fire, Road Accidents, Heat Wave, and Cold Wave. There were also less reported disasters in the media—earthquakes, lightning, dust storms, and building collapse.

11.4 Key Findings

The results point to the fact that journalists wrote extensively on the effect of seasonal disasters on people and infrastructure. The most popular disasters covered by the media were heat strokes, urban flooding, fog, and dust that have dangerous consequences especially on the poorer sections of the society.

Other findings indicated that journalists have increased their coverage in response to the intensifying impact of disasters on the city that is creating more suffering and loss. Journalists in their reports referred to the history of these catastrophes such as the past episodes to show the rising threat and its causes. Their stories also spotlighted the human suffering among vulnerable populations while describing the economic losses from the disaster applicable for individuals and communities. Published reports called for urgent reforms and tended to blame the authorities for pointing out slow or lack of actions to implement new policies that will make the city less prone to disaster risks.

Notably absent were journalist stories published after the disaster. Anniversary stories were scarce, particularly, on the smaller scale disasters. In addition, it was found that there was a lack of news covering disaster risk reduction (DRR) topics published before the seasonal disaster as a warning or information to prevent loss. Journalists also face the challenge of finding sufficient time and systematic editorial support to help them write in-depth stories. The priority in media offices is to make the disaster a routine seasonal story unless the tragedy has far-reaching consequences.

The book identifies the five major local disasters that strike Varanasi regularly—flood and urban flood, fire, road accidents, heat wave, and cold wave. The project also identified disasters that were less frequently reported in the media—earthquakes, lightning, dust storms, and building collapse. Emerging from the analysis was that floods received prime coverage with countless headlines written in 1993 to mark one of the most dangerous floods in Varanasi after the waters in the Ganges rose to as much as 10 feet in certain areas flooding the overall ancient city. There was also extra media reporting on the floods in August 2016 when some parts of the low-lying areas in the city were covered with 5 feet of water that forced hundreds of people to evacuate their homes. Schools and public halls were turned into temporary displacement shelters and the city grappled with health issues, tons of washed garbage, and heavy transport blocks over several weeks until the water receded.

The booklet includes safety tips for protection from seasonal disasters with the intent of providing hands-on DRR education source for the public. The books were distributed free to media houses, schools, libraries, and official disaster management organizations including in New Delhi and other cities.

Examples of content of disaster stories as reported in the media:

- Disasters in Varanasi are seasonal and thus mostly predictable.
- Floods occur during the rainy season when the Ganga overflows into low-lying areas destroying homes, shops, and crops.
- In the city, urban disasters are linked to unplanned construction, irresponsible garbage disposal, and population density. Waterlogging is a serious issue for the city causing civilian displacement, loss of jobs and industry, and life-threatening viral and vector-borne diseases.
- Fire can be particularly lethal in Varanasi where populations live in narrow and congested ancient streets making access difficult or even impossible for fire engines. Fire disasters are reported mostly during April and May when dry temperatures can reach over 45 centigrade. January and February are also fire hazard

months because poor communities light fires on the roadside to keep warm raising the risk of fire and smoke spreading to cause accidents when fanned by winds or human accidents. Regular fire drills are not conducted by public authorities and building owners are lax in investing in emergency escape infrastructure.

- Air pollution makes Varanasi one of the six most polluted cities in India.
- Journalists report the loss of greenery as a major cause followed by fumes from vehicle traffic and factories in the city.
- Reports on building collapse educate readers about the vulnerability of ancient buildings in Varanasi.

11.5 Other Findings

Following are some of the other findings.

1. Flood stories are a top priority for journalists covering the environment and disasters in Varanasi.
2. Editors publish the Ganga River level changes by gathering data from the Central Water Commission. The Times of India publishes the water level figures daily in the newspaper.
3. The disaster impact of the flood on vulnerable populations such as injury and death, loss of houses and belongings.
4. The fear of theft targeting vacant houses during flood.
5. Relief measures taken by the authorities—providing rescue, shelters, food, and water.
6. Displacement and hardship in the shelters
7. Response of the authorities—such as the availability of emergency food and water and medical help.
8. The impact of the flood on business and the economy. The losses faced by small vendors and shops in the flood-affected areas.
9. The effect of the flood on Varanasi's many boatmen—they face economic loss when they cannot operate their boats on the river during the flood. Also their role in rescue operations for people in flood marooned areas.
10. Urban flood—articles highlight the poor city infrastructure, administration negligence, garbage blocking drains, deaths, or accidents from falling into open manholes to water-borne diseases. Table 11.2 shows the analysis of news reports on urban floods.

11.6 Results and Discussion

The booklet stressed the role of the media acting as a partner to create a culture of preparedness in disaster management. Traditionally relations between media and emergency organizations are strained, often because of the conflict that arises between

Table 11.2 Analysis of news reports on urban floods

Scientific facts	Insufficient in data
Interviews	Officials and survivors
Anniversary story	Rare and restricted to major floods
Flood topics	Survivor statistics, response and relief, loss of infrastructure, disease, displacement
DRR	Even though urban floods are seasonal, few DRR news were published

the needs of the media to report speedily during a disaster in contrast to authorities who are fearful of inaccurate reporting, and therefore rely on sharing selected information. Moreover, the media views itself as a watchdog using its reports to blame or pressure authorities to implement disaster protection policies. Against this backdrop, the booklet stresses the important message that the media can make disasters relevant through a partnership with authorities. The main goal for journalists in disaster reporting is to inform people through the dissemination of correct information widely. During an emergency, it is the fact that the media remains the most crucial source of information for the public. In this way, journalists can use their communication strength to promote public actions that can save lives and protect the rich cultural legacy of Varanasi for future generations.

11.7 Sample Interviews with Local Journalists

11.7.1 Flood Disasters

Senior Journalist, Times on India, Varanasi version. Flood 2016.

My reports on flood disasters focus on the number of affected people in their villages and evacuation. I rely on data issued by the administration. I also report on "miraculous" stories from the field such as people showing exceptional courage or resilience. I also cover post-flood health issues when people suffer from vector-borne diseases are common. Especially the people living in the low-lying areas are vulnerable to this risk. Urban floods enter their houses carrying human waste and other garbage that cause infections such as high fevers. Lack of clean water for the affected people is the main issue and proper drainage facilities must be installed for safety. My stories have shown that people are aware of the risk from seasonal floods but they take the attitude that the rains will recede after one and half months. Therefore, this is the prime reason they are not prepared for the disaster. Despite knowing the risk, the people are reluctant to move away from their fields or homes because they worry about theft when their homes are left empty. My reports have also shown that people who live in the city prefer to move to the second floor of their houses to escape the flood. They ignore requests issued by the authorities to leave to evacuation sites. My reports also focus on the lack of relief goods that are distributed unevenly leaving some people without any help. Included in my reporting is coverage of the relief work conducted by the National Disaster Relief Forces personnel that has saved many lives.

Correspondent: Hindustani Times.

It is important for journalists to travel to the affected site to get the proper information. The huge earthquake that hit Nepal in April 2015 impacted Varanasi and Uttarakhand. My office had a small fund so I covered small villages that are on the border with Nepal. My stories showed that the majority living there had no knowledge about earthquakes and were not aware of the steps they could take to protect themselves. My story stressed that prevention is always better than cure.

Senior journalist, the Hindustani Times.

During my career, the most important disaster story is on the floods that affect Varanasi, especially the villages that have developed on the banks of the river Ganges. This is a seasonal story and reporters are prepared. My stories are usually about the problems faced by the people such as the lack of food, evacuation sites, medicines, toilets, and proper information from the authorities. My stories focus on fostering aid to the people who need it the most. I also highlight the importance of community in disaster management by writing about people helping each other before official relief arrives. I also point out that the city has too many narrow streets making it difficult for rescue boats to enter. Disaster losses are related to illegal construction by people who arrive to Varanasi from poorer areas from neighboring states to earn a better livelihood. They reside in areas that are landfilled that can flood easily.

11.7.2 Cold Wave

Special Correspondence, Times of India, Varanasi edition.

Stories on cold waves are a regular beat in our newspaper during the winter times. We look at whether shelters are providing adequate warmth for the affected people. Our reporting aims to keep pressure on the authorities who are responsible for providing adequate care to the people in the city. As a bureau chief, I believe that newspapers can highlight disasters and other environment-related issues facing the city. Our stories put pressure on the decision-makers to bring solutions and reduce hardship.

11.7.3 Heat Wave

Reporter, Dainik Jagaran Newspaper.

April, May, and June are the hottest months for heatstroke and I cover this topic often focusing on the unpredictability of the weather. I also write about the problem of rapidly vanishing greenery in the city that is contributing to heat wave conditions. My articles include interviews of doctors who explain the dangers of heatstroke that can even lead to death, and I publish medical advice to inform the readers about the need to prepare and prevent the risk by drinking extra water and staying indoors when the temperature reaches peak periods.

11.7.4 Road Accidents

Senior sub-editor, Aj, a Hindi daily.

Coverage of road accidents is a local disaster and is an important news beat that gets coverage throughout the year. But the issue becomes particularly important for the editorial desk during fog in the winter and dust storms in the summer which lead to poor visibility for the drivers and causes road accidents to occur more frequently. It is important to raise public awareness on the issue as Varanasi gets more traffic congested.

11.7.5 Dust Storms

Senior sub-editor, Aj Hindi daily.

"Dust storms are linked to traffic accidents that are leading stories in my newspaper. Poor management of land and late monsoons are contributing to heavier dust storms. Journalists need to have better access and understanding of the scientific cause of dust storms."

11.8 The Way Forward

The chapter compiles critical information about local disasters and their importance to smaller communities. The research data provides information on the reporting of disasters by local journalists leading to lessons that can improve content and safety messages. Interviews with journalists showcase the importance of local disasters for the public and that reports highlight the local hazards adding pressure on authorities to implement measures to reduce loss. The research is also important for developing a media partnership in communication strategies in the planning and operation stages of official disaster management.

Acknowledgements The SEEDS Asia disaster reduction project—A three-year project: Participatory Community Based Disaster Risk Reduction (DRR) Approaches in Varanasi—was conducted to foster developing DRR education in local schools.

References

Chatterjee R, Verma P, Shaw R, Raghubanshi AS (2015) Climate and disaster resilience of Varanasi: city, zone and ward profile. Kyoto University, Benaras Hindu University, Varanasi Nagar Nigam study, Kyoto, Japan, 76 pp

SEEDS Asia (2017) Media reporting disasters: voices and experiences from Varanasi. SEEDS Asia Publication, Kobe, Japan, 24 pp

Chapter 12
Challenges of News Gathering in a Disaster Zone: A Study of Jammu and Kashmir Floods

Himanshu Shekhar Mishra

Abstract Disasters are one of the most difficult and complex assignments news correspondents have to manage and cover in their professional careers. It involves managing high level of risks and hardship, as it entails gathering news in an environment of uncertainty and social dislocation caused by a given disaster. This paper attempts to critically analyze the challenges news reporters have to face in a Disaster Zone. Based on a first-hand field experience of covering the devastating floods in Jammu and Kashmir in September 2014, the worst in India's recent history in terms of scale and the quantum of economic losses it caused, the paper delineates the logistical challenges and ethical and moral questions news correspondents have to face while working in a Disaster Zone. It proposes a Code of Conduct for disaster-sensitive reporting and highlights the significance of an ethical and humanitarian approach in Disaster Journalism. The paper outlines a Standard Operating Procedure news correspondents should adhere to while gathering news in a Disaster Zone, including an ethical protocol for interviewing disaster victims. At the larger level, the primary objective is to develop a normative framework for Disaster Reporting which is becoming increasingly important, especially in the context of a rise in frequency and scale of climate-related disasters in the last two decades. Disasters destroy critical infrastructure like rural roads and highways, bridges, power and water supply lines, and communication infrastructure (including mobile towers) in and around Ground Zero. This makes it challenging for news correspondents to travel inside a disaster-affected zone and gather and transmit news from there. The unprecedented deluge in Jammu and Kashmir and the landslides that followed made it difficult for reporters to travel by road to Srinagar and other flood-affected areas for several days. Disasters also disrupt social processes: they create a social circle of fear in the affected areas, as the victims suffer from an acute sense of loss of life and property around them. This makes it imperative for Reporters to develop a Protocol to manage risk and gather news in a climate of fear and insecurity. They also need to protect themselves from the possible outbreak of an epidemic in a given disaster zone. At a broader level, the chapter argues the outflow of credible information from a given disaster zone is largely conditioned by the ability of news correspondents to access and gather critical

H. S. Mishra (✉)
New Delhi Television Limited (NDTV), New Delhi, India
e-mail: h_mishra@yahoo.com

© Springer Nature Singapore Pte Ltd. 2021
R. Shaw et al. (eds.), *Media and Disaster Risk Reduction*, Disaster Risk Reduction,
https://doi.org/10.1007/978-981-16-0285-6_12

information in a disaster zone. Credible news reporting on the nature and scale of damages and the status of rescue and relief work in a disaster-affected zone can help direct relief and rescue operations in the right direction and also strengthen them. This is especially significant in situations, where disasters impair the institutional flow of information from official channels, mainly because of the sudden collapse of communication structures.

Keywords Jammu and Kashmir floods · Disaster journalism · Crisis communication · Disaster management · Media ethics · Sendai framework

12.1   Introduction

The rise in intensity and scale of climate-related disasters is increasingly threatening the lives of hundreds of millions of people in almost every part of the world. This has followed significant changes in the global climate as greenhouse gas emissions have gradually altered weather patterns often leading to extreme weather events like a high-intensity rainfall, flash floods and heatwaves. The Intergovernmental Panel on Climate Change (IPCC) has warned in its report "Global Warming of 1.5 Degree" that global warming might reach 1.5 °C between 2030 and 2052 if greenhouse gas emissions continued to rise at the present pace (IPCC 2018). This is bound to further intensify the scale of extreme weather events often leading to more frequent climate-related disaster incidents in future. A global study by the United Nations Office for Disaster Risk Reduction (UNDRR) and Centre for Research on the Epidemiology of Disasters (CRED) has revealed the number of climate-related disaster events like floods, storms, and heatwaves more than doubled from 3,017 events recorded between 1976 and 1995–6,392 events recorded during the subsequent two decades between 1996 and 2015 (UNDRR and CRED 2016).

   The two consecutive years of devastating floods in Kerala in 2018 and 2019 are broadly reflective of this disturbing trend in India. Indian Meteorological Department has argued that these unprecedented flood incidents followed exceptionally high rainfall in Kerala, which was an outcome of the impact of Climate Change (New Delhi Television 2018). Ministry of Environment, Forest and Climate Change too has informed the Indian Parliament that climate model simulation studies done by IPCC and other agencies "project possible linkages of climate change with frequency and intensity of weather related events" (Lok Sabha 2019). To combat this challenge at the global level, the United Nations has initiated institutional steps under the ambit of Sustainable Development Goals (SDGs) and Sendai Framework for DRR 2015–30 through a global consensus. Significantly, 10 of the 17 SDGs and 25 of the 169 Targets identified are related to disaster risk reduction (United Nations 2015a, b). To create an informed public discourse on this issue, Sendai Framework has outlined a global roadmap for the usage of traditional and social media in disseminating knowledge about disaster risk communication measures at local, national, and global levels. This has brought into sharp focus the critical role of Disaster Journalism—in both highlighting and sensitizing the global community—to the dangers posed by climate-related disasters. Based on my field reporting as a TV news correspondent in Srinagar, during the unprecedented floods of September 2014, this paper highlights the logistical challenges, security issues, and moral/ethical questions journalists have to face in a disaster zone.

12.2 Kashmir Deluge (September 2014)

India figures among the most disaster-prone countries in the world. According to the latest data on international disasters released by the Emergency Events Database (EM-DAT), India accounted for the second worst disaster event globally in 2019—a series of flood incidents across 13 States in Northern India between July and October 2019—which killed 2000 people (CRED 2020). It showed India's growing vulnerability to flood incidents in recent years. For instance, the devastating floods in Jammu and Kashmir in September 2014 is one of the worst flood incidents to hit India. The Parliamentary Standing Committee on Home Affairs informed the Indian Parliament that the flood crisis of this scale had not been witnessed in Jammu and Kashmir since 1902. As per official figures, 287 people had died in the flood tragedy. The scale of devastation was so huge that parts of Srinagar city remained submerged in floodwaters for more than two weeks. Around 2.54-lakh houses were fully or partially destroyed and 6.51-lakh hectares of cropped area was badly affected across 5,642 villages in the Jammu and Kashmir region (Rajya Sabha Secretariat Report 2014). It turned out to be the costliest disaster of the year in the world causing damages worth USD 16-billion (Guha-Sapiret et al. 2016). Considering the strategic significance of Jammu and Kashmir, India's most sensitive border region it shares with Pakistan, it attracted global attention. The scale of devastation caused by floods was so huge on both sides of Line of Control that Prime Minister of India, Narendra Modi and the then Prime Minister of Pakistan, Nawaz Sharif offered to help each other in relief and rehabilitation work (The Economic Times 2014; Live Mint 2014).

12.3 Flight to 'Apocalyptic' Disaster Zone

As horrifying images of the flood tragedy began to be relayed on national and international television channels and news media platforms, it shook the national imagination. The picturesque Kashmir valley, considered one of the most exquisite and scenic places on earth and an international tourist hotspot, had been severely ravaged by raging floodwaters for several days. All the major highways leading to Jammu and Kashmir were badly damaged following unprecedented rainfalls and landslides. With commercial flight services disrupted, the fastest way to reach Srinagar, the ill-fated capital city, was to fly in an Indian Air Force aircraft. When I reached the Palam Air Force station in South Delhi early in the morning on September 11, 2014, the Sun was yet to rise. We had been called by the National Disaster Response Force (NDRF) officials to board one of the Indian Air Force transport aircraft, which had been deployed to airlift relief materials to the flood-ravaged Kashmir valley. Even at 4.30 am in morning, a 24-h loading of relief and rescue materials on Indian Air Force transport aircraft was on at a war scale. They were making round-the-clock relief sorties to flood-affected Jammu and Kashmir state, airlifting Tentage, medicines, medical equipment, food packets, and medical workers, including doctors and NDRF personnel.

Indian Air Force Pilots were under strict orders from the Prime Minister's Office to give first priority to airlift relief and rescue materials from Delhi and other parts of India to the flood-affected zones and evacuate thousands of flood victims stranded there on their return flight. As we waited for our turn to fly and the day slowly progressed, the flood tragedy began to unfold in front of our eyes at the Palam Air Force station. Indian Air Force aircrafts landed in close succession from Jammu and Kashmir with hordes of disheveled and distraught flood victims, some seriously injured and in urgent need of medical attention. They were mostly tourists, migrant workers, and families of government officials stationed in Jammu and Kashmir when the flood crisis stuck. Some flights carried dead bodies of flood victims. It was the first indication of the complex challenges that awaited us on Ground Zero in the flood-ravaged valley.

After waiting for almost sixteen hours at the Palam Air Force Station, we finally got the permission to fly in an Antonov AN-32 twin-engine turboprop light military transport aircraft shortly after sunset. A team of five doctors had failed to turn up at their designated time, and we finally got an opportunity to board the transport aircraft and fly to Srinagar. The military transport aircraft was loaded with tons of flood relief materials. The payload included tentage, thousands of packets of food and medicines mainly for common water-related diseases like diarrhea, vomiting, etc., for distribution in disaster-affected areas. A senior Air Force doctor, Wing Commander Bhupinder Singh was also on board the AM-32 transport aircraft. Within minutes of take-off, we began to shoot inside the transport aircraft with an interview with Wing Commander Bhupinder Singh on the list of medical equipment on board which included a Patient Transfer Unit ("Mini ICU") fitted with ventilators and oxygen cylinders to airlift critically ill patients to big hospitals (New Delhi Television 2014a, b, c, d, e, f, g, h, i, j).

12.4 First Lessons in Disaster Reporting

When we landed in Srinagar Air Force Station after nearly an hour and a half long flight, the night was falling. As we disembarked from the AN-32 transport aircraft, a horde of flood victims were standing in a serpentine queue near another transport aircraft. They all seemed desperate to fly out of the flood-ravaged valley. They had got stranded in the valley as the unprecedented floods had given them no time to escape nature's fury. In the silhouette of the dim tail light of the AN-32 aircraft, I could hear shrieks of women screaming for help, children crying in their mothers' lap as they all anxiously waited for their turn to fly out of the disaster zone. There was a large crowd of flood victims lined up just outside the tarmac, restless and almost jostling to get the first opportunity to get onto an aircraft and fly out of Srinagar. As we walked past them, a distraught lady told us her child had not had milk for more than 24 h, and requested us if we could help her. As I tried to explain my helplessness to her, I initially thought of taking out our camera equipment to interview the irate flood victims on their plight but soon realized they were emotionally too disturbed to give any interview. As we walked away from the tarmac, we realized the line of flood victims inside the Srinagar Air Force station was more than a kilometer long, as hundreds of them waited anxiously late in the night for an opportunity to fly out of the disaster-affected region. My first hour after landing at the Srinagar Air Force Station had exposed me to the challenges that lay ahead.

An Air Force official asked us where we had planned to stay in the Srinagar city which was flooded, how we planned to commute to collect news and report and what was the alternative mechanism we had planned to communicate with our news headquarters if the mobile networks did not work in the heart of Srinagar. We had no idea where we would stay at night, how we will charge our camera equipment to shoot tomorrow. There were no vehicles in sight to help us move out of the Air Force Station as well. The first lesson in disaster reporting had been learnt. We felt stranded in a city under floodwaters. I had carried just a small bag with a handful of clothes and two new SIM cards in case my mobile network did not work in the flood-affected zone. It was just a routine planning I had learned to make while travelling to a routine outstation shoot. A strong urge to understand and witness how disasters incapacitate and destroy lives, property, and livelihood opportunities had pushed me to fly to Ground Zero without any requisite planning to work in a disaster zone. The next few hours were to unravel a whole new world of disaster journalism.

12.5 Breakdown of Communication Network

As my mobile phone network remained dysfunctional and both the new SIM cards failed to activate, we realized we had landed in a no-communication zone. The collapse of mobile towers and phone networks had incapacitated the communication infrastructure in Srinagar and nearby districts in the immediate aftermath of the flood tragedy. It had severely constricted the ability of news reporters to collect credible first-hand information from primary sources and transmit them to their news headquarters. I had no alternative mechanism to communicate with my news headquarters in Delhi and transmit the video content from Ground Zero. Within the first hour of landing at the Srinagar Air Force Station, I realized how ill-equipped I was for Disaster Reporting. We were taken in a police vehicle to the residence of a Deputy Inspector General (DIG) of Central Reserve Police Force (CRPF), a leading paramilitary force, to spend the night. When we reached there, we found that around ten reporters had already taken refuge there. It was an ad hoc arrangement since there were few safe accommodation facilities available in Srinagar for outstation journalists with necessary infrastructure like 24-h water and power supply. We were fortunate to get an opportunity to charge our camera and other TV equipment and spend the night at a safe place with both 24-h power and water supply facility.

As we readied ourselves for a challenging day at work, senior paramilitary officials informed us that many colonies in Srinagar were flooded and it would be extremely difficult for reporters to commute and shoot there. Floods had choked the water supply lines in large parts of Srinagar city, and power supply too had been cut off in flooded sections of the city. Collapse of communication infrastructure had seriously impaired the reporter's ability to seek credible information from the government's official information managers and representatives of government and private aid agencies involved in rescue and relief work on the larger tragedy that was unfolding in the Kashmir valley. Directors General of paramilitary forces—Central Reserve Police Force (CRPF) and National Disaster Response Force (NDRF)—strongly advised us to move around in the flooded city in vehicles manned by CRPF paramilitary personnel. There were reports of protests in the worst flood-affected parts of Srinagar; the situation was becoming volatile as floods had caused large-scale damage and the official relief and rehabilitation work was allegedly delayed and not commensurate with the losses incurred.

12.6   Flood Apocalypse in Kashmir

The unprecedented rainfall in Jammu and Kashmir region had caused havoc on the ground. 10 districts had been among the worst-affected—five each in Jammu and Kashmir divisions. The enormity of the tragedy can be gauged from the fact that the Shopian district recorded an excess rainfall of 2953% while the Srinagar district registered 1410% above normal rainfall between September 04 and September 10, 2014 (Rajya Sabha Secretariat Report 2014). As the humanitarian tragedy unfolded on the ground, one of the largest rescue and disaster relief operations in India's post-independence history was launched. Indian Army deployed nearly 30,000 troops along with 224 boats and 17 aircraft; Indian Air Force deployed 30 transport aircraft and 53 helicopters; while the National Disaster Response Force sent 22 teams consisting of 955 personnel to assist the State Government in search and rescue operations. Indian Air Force and Army aircrafts together carried out 3000 sorties between September 06, 2014, and September 25, 2014. An estimated 2.92-lakh people had to be evacuated (Rajya Sabha Secretariat Report 2014).

As the scale of devastation caused by floods was huge, flood victims scrambled to get immediate flood relief. Security and disaster relief/aid agencies had to struggle hard to supply relief to lakhs of affected people. The alleged delay in supply of relief materials in some flood-affected areas led to incidents of an irate mob of flood victims even attack security personnel. The then NDRF Director-General, OP Singh told me in an interview that around 40 boats of NDRF were badly damaged during the rescue and relief operations, some of which were damaged by an irate mob of relief seekers

(New Delhi Television 2014a, b, c, d, e, f, g, h, i, j). Some Indian Air Force choppers involved in relief and rescue operations were also pelted with stones. A footage shot by a video journalist, onboard an Indian Air Force's Cheetah helicopter, showed a few young people throwing stones at the relief helicopter as it moved closer to the ground to drop relief materials (New Delhi Television 2014a, b, c, d, e, f, g, h, i, j). The incident highlighted the dangers both relief workers and journalists can be exposed to while working in a disaster zone.

12.7   Reporting in a Climate of Fear

As we traveled to the flood-affected colonies in a security vehicle guarded by paramilitary personnel, a climate of fear was palpable everywhere—a sense of loss and tragedy all-pervasive. Thousands of flood victims had been forced to abandon their flooded homes. With limited space available in relief camps and disaster shelter homes to house these displaced flood victims, many families were forced to take shelter in makeshift tents along the banks of the Jhelum River. Jawahar Nagar was the first flooded colony we visited, one of the worst-affected areas in Srinagar city. Some homes in the colony had been flooded up to two floors, and affected residents had assembled in an elevated area just a few meters away. The residents were in acute anguish and pain, as the flood tragedy unraveled right in front of their eyes. Most of the household goods on the first two floors of their homes had been destroyed. Some had managed to shift important household goods to the terrace with lots of difficulties. It was dangerous to live in a flooded home, so they had sought shelter in a makeshift tent.

The first flood victim I approached for a conversation seemed composed. He narrated the horrifying moment his family first saw the water level rise in their home and the desperate attempt they made to save the precious goods before deserting their flooded home. The second person I approached had undergone a bigger tragedy. His sister was a cancer patient. With all major hospitals in Srinagar badly affected by floods, he was struggling to shift her to a hospital for immediate care. By then, a small crowd of flood victims had gathered around us. As I tried to gather facts and data from common flood victims, a man suddenly shouted at us, alleging that national media was distorting the reality and the news channels were neglecting the plight of the common flood victims. Soon, the crowd of flood victims which had gathered there surrounded us, as they got agitated and restless. Before we could respond to the situation, one agitated flood victim walked towards me and threatened to throw me in the floodwaters if I tried to interview any flood victim in the locality. The paramilitary personnel soon told us to leave the place and quickly escorted us into their security vehicle and moved us out to a safer locale. We could not interview a single person there. We faced the wrath of flood victims suffering from psychological trauma and an acute sense of loss at least at two other locations as well.

12.8   A Protocol to Interview Disaster Victims

These incidents highlight the importance of developing a special code for inter-viewing victims in a disaster zone. Journalists must be sensitive to the plight of flood victims: they must first learn to empathize and gain the confidence of their subject, ascertain his or her state of mind before making any request for an interview. Reporters must be very careful in selecting the subject and location for conducting such interviews. The disaster victims are distressed on the ground. Many of them suffer from a sudden sense of loss of social power—both in terms of losing prop-erty, livelihood opportunities and in worst cases, losing their loved ones. They suffer from psychological stress and psychiatric problems, and are largely traumatized and psychologically unstable subjects. Journalists must be sensitive to this factor while interacting and interviewing disaster victims. Reporters must realize they interview people who face a high degree of uncertainty and insecurity. They should be sensitive to the anger, agony, pain, and misery of flood victims. This brings to fore the impor-tance of developing a Protocol to interview victims in a disaster zone. The global journalistic community must collectively work to develop such a protocol based on their shared experience of covering disasters in different parts of the world. It should be based on a humanitarian approach in newsgathering. Journalists also need to develop a Reflective Approach in this regard to constantly innovate their approach in this regard. Also, in the light of the threats and anger we faced on Ground Zero, it is imperative for journalists to move around in small groups and work in close coordination with each other in a disaster zone. This would help manage the risks and challenges they may have to face while gathering news in an environment of fear and uncertainty.

12.9   Fear of an Epidemic

As we traveled from one flooded colony to another, the damages caused by floods were visible everywhere. Critical infrastructure like power and drinking water supply had been severely crippled; a large number of homeless flood victims had no access to safe basic shelter facilities. Thousands of families were forced to take shelter in open makeshift tents along the roadside, some even on the banks of the overflowing Jhelum River. I saw dead bodies of animals floating in the Jhelum River at several locations, including in Jawahar Nagar locality situated along the banks of the Jhelum River. In one instance, the carcass of an animal was floating just a few meters behind a makeshift tent setup by a family on the river bank. With many localities flooded for more than two weeks, the fear of an epidemic was looming large. Director-General of CRPF, Dilip Trivedi told me in an interview that floating animal carcasses posed the biggest challenge before the relief and rescue agencies involved in relief and rescue work (New Delhi Television 2014a, b, c, d, e, f, g, h, i, j). As government agencies intensified efforts to stop any epidemic from spreading, Union Health Minister Dr.

Harsh Vardhan flew to Srinagar to take stock of the flood crisis. In an interview to NDTV, Dr. Harsh Vardhan categorically said the possibility of diseases like Diarrhoea, Gastroenteritis, Hepatitis, and Typhoid spreading because of stagnant water was high and urgent steps were needed to fight this threat (New Delhi Television 2014a, b, c, d, e, f, g, h, i, j).

But the collapse of healthcare infrastructure at several places incapacitated the health services for several days, making it difficult for injured and ill patients to seek medical assistance. Considering that journalists were working on ground zero and traveling to the worst disaster-affected localities, they were equally vulnerable and exposed to the dangers posed by stagnant floodwaters. While reporting on the plight of flood victims who had fallen ill, I realized how much vulnerable and ill-prepared I was to work in a disaster zone. None of the journalists working in our group had any medical kit or even essential medicines for water-borne diseases. We had no wherewithal to fight any personal medical emergency in a crisis zone. In the wake of our experience, it is important for a news correspondent to prepare for any healthcare emergencies he or she may have to face before traveling to a disaster zone. In fact, journalists traveling to report from a disaster zone must codify the risks they may have to face in a disaster zone. They must prepare themselves to live and work in a crisis zone; they need to develop their own standard operating procedure to manage risks they might face in a disaster zone. This would necessitate developing a risk assessment plan according to the nature of the disaster they have been assigned to cover.

12.10   A Disaster-Sensitive Code for Reporting

Disasters destroy life and property. They disrupt life processes and significantly increase the economic vulnerability, especially of the underprivileged and poor people. The reporter's primary responsibility is to highlight the debilitating impact disasters have on local economies and livelihood opportunities of common people. In this context, it is important for reporters to highlight the degree of efficacy of relief and rescue operation from ground zero. They have to broadcast the first report to the world about the scale of devastation caused by a disaster in a given zone and whether the relief and rescue operations are moving in the right direction. This means working in an extremely challenging social environment, where thousands of people are insecure and living in fear. This makes it imperative for the journalistic community to devise a disaster-sensitive code for Reporting in a disaster zone. It must incorporate a methodology for disaster-sensitive journalism, including a humanitarian perspective in newsgathering. Journalists need to develop a protocol for managing their professional conduct in a given disaster zone. In fact, disaster coverage would require a special approach and a specialized training to manage logistical challenges and ethical and moral questions journalists have to face in a disaster zone.

12.11   Conclusion: The Road Ahead

As the global community grapples with the challenge posed by a rise in frequency and scale of climate-related disasters, the role of Disaster Journalism is becoming more and more crucial. It is imperative for Journalists to work collectively at the global level to strengthen their capability and develop a Code of Conduct for Disaster Reporting. They need to develop a protocol to address the moral/ethical and logistical challenges they have to face in a disaster zone. They also need to devise a risk assessment plan to help the body of journalists prepare better and strengthen their ability to gather news in a climate of fear and uncertainty. Importantly, the global community has initiated steps toward strengthening disaster risk and emergency communication measures and enhance the media's role in disseminating disaster-related information in this regard. The Sendai Framework for Disaster Risk Reduction, 2015–30 released after a global consensus at the Third United Nations World Conference on Disaster Risk Reduction in Sendai, Japan has outlined a roadmap to strengthen disaster risk and emergency communications mechanisms, including improving the resilience of telecommunications infrastructure. Section 36 (d) of 'Sendai Framework' categorically outlines this objective as it urges:

"Media to take an active and inclusive role at the local, national, regional and global levels in contributing to the raising of public awareness and understanding and disseminate accurate and non-sensitive disaster risk, hazard and disaster information, including on small-scale disasters, in a simple, transparent, easy-to-understand and accessible manner, in close cooperation with national authorities; (and) adopt specific disaster risk reduction communications policies…". (United Nations 2015a, b).

References

Centre for Research on the Epidemiology of Disaster and UN Office for Disaster Risk Reduction (2016) Poverty & death: disaster mortality, 1996–2015

Centre for Research on the Epidemiology of Disasters (CRED), UC Louvain and USAID (2020) Disaster year in review 2019. Cred Crunch. Issue no 58, p 1, Apr 2020

Guha-Sapir D, Hoyois P, Wallemacq P, Below R (eds) (2016) Annual disaster statistical review 2016, the numbers and trends. CRED, Brussels, p 21

Intergovernmental Panel on Climate Change (2018) P-4. https://www.ipcc.ch/site/assets/uploads/sites/2/2019/05/SR15_SPM_version_report_LR.pdf. Accessed 8 Oct 2018

Lok Sabha Secretariat (2019) https://loksabhaph.nic.in/Questions/QResult15.aspx?qref=10906&lsno=17. Accessed 13 Dec 2019

Live Mint (2014) https://www.livemint.com/Politics/BxJeONt39Bprcp1TUyusnO/Floods-in-Pakistan-kill-over-200-people-Nawaz-Sharif-survey.html. Accessed from 08 Sept 2014

New Delhi Television (2014a) 3000 flood victims take shelter in Srinagar Gurudwara. https://khabar.ndtv.com/video/show/news/three-thousand-flood-victims-take-shelter-in-srinagar-gurudwara-337948. Accessed 13 Sept 2014

New Delhi Television (2014b) NDRF chief on rescue operations in Jammu Kashmir. https://khabar.ndtv.com/video/show/news/ndrf-chief-on-rescue-operations-in-jammu-kashmir-337938. Accessed 13 Sept 2014

New Delhi Television (2014c) After floods threat of diseases in JK: CRPF DG. https://khabar.ndtv. com/video/show/news/after-floods-threat-of-diseases-in-j-k-crpf-dg-337920. Accessed 13 Sept 2014

New Delhi Television (2014d) Fear of epidemic in Kashmir. https://khabar.ndtv.com/video/show/ news/fear-of-epidemic-in-kashmir-338107. Accessed 14 Sept 2014

New Delhi Television (2014e) Health Minister Harsh Vardhan visits flood-affected Srinagar. https://khabar.ndtv.com/video/show/news/health-minister-harsh-vardhan-visit-flood-affected-sri nagar-338048. Accessed 14 Sept 2014

New Delhi Television (2014f) Stone pelting on army chopper in Srinagar. https://khabar.ndtv.com/ video/show/news/stone-pelting-on-army-chopper-in-srinagar-338045. Accessed 14 Sept 2014

New Delhi Television (2014g) Stone pelting stalls food drops in parts of Srinagar. https://www. ndtv.com/cheat-sheet/stone-pelting-stalls-food-drops-in-parts-of-srinagar-10-latest-developme nts-666418. Accessed 14 Sept 2014

New Delhi Television (2014h) https://www.ndtv.com/video/news/news/himanshu-prerec-air-force- base-338228. Accessed 15 Sept 2014

New Delhi Television (2014i) Kashmir floods: Air Force arranges for mini ICU. https://khabar.ndtv. com/video/show/news/kashmir-flood-air-force-arranges-for-mini-icu-338144. Accessed 15 Sept 2014

New Delhi Television (2014j) Rescue works in JK biggest operation launched by Centre: Cabinet Secretary. https://khabar.ndtv.com/video/show/news/rescue-works-in-j-k-biggest-operat ion-launched-by-centre-cabinet-secretary-338577. Accessed 18 Sept 2014

New Delhi Television (2018) Kerala floods because of climate change, top weather official tells NDTV. https://www.ndtv.com/video/news/news/kerala-floods-because-of-climate-change- top-weather-official-tells-ndtv-499745. Accessed 24 Nov 2018

Rajya Sabha Secretariat (2014) Rescue, rehabilitation and reconstruction in the aftermath of the floods and landslides in Jammu & Kashmir. Rajya Sabha Secretariat, New Delhi

The Economic Times (2014) Kashmir floods: PM Narendra Modi extends help to Pakistan PM Nawaz Sharif. https://economictimes.indiatimes.com/news/politics-and-nation/kashmir-floods- pm-narendra-modi-extends-help-to-pakistan-pm-nawaz-sharif/articleshow/41972964.cms?fro m=mdr. Accessed 08 Sept 2014

United Nations (2015a) Sendai framework for disaster risk reduction 2015–30. United Nations, New York, p 24

United Nations (2015b) Sustainable development goals. United Nations, New York

Chapter 13
Disaster Broadcasting: Challenges, Evolution and Lessons from Japan

Sayaka Irie

Abstract Japanese broadcasters have made great efforts to report disasters over the past 100 years. The role of broadcasting is not only to report the damage when a disaster occurs. When there is a risk of a disaster, to convey correct information and encourage rapid evacuation, to support the recovery and reconstruction of the affected area after a disaster, to deepen understanding of disaster risks in normal times and to raise awareness of disaster prevention. There are roles to be played before, during, after disasters and normal times. Since the Great East Japan Earthquake that killed more than 20,000 people on March 11, 2011, coverage of disasters in Japan has increasingly focused on hazard mitigation. Broadcasters have been making progress in improving both the software and hardware for encouraging early evacuation in disasters. This chapter describes the challenge and issues of disaster broadcasting in Japan in recent years.

Keywords Disaster-broadcasting · NHK · Evacuation · Great East Japan Earthquake

13.1 Background of Disaster Broadcasting in Japan

Japanese broadcasters have invested a great deal of human and material resources in broadcasting natural disasters such as earthquakes, volcanic eruptions, typhoons, and heavy rains. It is not only because Japan is a disaster-prone country, but also the historical background and the role of disaster broadcasting in the government's disaster prevention plan (Table 13.1).

Although Japan's land area is only 0.25% of the world's, 18.5% of the world's earthquakes of magnitude 6.0 or greater occur in Japan. 7.1% of the world's active volcanoes are in Japan (Japan Meteorological Agency 2019). There are many weather disasters such as typhoons, heavy rains, and heavy snowfalls. Japanese broadcasting,

S. Irie (✉)
NHK Broadcasting Culture Research Institute, Japan Broadcasting Corporation (Nippon Housou Kyoukai), Tokyo, Japan
e-mail: irie.s-hs@nhk.or.jp

© Springer Nature Singapore Pte Ltd. 2021
R. Shaw et al. (eds.), *Media and Disaster Risk Reduction*, Disaster Risk Reduction,
https://doi.org/10.1007/978-981-16-0285-6_13

Table 13.1 History of disaster broadcasting in Japan

Year	Name of disaster (number of death and missing)	Events related to disaster broadcasting
1923	Great Kanto Earthquake (over 100,000)	Phone and newspaper lost functions False information and rumors spread Expectations for radio are rising
1925		First radio broadcast in Tokyo
1928		First nationwide radio broadcast
1950		The Broadcast Law
1953		First TV broadcast from NHK's television studios in Tokyo
1959	Typhoon Vera (Isewan Typhoon) (5,098)	First live broadcast of typhoon from Meteorological Agency Huge damage throughout the country Trigger the enactment of the Disaster Countermeasures Basic Law
1960		First television broadcasts in color
1961		The Disaster Countermeasures Basic Act NHK became a designated public organization
1962		Central Disaster Management Council established
1964	Niigata Earthquake (26)	NHK holds "safety broadcast (Person Finder)" Portable radio was useful
1985		Introduction of emergency warning system
1991	Mt. Unsen Eruption (44)	44 Dead or Missing, including Journalists Safety management in disaster reporting was required Remote-controlled cameras became widespread
1993	Hokkaido Nansei-oki Earthquake (230)	The tsunami warning was too late Improvement of tsunami warning was required
1995	Great Hanshin-Awaji Earthquake (6,437)	Severely damage urban area "Living information" for victims was required
1996		Japan Meteorological Agency revised seismic intensity scale NHK sets up seismic intensity meters at stations nationwide

(continued)

Table 13.1 (continued)

Year	Name of disaster (number of death and missing)	Events related to disaster broadcasting
2007		Japan Meteorological Agency introduced Earthquake Early Warning System
2011	Great East Japan Earthquake (21,839)	Largest earthquake on record in Japan Using SNS for Disaster Reporting Shift to broadcasting for disaster reduction Improvement of broadcasts during tsunami warnings
2016		NHK Launches Disaster Information App

which began in 1925, has progressed in tandem with natural disasters. Today's disaster broadcasting in Japan cannot be discussed without its history.

13.1.1 The Great Kanto Earthquake and Radio Broadcasting

The Great Kanto Earthquake that occurred on September 1, 1923, caused devastating damage to the capital, Tokyo and its surrounding areas (Fig. 13.1). A large number of wooden houses collapsed due to the strong earthquake motion, and a large-scale fire broke out. More than 150,000 people were killed or missing, more than 220,000 houses were completely or partially destroyed, and more than 212,000 houses were destroyed by fire (National Astronomical Observatory 2020; Central Disaster Management Council 2011).

Traffic, mail and telephone services were suspended due to the disaster. Of the 22 newspaper and news agencies in Tokyo at the time, 18 were destroyed by fire. Four companies, including the English-language "Japan Times" lost their newspaper

Fig. 13.1 Devastating damage by the Great Kanto Earthquake in 1923 (From "Actual damage by the Great Kanto Earthquake in Tokyo" Tambasasayama City Audio Visual Library)

publishing functions due to power outages and telephone service disruptions (Japan Newspaper Museum 2003). The failure of mass communication to accurately convey information such as the extent of damage and the government's response has led to false information and rumors, resulting in serious social confusion (NHK Information Service 2002).

At the time of the Great Kanto Earthquake, radio broadcasting was being tested in Japan. The loss of telephone, postal, and mass communication functions led to the spread of erroneous information, and there was growing momentum for the practical application of radio broadcasting, which quickly transmits accurate information in the event of a disaster (Hiroi 1996). As a result, radio broadcasting began in 1925 in 3 cities: Tokyo, Osaka, and Nagoya. The following year, these three broadcasting stations merged into NHK. Japanese broadcasting stations were born with the role of disaster broadcasting (NHK 2011).

13.1.2   Disaster Countermeasures Basic Act and Broadcasting

In 1958, NHK started broadcasting on TV. In September 1959, 4 years later, a violent typhoon hit Japan, causing tremendous damage to 5,098 people who died or went missing. This disaster led to the establishment of "Disaster Countermeasures Basic Act" in 1961 (Cabinet Office 2015). The "Disaster Countermeasures Basic Act" stipulates the government's disaster prevention system, disaster prevention plans, responsibilities of local governments and measures to protect disaster victims.

The Disaster Countermeasures Basic Law establishes the "Central Disaster Management Council" as the government's highest decision-making body for disaster prevention measures. The Central Disaster Management Council is chaired by the Prime Minister and consists of all cabinet ministers, academic experts, and representatives of the designated public corporation. Designated public corporations are organizations that cooperate with the national and local governments in disaster response and disaster prevention measures. They include the Japan Red Cross, the Bank of Japan, utilities such as telecommunications, and NHK. Under the Disaster Countermeasures Basic Law, NHK is obliged to contribute to disaster prevention through broadcasting.

However, this does not mean that NHK broadcasts are subject to government control in the event of a disaster. The Disaster Countermeasures Basic Act does not limit the independence and autonomy of NHK as a news organization. Without the government's instruction, disaster broadcasting is directly linked to the protection of people's lives and property.

NHK has its own "broadcasting guideline". In it, he stated that "NHK's Mission to Report on Disaster Prevention and Mitigation" and that "Make every effort to provide information to protect lives and livelihoods in times of disaster"(NHK 2020).

13.1.3 Current Status of Broadcasting Stations in Japan

NHK is a "public broadcaster" which is operated with subscription fees from viewers. It has 54 broadcasting stations nationwide and about 10,000 employees. There are 2 terrestrial channels (general and educational), 4 satellite channels (First, Premium, 4K, 8K), and 3 radio channels (AM1, AM2, FM) (NHK 2019).

There are 127 private TV stations nationwide. Each of the five key stations in Tokyo has a news network. Each station broadcasts programs sent over the network or independently produced programs. There are 13 private broadcasting stations that do not join the network (NHK Broadcasting Culture Institute 2020). Commercial radio broadcasters include 47 AM stations, 52 FM stations, 320 community stations, and 1 shortwave station.

Based on the Disaster Countermeasures Basic Act, only NHK is designated as a national public organization. Private broadcasting stations exist throughout Japan. These broadcasting stations are each prefecture's designated public corporation. In the event of a disaster, they will broadcast the program in cooperation with local governments.

13.2 Role of Disaster Broadcasting

Here, the definition of the disaster broadcast should be confirmed. In general, a disaster broadcast is often regarded as a broadcast to convey "damage" in the event of a disaster. Actually, we have to consider the following 4 steps: "Before the disaster" "During disaster" "After the disaster", and "Normal time".

13.2.1 Before the Disaster

In the case of natural disasters that can be predicted in advance, such as typhoons, heavy rains, heavy snowfalls, and volcanic eruptions, life and property can be protected if appropriate preparations and evacuation are made in advance. In Japan, the Meteorological Agency issues advisories and warnings about meteorological disasters and volcanic eruptions. For local governments, the information provided evacuation advisories and evacuation orders will be issued based on the guidelines. Broadcasters quickly transmit this information with verbal messages of newscasters, alarms, subtitles, maps, and images from remote control cameras to call on residents to encourage early evacuation.

13.2.2   During the Disaster

When a disaster actually occurs, the broadcasters report the damage. Information and live footage from the affected areas will encourage evacuation and prevent secondary disasters. In addition, broadcasting early information on the situation in the area will lead to rescue efforts by the central and local governments.

Basically, reporters and cameramen rush to the site for reporting the damage. If they cannot access the site, remote control cameras or helicopter footage are used. In recent years, broadcasters often use images taken with smartphones and images uploaded to SNS by residents in disaster-stricken areas.

13.2.3   After the Disaster

Disaster broadcasting also plays a role in supporting areas that have suffered great damage after a disaster. In the immediate aftermath of a disaster, lifelines such as electricity and communications were lost, and supplies such as water and food were shorted. Medical services may not be available. For such disaster-stricken areas, broadcasters provide detailed information on the distribution of supplies and medical care will be provided.

It will take a long time for the disaster areas to recover. As time passes, the public's interest fades. It is an important role of disaster broadcasting to look at the situation in the disaster-stricken areas from a long-term perspective and communicate widely the situation and issues of recovery and reconstruction of the area. Such broadcasting not only supports disaster victims but also help prepare for future disasters nationwide.

13.2.4   Normal Time

In order to build a disaster-resilient society, it is essential to broadcast disaster information even during normal times. A special program will be set up on the day of major disasters in the past to raise people's awareness of disaster prevention and encourage them to prepare for the next one. Typical examples are the Great Hanshin-Awaji Earthquake (January 17), the Great East Japan Earthquake (March 11), and the Great Kanto Earthquake (September 1). The program not only looks back on past disasters, but also on potential disasters and disaster prevention measures in the region. Awareness of disaster risks in each area has a major impact on residents' behavior when a disaster occurs. Disaster broadcasting during normal times is an important form of risk communication.

13.3   Disaster Broadcasting of NHK

In this section, we look at the procedure of NHK's disaster broadcasting in the case of earthquakes and typhoons. The response to the Great East Japan Earthquake in 2011 is also introduced.

13.3.1   Earthquakes

As I mentioned at the beginning, Japan is an earthquake-prone country. When an earthquake occurs, the Meteorological Agency immediately sends out various information. This section describes the measures taken by NHK in the event of an earthquake with a seismic intensity of lower 5 or higher on the Meteorological Agency scale.

Earthquake Early Warning

When an earthquake with a seismic intensity of lower 5 or more occurs, the Meteorological Agency announces "Earthquake Early Warning". Earthquakes consist of a small shake called primary waves (P-waves) followed by a large shake called secondary wave (S-wave). Earthquake Early Warnings capture the primary wave and instantly predict the scale and epicenter of the quake, releasing it seconds to 10 s before a secondary wave of major tremors (Fig. 13.2).

The Japanese seismic intensity scale ranges from 0 to 7. The Meteorological Agency announces emergency earthquake warnings when it predicts an earthquake with a seismic intensity of lower 5 or higher.

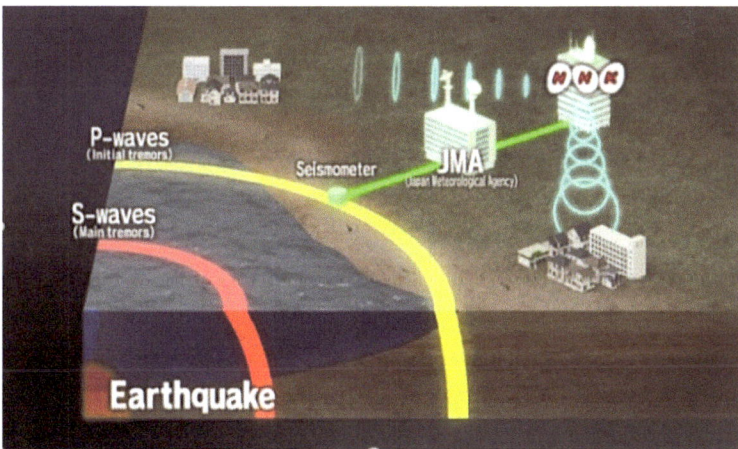

Fig. 13.2 Earthquake Early Warning System (NHK)

Fig. 13.3 Broadcasting Earthquake Early Warning (NHK)

The purpose of the earthquake early warning is to make people take actions to protect themselves before a strong ground motion strikes. They crawl under tables at home and stay away from buildings outside to avoid falling objects.

When NHK receives an earthquake early warning from the Meteorological Agency, it automatically broadcasts it on all TV and radio channels. Of all the NHK broadcast content, the Earthquake Early Warning is the only one that does not involve anyone, because even one second cannot be wasted.

On TV, the chime sounds and subtitles with maps appear (Fig. 13.3). On the radio chime sounds and artificial voice read the moment. This chime sound is exclusively for Earthquake Early Warnings developed by NHK. The sound is not similar to existing alarms or electronic sounds and easy to hear for the elderly. NHK provides the chime sound to private broadcasting stations free of charge and it is commonly used on TV and radio nationwide.

Seismic Intensity Information

The Meteorological Agency announces the "seismic intensity information" about 1 min and a half after an earthquake occurs. Seismic intensity information consists of areas, where a seismic intensity of 3 was observed and the intensity. NHK and private broadcasting stations will display the intensity information on their screens with maps and subtitles.

NHK has set standards on whether to stop broadcasting programs and switch to emergency news programs depending on the intensity of the quake. NHK usually switches to emergency news when the seismic intensity is lower 5 or more.

Tsunami Warning and Advisory

In the case that the epicenter of the earthquake was at the seabed, a tsunami could occur. The Meteorological Agency issues tsunami warnings and advisories about three times after the earthquake. If a tsunami warning or major tsunami warning is issued, NHK will issue an "emergency warning". A special signal is built into the alarm sound of the emergency warning broadcast. The signal automatically activates the system even if the TV or radio is off. The system was developed by NHK Technical Research Laboratories and has been in operation since 1985. It is a useful system that enables people to be aware of tsunami warnings and major tsunami warnings even when they are asleep, but unfortunately, not all TV sets and radios have built-in devices that can receive emergency warning broadcasts.

Even after tsunami warnings and advisories are issued, the Meteorological Agency continues to issue information on the expected arrival time of tsunamis, the expected height of tsunamis, and the observed height of tsunamis. In the Great East Japan Earthquake (2011), about 20,000 lives were lost by the tsunami. People near the sea must evacuate to higher ground as soon as possible. When a tsunami advisory or warning is issued, NHK will give top priority to the announcement of evacuation. The newscaster calls in a strong tone. It will also use a remote- controlled camera installed along the coast and relay images from helicopters. In Japan, where natural disasters are becoming more severe, rapid evacuation in the event of tsunamis or floods has become a major issue, NHK's Tokyo headquarters and the Osaka station have been training in emergency reporting on earthquakes and tsunamis every midnight.

Reporting Damages

News coverage and broadcasting of the damage will begin immediately after the earthquake. In the initial stage, remote control cameras and helicopter images are effective.

In the 2011 Great East Japan Earthquake, coastal cameras provided real-time images of major tsunamis. NHK has installed remote control cameras at about 750 locations nationwide. They are installed not only in coastal areas, but also in stations, airports and downtown areas where people gather. Since most camera footage is sent to a dedicated server in real time and stored for 72 h, it is also possible to replay footage of earthquakes.

There's a reason NHK has so many remote-controlled cameras. On June 3, 1991, a large pyroclastic flow occurred at a volcano called Mt. Unzen-Fugendake in Nagasaki Prefecture. This volcano has been erupting since the previous year. News crews from NHK, a commercial broadcasting station and a newspaper company were holding a camera every day to take pictures of pyroclastic flow on the small hill called "fixed point". The huge pyroclastic flow reached the point and killed 43 people including cameramen, reporters, taxi drivers, and volcanologists (NHK 2001). Based on this lesson, the importance of safety management in disaster reporting was reaffirmed, and the installation of remote-controlled cameras was promoted to prevent the risk to reporters. Private broadcasters also have remote-controlled cameras (Fig. 13.4).

NHK has 15 helicopters at 12 bases nationwide. At bases in Tokyo and Osaka, the camera crew and pilot are on standby 24 h a day, and at other bases during the day. In the event of a major earthquake, helicopters take off immediately and report damage that cannot be detected on the ground. In order to quickly report the scale and seriousness of a disaster and lead to a rescue, helicopter images are extremely important.

Fig. 13.4 Huge tsunami captured by remote-controlled in the Great East Japan Earthquake (NHK)

In the Great East Japan Earthquake, an NHK helicopter that took off from Sendai Airport captured images of tsunamis hitting the city. The video was broadcast by 2,000 broadcasting stations around the world.

In the disaster-stricken areas, media coverage activities will be conducted under the direction of local desks. Sufficient consideration must be given to the feelings of disaster victims when conducting interviews. They have lost their families and homes and have been forced to live in severe shelters. When reporting at shelters, obtain permission from the responsible person and follow the rules. Even a collapsed house is a valuable asset to its owner. We should not step on the roof to take pictures.

As mentioned above, safety management is also important. Aftershocks often follow major earthquakes. It is necessary to prevent our staffs from entering buildings that are likely to collapse, and to evacuate to higher ground immediately in the event of a tsunami.

Supporting the Victims

In disaster-stricken areas, lifelines such as electricity, gas, and water may have lost their functions, and daily necessities may not be available. Victims want information about where and how they can get help. When a disaster occurs, NHK immediately sends out "lifeline information". A special team, which is different from the news coverage, is in charge of collecting and disseminating information for daily life. The information is transmitted not only through TV and radio, but also through all NHK media such as data broadcasting and the Internet. As time passes since the disaster, the information needs of victims also change. Immediately after the quake, people showed a strong interest in water, food, and medical treatment, but within a few days, people turned to restoration of railways and roads and disposal of debris. From one week to one month, they will need information to rebuild their lives, such as subsidies for disaster victims and applications for temporary housing by the local governments. It is also an important role of disaster broadcast to pay attention to the lives of victims and convey necessary information in detail. Such measures are taken not only in the case of earthquakes but also in the case of meteorological disasters such as typhoons and heavy rains and so on.

13.3.2 Typhoons and Torrential Rains

According to the Japan Meteorological Agency, an average of 25.6 typhoons strike Japan every year, with 11.4 approaching and 2.7 landing. Heavy rain disasters also occur almost every year. Unlike earthquakes, typhoons and heavy rains can be predicted to some extent in advance. Therefore, NHK is focusing on broadcasting to inform people of the risks of disasters and reduce the damage.

The Japan Meteorological Agency issues various information as follows;

- "Warning/Advisory" (heavy rain, floods, windstorms, blizzards, storm surges, waves).
- "Emergency Warning" issued when the increased risk of a serious disaster far exceeding the warning.
- "Information on record short-term heavy rain" released when violent rain of around 100 millimeters per hour is observed.
- "Sediment disaster warning information" released when the water content in the soil exceeds a certain level.
- "Flood warning information" released when there is a risk of flooding of rivers.

The information issued by the Japan Meteorological Agency is provided online to NHK and other broadcasting stations and local governments. NHK has detailed standards for breaking news reports, and the information is quickly conveyed to the target areas by TV subtitles and radio comments. In the event that "Emergency warning", it will be announced on all channels nationwide. If there is a risk of disasters due to typhoons or heavy rains, the Japan Meteorological Agency will hold an extraordinary press conference a few days in advance to call for caution. At a press conference held by the Japan Meteorological Agency, the agency will not only explain the forecast of typhoons and heavy rains in detail, but also emphasize points to be noted in disaster prevention. NHK puts a great deal of emphasis on broadcasting news conferences by the Meteorological Agency and shows it on top of news programs.

Commentary by Weather Forecasters

Japan has a system of "weather forecaster" authorized by the Japan Meteorological Agency. The "weather forecaster" is allowed to forecast by analyzing meteorological data and satellite images provided by the Meteorological Agency. Many weather forecasters work for NHK and private broadcasting stations. In the event of a typhoon, torrential rain, or other weather disasters, NHK will set up special weather information programs in addition to regular programs to provide easy-to-understand explanations of the expected amount of rain, wind speed, and the time of day when caution is needed.

When there is a risk of a typhoon or a torrential rain disaster, NHK calls for caution in a news program a few days in advance (Fig. 13.5). Once a typhoon hits or heavy rainfalls, people cannot go to evacuation shelters safely.

When a local government issues "evacuation advisory" or "evacuation order", NHK will promptly inform on TV and radio. Reporters will broadcast the current situation from the site, and remote control cameras will be used to broadcast the rain and wind conditions in real time to urge residents to evacuate at the early stage.

The Ministry of Land, Infrastructure and Transport, which is in charge of river administration, has installed about 3,000 river monitoring cameras nationwide. NHK receives real-time images from the cameras and uses them for broadcasting. It also receives real-time information on the water-level data of rivers observed by the Ministry of Land, Infrastructure and Transport. Information on the water levels of rivers can also be found on data broadcasts and on NHK's website.

Reporting the Damage

As in the case of an earthquake, reporters, reporters and cameramen rush to the affected areas to report the damage in detail. Sometimes they are not able to enter the site due to floods and landslides. If the weather condition is bad, helicopters can't fly either. In such cases, NHK receives photos and videos taken by residents of the disaster-stricken areas and try to communicate the damage situation by telephone.

Fig. 13.5 Commentary of a weather forecaster in the case of typhoon (NHK)

Depending on the extent of the damage, regular programs will be canceled and special disaster broadcast programs will be launched.

13.4 Disaster Broadcasting in the Great East Japan Earthquake

The Great East Japan Earthquake, which occurred at 2:46 PM on March 11, 2011, had a magnitude of 9.0 and was the largest earthquake ever recorded around Japan. The Pacific coast of the Tohoku region was hit by a powerful quake on the Japanese seismic intensity scale 7 and a massive tsunami. The accident at TEPCO's Fukushima Daiichi Nuclear Power Station also occurred. The earthquake and tsunami killed more than 20,000 people. In the wake of this unprecedented disaster, NHK's all-out disaster broadcast was conducted (NHK 2019).

When the quake struck at 2:46 PM, emergency earthquake warnings were broadcast on all TV and radio channels. Two minutes after the outbreak, the newscasters entered the studio and started the emergency news on all channels, which continued for three days. NHK TV, Satellite 1 and Radio 1 continued emergency broadcasts for 1 week and 24 h.

Immediately after the earthquake, more than 600 people, including reporters, cameramen, directors, and announcers, 4 helicopters, and 17 relay vehicles, were dispatched to the affected areas (Fig. 13.6). NHK provided broadcasting services to the fullest extent possible, including non-broadcasting departments. 571 h of news and programs on the Great East Japan Earthquake were broadcast on national television 1 month after the quake.

The accident at the Fukushima Daiichi Nuclear Power Station was serious. The situation was constantly changing, so the accuracy and speed of information were particularly important. NHK used elaborate models and computer graphics to explain

Fig. 13.6 Huge tsunami captured by NHK helicopter on March 11, 2011 (NHK)

the structure of nuclear power plants, damage to them, and the meaning of technical terms. In addition, the government and Tokyo Electric Power Co. have set up a system that allows them to broadcast news conferences at any time.

"Safety information (person finder)" and "lifeline information" were also provided. In the tsunami-hit areas, communications were cut off, leaving many people unaccounted for. NHK broadcast lists of people at evacuation shelters around the country. Telephone reception centers have also been set up in Tokyo and Osaka. The center responded to inquiries by registering information received from disaster-hit areas and inquiries from family members and relatives. NHK has partnered with Google's Person finder to make it possible to search people on NHK's website.

We subtitled as much news about the disaster as possible for hearing-impaired people. The program was also expanded to include "NHK Sign Language News" which is normally broadcasted. In order to provide accurate information to foreigners living in Japan, a news program was broadcast with simultaneous interpretation in English.

The Great East Japan Earthquake accelerated the use of the Internet in NHK. As mentioned above, it was one of them that provided safety information in cooperation with Google. At the time, legal restrictions prevented NHK from streaming live TV broadcasts. However, the disaster-hit areas were not able to watch television. As a special measure, on external video sites, "Ustream" "Yahoo!" and "niconico namahousou (live broadcast) ", NHK news live streaming was performed for the first time at. Also the NHK first radio broadcast was made available on the NHK website.

13.5 Current Issues of Disaster Broadcasting

Since the Great East Japan Earthquake, the media environment in Japan has changed dramatically. With the spread of smartphones and the advancement of the communications environment, the younger generation has become dependent on the Internet and has stopped watching TV. What kind of existence is disaster broadcasting by television and radio in Japan today?

13.5.1 Presence of Disaster Broadcasting

In a nationwide survey of 3,600 men and women aged 16 or older conducted by the NHK Broadcasting Culture Research Institute we asked a question "From what do you want to get information in a disaster?". 89.9% of the respondents said, "TV" (Yoshizawa, Nakayama and Kono 2020). The percentage of those in their 20s was 80%, which is lower than that of other generations. But in all generations, "TV" was far ahead of other media. "TV" was followed by "SNS" and "Internet" for those in their 20s and younger, the Internet for those in their 30s and 40s, and "Radio" and "Wireless Communication system managed by local governments" for those in their 60s and older. "TV" still seems to have a presence as a means of obtaining information in the event of a disaster.

In recent years, a series of disasters have increased the presence of radio. According to "Hokkaido Eastern Iburi Earthquake" (Mj 6.7), which occurred on September 6, 2018. Power supplies were cut throughout most of Hokkaido, with up to 2.95 million households without power.

TV, smartphones are no longer available. Under these circumstances, battery-powered or manually rechargeable "Radio" worked so much (Irie and Nishi 2019). In a survey of residents conducted by the Hokkaido prefectural government after the earthquake, many said they had prepared rechargeable or manually rechargeable radios. In September 2019, a record storm caused by Typhoon No. 15 (faxai) caused a massive blackout in the Tokyo metropolitan area. At that time, the role of radio was once again recognized.

13.5.2   Can the Broadcast Deliver "Sense of Crisis"?

On the other hand, there are major challenges facing broadcasting. It is the "evacuation" of the residents. Recently, Japan has been experiencing tremendous disasters caused by typhoons and torrential rains almost every year. Many people have been killed by river flooding and landslides. The Meteorological Agency has issued warnings, while local governments have issued evacuation advisories and instructions. NHK also releases the information to the target areas. However, many residents have not been informed of the "sense of crisis" and have not taken evacuation actions. As a result, they have lost their lives or have been isolated for long periods in flooded areas.

The Great East Japan Earthquake taught us a lesson. The newscasters of NHK, a public broadcaster, have always read news calmly. Comments calling for evacuation were also objective, such as "There is a risk of tsunami." and "Please evacuate to higher ground immediately.". During the 30 min period between the earthquake and the tsunami, NHK anchors repeatedly called for people to evacuate, but many of them did not or returned home, resulting in the loss of many lives.

One of the reasons why people do not evacuate is psychological "normality bias" who believe that "I am the only one who's okay". There are also cases in which people believe that disasters will no longer occur after the construction of seawalls and river embankments in the past 10 years. The area near the river and the steep slope was developed for residence, but new residents were not aware of the disaster risks in the area. This is precisely a problem of risk communication. How can we convey the message that "have a disaster on one's mind"? NHK has made various attempts over the past 10 years.

Improvement of Comments Calling for Evacuation

Immediately after the Great East Japan Earthquake, NHK started to improve news-casters' calls for evacuation. Instead of using conventional calm and objective expressions "There is a possibility of a tsunami coming" "Please evacuate to a hill", he switched to imperative expressions, assertive expressions and emotional expressions. For example, he states that "A huge tsunami is coming! Please evacuate immediately!". He said in a strong tone of command. In the event of a typhoon or torrential rain, NHK uses strong expressions such as "Your experience doesn't work. Take maximum precautions." to convey that "emergency situation".

Improvement of Subtitles and Map

The subtitles used when tsunami warnings were issued were also drastically revised. NHK added a big red sign "Tsunami! Evacuate!" on the screen (Fig. 13.7). When a tsunami warning is issued, the target area is shown on the map, but some people have pointed out that the conventional color scheme is difficult for people with color blindness to see. With the cooperation of NPOs and experts engaged in color universal design, the color of the screen was completely reviewed. The new color scheme is shared by NHK and private broadcasters.

Automatic Display of Evacuation Information

In recent years, when we asked the question "What kind of TV contents should be broadcast to encourage early evacuation?" in public opinion surveys in the disaster-stricken areas, many answered "names of areas where evacuation advisories have been issued" and "water level of a nearby river" (Irie 2019). Residents want to know

Fig. 13.7 Improved tsunami subtitles and map. "Tsunami! Evacuate!" sign (*white circle*)

exactly what "whether or not one is in danger" is. Television and radio are good at delivering the same content to many people at once, but it is difficult to deliver personalized information.

Advanced efforts have emerged to solve this problem. It is "limited area display of disaster information", which was introduced by a private broadcasting station (ABC) in Osaka in 2017. If an evacuation advisory or evacuation order is issued, automatically display "evacuation advisory" and "evacuation order" only on a television screen of a target region. You have to press the blue button on the remote controller to erase it, so you won't miss it. Press the red button for more information. The system linked a preregistered TV zip code and evacuation information. NHK, an Osaka broadcasting station, introduced a similar system in 2019. When an evacuation advisory is issued, a notice "Evacuation information was announced to the area where you live." will be appeared on TV screen.

13.5.3 Utilization of the Internet

There is a limit to how much personalized evacuation information and the diverse information needs of disaster-stricken areas can be satisfied by TV and radio alone. NHK is working to make up for this by using the Internet. One of them is the "NHK News and Disaster Prevention App". It is a free smartphone application provided by NHK and specializes in disaster prevention information. If local governments issued warnings and evacuation information, they will be pushed. It also has a function to check the degree of flood risk of rivers and the degree of landslide risk on a map. When a disaster occurs, you can watch the disaster broadcast on NHK TV on the phone. It will also stream images from remote control cameras in disaster-hit areas and emergency press conferences from JMA.

In addition, NHK displays a QR code at the bottom left of the TV screen to guide viewers to an app or to NHK's disaster prevention information site, so that they can get detailed information on evacuation areas and evacuation sites (Fig. 13.8). QR codes also direct users to NHK's foreign language information site. NHK is in the process of making a major shift from "public broadcast" which is only for TV and radio to "public media" which includes the Internet.

13.6 Conclusion

In Japan, a country prone to disasters, improvements in disaster broadcasting have continued over the past 100 years. In particular, since the Great East Japan Earthquake of 2011, Japanese broadcasters have put more effort into broadcasting in order to reduce human damage. NHK is encouraging residents to evacuate as soon as possible by providing a variety of information, including video relays from remote-control

Fig. 13.8 QR code guide to app (*white arrow*) (NHK)

cameras nationwide, comments from newscasters, and information on water levels in rivers.

According to NHK survey, viewers want personalized information such as images of rivers near their homes, as triggers for evacuation. It is difficult for television and radio to convey personalized information to all regions. NHK and other broadcasters are trying to attract viewers to their Web sites and smartphone apps to convey detailed images and information tailored to the region.

There is also the digital divide. The ratio of the elderly aged 65 or older to the population of Japan is 28.4% (Ministry of Internal Affairs and Communications, 2019), the highest in the world. Many elderly people have been killed by typhoons and floods in recent years. For older people who don't use smartphones or other digital devices, television and radio are the "lifeline" of information for them. In order to encourage elderly people to evacuate early, it is necessary to examine what kind of broadcasting is effective on TV and radio.

On the other hand, an increasing number of young people do not own TVs or PCs and rely only on smartphones. Another important issue is how to provide disaster prevention information and images that have been transmitted through television.

References

Cabinet Office (2015) Disaster management in Japan. Cabinet Office, Government of Japan, Tokyo
Central Disaster Management Council (2011) Learn from the history of disasters. Central Disaster Management Council, Government of Japan, Tokyo (in Japanese)
Hiroi O (1996) Historical development of disaster broadcasting, vol 32. Studies of broadcasting. NHK Broadcasting Culture Research Institute, Tokyo, pp 7–31 (in Japanese)

Irie S (2019) Recurrent rainfall disasters: how and what should broadcasters report? From the internet survey on the heavy rain event of July 2018 conducted in Ehime prefecture. NHK Monthly Report on Broadcast Research, Oct 2019. NHK Broadcasting Culture Research Institute, Tokyo, pp 78–99 (in Japanese)

Irie S, Nishi K (2019) Which media worked in the 2018 Hokkaido Blackout? From the internet survey on media use at the Hokkaido Eastern Iburi Earthquake. NHK Monthly Report on Broadcast Research, Feb 2019. NHK Broadcasting Culture Research Institute, Tokyo, pp 38–47 (in Japanese)

Japan Meteorological Agency (2019) Earthquakes and tsunamis observation and disaster mitigation. Japan Meteorological Agency, Tokyo

Japan Newspaper Museum (2003) The Great Kanto Earthquake and the press. The Japan Newspaper Museum, Yokohama, Kanagawa (in Japanese)

Ministry of Internal Affairs and Communications (2019) Population census. https://www.stat.go.jp/data/topics/topi1211.html

National Astronomical Observatory (2020) Chronological scientific table. National Astronomical Observatory of Japan, Tokyo

NHK (2001) Broadcast history of the 20th century. Japan Broadcasting Corporation (NHK), Tokyo (in Japanese)

NHK (2011) Annual report 2011–2012. Japan Broadcasting Corporation (NHK), Tokyo

NHK (2019) Corporate profile 2019–2020. Japan Broadcasting Corporation (NHK), Tokyo

NHK (2020) Broadcasting guideline 2020. Japan Broadcasting Corporation (NHK), Tokyo (in Japanese)

NHK Broadcasting Culture Institute (2020) NHK data book: the world's broadcasting. NHK Publishing Inc., Tokyo (in Japanese)

NHK Information Service (2002) Records of the great disasters of Japan in the 20th century. NHK Publishing Inc., Tokyo (in Japanese)

Yoshizawa C, Nakayama J, Kono K (2020) Public attitudes towards disaster, preparedness, and evacuation behavior from the attitude survey on disaster. NHK Monthly Report on Broadcast Research, Apr 2020. NHK Broadcasting Culture Research Institute, Tokyo, pp 28–49

Chapter 14
Disaster Awareness and Risk of Foreign Residents and Tourists in Japan: Impact on Society and Role of Media

Midori Kusagaya, Shodai Honzawa, Shunya Hosokawa, and Rajib Shaw

Abstract In Japan, the number of foreign tourists and residents is steadily increasing which requires urgent attention in a strategic risk communication process. However, social infrastructure in Japan, including media communication, is not yet sufficient for foreigners due to lingual, cultural, and social gaps. While the tourists need customized emergency information, foreign residents need more local risk information to enhance their daily life preparedness. To find an effective strategy, this chapter will analyze disaster awareness and risk communication of foreign tourists and residents in Japan through a first-hand survey, data analysis, and interviews. The survey focuses on four language groups, Chinese, Portuguese, Vietnamese, and Indonesian speaking communities, which have different historical and social backgrounds in Japan. This chapter also discusses countermeasures through a local activity which involved foreign and Japanese residents and proved to be effective communication in the time of disaster.

Keywords Foreign tourist · Foreign resident · Risk awareness · Community interaction · Multi-lingual broadcasting

14.1 Introduction

Ethnic diversity has become more visible in Japan than it used to be. It is easy to find tourists from overseas everywhere in Japan. It's common that non-Japanese workers serve you at convenient stores or restaurants. This is due to a change in the policy of the Japanese government to increase the number of both foreign tourists and residents. In 2016, the Japanese government set a goal of welcoming 40 million foreign tourists in

M. Kusagaya (✉)
NHK Educational Corporation, Tokyo, Japan
e-mail: kusagaya.m-fc@nhk-ed.co.jp; kusagaya.m-fc@nhk.or.jp

S. Honzawa · S. Hosokawa
Faculty of Policy Management, Keio University, Fujisawa, Japan

R. Shaw
Graduate School of Media and Governance, Keio University, Fujisawa, Japan

© Springer Nature Singapore Pte Ltd. 2021
R. Shaw et al. (eds.), *Media and Disaster Risk Reduction*, Disaster Risk Reduction,
https://doi.org/10.1007/978-981-16-0285-6_14

221

2020, when Tokyo was scheduled to host the Olympic and Paralympic games (MLIT 2016). Local governments and businesses are promoting themselves by providing information and service in several languages.

The number of residents from overseas is also increasing, totaling 2,829,000 in June 2019 (MOJ 2020a). These people include workers, students, and spouses of Japanese. Among them are a relatively new group of foreigners called "technical intern trainees" (MOJ 2017). They are mostly from Asian countries and work in the manufacturing, construction, service, and agriculture–fisheries industries, filling labor shortages caused by the shrinking and aging population. With the new Immigration Control Act of 2019, Japan has renewed its immigration policy opening up more positions for more foreign residents of specific countries in specific job categories (MOFA 2020). Both types of foreigners (tourists and residents) are increasing over years, and the government is also implementing an aggressive plan for this (MOJ 2020b). In spite of this trend, foreign tourists and residents are left behind in regard to disaster preparedness. Figure 14.1 shows that death rate was six times higher for foreigners at the Great Hanshin-Awaji Earthquake in 1995. The rate is eight times higher for injury (Hosokawa 2020).

Twenty-five years have passed since then. However, it is still unknown what kind of risks specifically foreigners face when disaster strikes. Japanese society needs to pay more attention to their safety and take measures to protect them. Media's role is crucial in making society more inclusive. Japan has nurtured a disaster preparedness culture through its long history of numerous disasters, but it is difficult for foreigners to promptly learn and adjust to the culture. Therefore, media is responsible to raise awareness of all members of the society, including foreign visitors and residents, as well as to provide emergency information in accessible ways during and after disasters.

Fig. 14.1 Comparison of Japanese and foreigners in terms of death and injury in The Great Hanshin-Awaji Earthquake

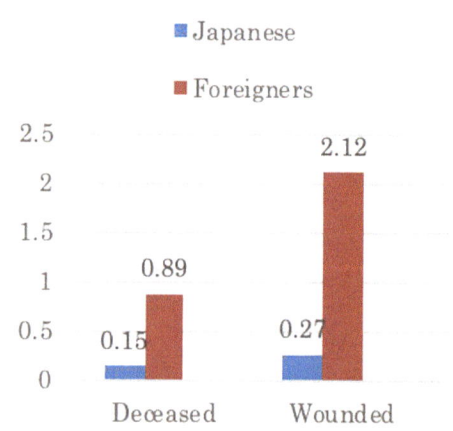

14.2 Foreign Tourist Risk Perception

In order to investigate the disaster preparedness awareness of foreign tourists who are traveling to Japan, a questionnaire survey was conducted in 2019 (Hosokawa 2020, Honzawa 2020). The survey was carried out two times. First, online questionnaire was spread on SNS such as Twitter and Facebook from June to July. The second was on-spot interview using the same list of questions, at places where many foreign tourists gather, such as Kamakura and Shibuya, Haneda airport from October to December 2019. Questionnaires had several parts: (1) general information (like age range, gender, nationality, first time or repeater in Japan, etc.), (2) whether they have experiences of disaster in their country, (3) their risk perception about Japan, source of information, basic needs of information, etc. Table 14.1 shows the characteristic of the respondent.

Even though 81.7% of respondents have had a disaster in their country, only 55.6% had actually experienced the disaster. Asked what disaster they had experienced using multiple choices, the answers were earthquake (33.8%), Flood (23.4%), Typhoon (29.9%), and Others (13.0%) in decreasing order. The survey results show that foreign tourists' disaster-risk perception is correlated with their disaster experience of the past. Tourists with disaster experience show more awareness of possible disasters during their trip. However, the tendency shrank when asked about their knowledge about Japan-specific disaster. In addition, among those who had experienced disasters, only 28.6% had taken any action to prepare. The figure dropped more for those who didn't have any experience. These results suggest that typical tourists are aware of disaster risk to some extent but did not prepare before visiting Japan.

The survey also found another risk, which was the lack of information or other resources. The actions respondents would take when they encounter disaster were "evacuate to a safe place" (53.2%), "try to get the correct information" (25.4%) "try to contact family or friends" (11.1%) in decreasing order (Fig. 14.2a). However, asked what they worry about most, the most common answer was "I don't know where should I go" (34.4%), followed by "Language problem" (25.6%), "I don't know the way to access correct information" (20.0%), and "I don't know how to contact my family" (18.4%) (Fig. 14.2b). There are gaps between need and reality.

The questionnaire also asked if the respondents had any specific suggestions for improving information for foreigners. The most frequent request was language support, while some respondents expressed the willingness to undertake simple training. Here are some examples from their answers:

- Have news programs, magazines, and posters in as many languages as possible.
- Leave multilingual pamphlets, which can easily be carried around, on the seats of airplanes, or at key points in the airport.
- Be able to watch videos summarizing disasters that can be seen during flight by air.
- Place signs (posters, etc.) at sightseeing spots, supermarkets, trains, and airports.

Table 14.1 Characteristics of respondents

		Total	Asia	North America	South America	Europe	Oceania
	Number of people	123(100%)	43(35%)	18(31%)	1(0.008%)	23(23%)	11(11%)
Age	~19	9(7.1%)	8	0	0	1	0
	29–29	71(56.3%)	32	21	0	17	1
	30–39	18(14.3%)	3	7	0	4	4
	49–49	9(7.1%)	0	2	1	4	2
	50–59	11(10.3%)	0	4	0	1	6
	Over 60	5(4.8%)	0	4	0	1	0
Gender	Male	69(54.8%)	19	23	0	16	11
	Female	54(45.2%)	24	15	1	12	2
Visit Count	Only once	53(42.4%)	12	13	1	19	8
	Several times	62(51.2%)	29	20	0	8	5
	Never	8(6.4%)	2	5	0	1	0
Who are you with?	Friends	49(39.7%)	21	11	0	14	3
	Family	36(28.6%)	10	11	1	6	8
	Colleague	5(4.8%)	1	4	0	0	0
	Alone	33(27.0%)	11	12	0	8	2
Length of stay	Less than 1 week	13(11.1%)	9	4	0	0	0
	1–2 weeks	52(42.9%)	14	15	0	17	6
	More than 2 weeks	58(46.0%)	20	19	1	11	7
Are there disasters in your country?	Yes	99(81.7%)	41	36	0	9	13
	No	24(18.3%)	2	2	1	19	0
Have you ever experienced a disaster?	Yes	67(55.6%)	27	24	1	7	8
	No	56(44.4%)	16	14	0	21	5
Have you prepared something, such as collected information for prevention disaster before visiting Japan?	Yes	28(25.4%)	12	12	0	2	2
	No	95(74.6%)	31	26	1	26	11

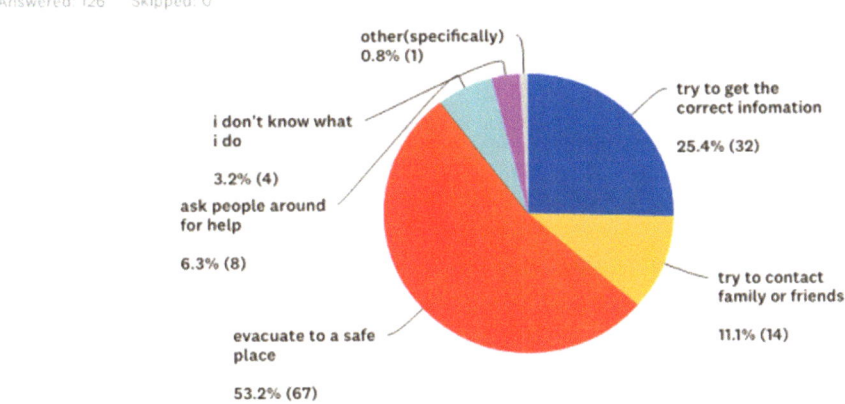

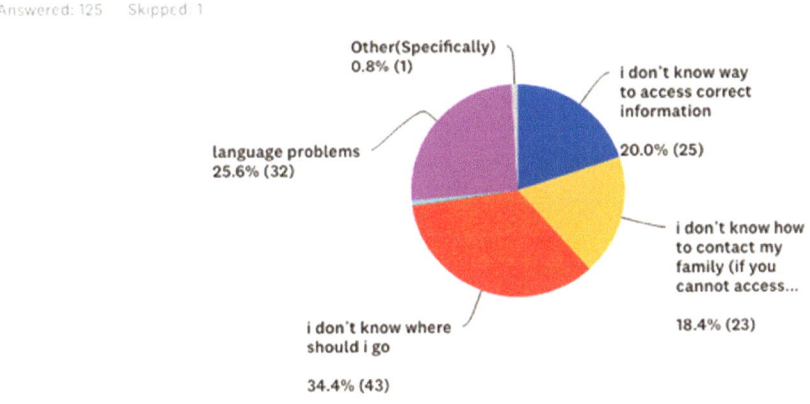

Fig. 14.2 **a** (left): What do you do first when you encounter a disaster and **b** (right): what are you most worried about when a disaster occurs

- Make a list of places where emergency contact can be made in the event of a disaster, such as hotels and tourism companies.

Most of the tourists are interested in acquiring knowledge and information quickly, in the places like hotel, airport, during transportation and sightseeing spots, etc.

Based on the survey, foreign tourists who need the most are those who have no disaster awareness. Therefore, "disaster prevention in phases" should be effective. Figure 14.3 illustrates this. The key point is that the information needs to be shared in different modes at several places so that it draws attention to the tourists.

Fig. 14.3 Possible role of media in raising awareness of tourists

Information on disaster preparedness would be provided in several places by different providers, so that tourists, who are not motivated will have maximum exposure to grasp disaster information. The information should be provided at places where many tourists visit, for example, videos in airplanes, limousine buses, and at hotels. Those videos should be short and provide basic information in different languages. Pamphlets are also useful and should be delivered to places like airports, tourist information centers, and sightseeing spots. In addition, it is indispensable to utilize popular tools such as social media and smartphone applications. Many sectors, including central and local governments, mass media, business, and citizens, have information using these tools. But most of them need better accessibility and usability. In order to reach every corner, QR code and URL to access information hub should be handed out at places like immigration.

14.3 Risk Perception Online Survey of Residents in Japan

Foreign residents in Japan have different needs for risk management from those of tourists. Therefore, a survey focusing on foreign residents in Japan was conducted through online questionnaires and face-to-face interviews in 2019 (Hosokawa 2020; Honzawa 2020). The research focused on four different language groups. First, Chinese, the largest population of non-Japanese in Japan. Second, Brazilians, who form condense communities in local areas. Third and fourth are Vietnamese and Indonesian, respectively, which are rapidly increasing mainly due to the Japanese government's policy to welcome the international workforce. Each group has a different history and different types of community in Japan.

Online questionnaires were conducted from October to December 2019 via Facebook, LINE, E-mail, using Survey Monkey in six languages (English, Japanese, Chinese, Portuguese, Vietnamese, and Indonesian). The questionnaire collected a total of 317 responses from people in 32 countries. The majority are in their 20s and 30s (79%). Work and study accounted for 70% of the qualifications in Japan. Japanese knowledge had an equal distribution from "Don't understand" to "Understand very well." When asked who they live with, couple or alone were the most common. Table 14.2 provides the basic data.

Factors correlating disaster preparedness awareness of foreign residents in general are analyzed. An index from 0 to 6 points was used in order to indicate the level of awareness. When respondents answered that they "Keep water in reserve," "Stabilize furniture," "Have decided evacuation route/place," "Have decided the method of contact (in the family)" or "Other," one point was given for each. The last question asked was "Do you know the location of your local evacuation site?" If the respondents answered "Yes," 1 point was added. In total the highest score was 6 points. Several following parameters were used in the correlation analysis:

- Age, years of living in Japan, how many generations living in Japan
- Whether experiences disaster in home country, whether experienced disasters in Japan
- Whether interacted with Japanese on daily basis, and
- Whether participated in disaster drills.

14.3.1   Factors Correlate Disaster Preparedness Awareness

From multiple regression, key influencing factors were identified: "participation in disaster drills" seems to be the most influencing factor. Disaster awareness is found to be highly correlated with three factors: (1) whether they experienced disasters in Japan, (2) whether they interact with Japanese on daily basis, and (3) whether they participated in disaster drills. Thus, from the survey, it is concluded that the above three factors affect the awareness of disaster prevention among the foreign residents in Japan.

14.4   Face-to-Face Interview to Investigate Details of Each Language Group

Face-to-face interviews were conveyed from November to December 2019 to four language groups: Chinese, Portuguese, Vietnamese, and Indonesian. The purpose was to investigate the details of their media usage, awareness, and preparation for disasters both in their daily life as well as during disaster. The research found that each

Table 14.2 Characteristics of the questionnaire respondents

		Total	%	Aisa		North America		South America		Europe		Africa		Oceania	
Gender	Number of people	315	100	232	74%	25	8%	14	4%	28	9%	6	2%	5	2%
	Male	140	44	110	47%	3	12%	4	29%	12	43%	5	83%	3	60%
	Female	170	54	121	52%	21	84%	10	71%	14	50%	1	17%	2	40%
	No answer/Other	5	2	1	0%	1	4%	0	0%	2	7%	0	0%	0	0%
Age	~19	7	2	6	3%	0	0%	1	7%	0	0%	0	0%	0	0%
	20–29	116	37	102	44%	2	8%	3	21%	8	29%	1	17%	0	0%
	30–39	129	41	100	43%	9	36%	5	36%	7	25%	4	67%	1	20%
	40–49	41	13	23	10%	3	12%	4	29%	7	25%	1	17%	2	40%
	50–59	10	3	0	0%	4	16%	1	7%	4	14%	0	0%	1	20%
	60–69	6	2	0	0%	4	16%	0	0%	1	4%	0	0%	1	20%
	70~	2	1	0	0%	2	8%	0	0%	0	0%	0	0%	0	0%
	No answer	4	1	1	0%	1	4%	0	0%	1	4%	0	0%	0	0%
Years lived in Japan	Less than 1 year	88	28	81	35%	2	8%	1	7%	4	14%	0	0%	0	0%
	More than 1 year, Less than 5 years	106	34	86	37%	4	16%	1	7%	8	29%	4	67%	2	40%
	More than 5 years, Less than 10 years	41	13	31	13%	4	16%	0	0%	4	14%	2	33%	0	0%
	Over 10 years	78	25	34	15%	15	60%	12	86%	11	39%	0	0%	3	60%
	No answer	2	1	0	0%	0	0%	0	0%	1	4%	0	0%	0	0%

(continued)

Table 14.2 (continued)

		Total	%	Asia		North America		South America		Europe		Africa		Oceania	
How many generations have you and your family been in Japan?	I am the first generation	297	94	226	97%	24	96%	5	36%	27	96%	6	100%	5	100%
	Since parents' generation	9	3	3	1%	1	4%	5	36%	0	0%	0	0%	0	0%
	Since grandparents' generation	4	1	1	0%	0	0%	3	21%	0	0%	0	0%	0	0%
	Before grandparents' generation	2	1	1	0%	0	0%	1	7%	0	0%	0	0%	0	0%
	No answer	3	1	1	0%	0	0%	0	0%	1	4%	0	0%	0	0%
Visa status	Work	109	35	75	32%	6	24%	8	57%	9	32%	4	67%	2	40%
	Study	110	35	97	42%	1	4%	0	0%	10	36%	2	33%	0	0%
	Spouse or Child of Japanese national	26	8	12	5%	9	36%	1	7%	2	7%	0	0%	2	40%
	Training	11	3	11	5%	0	0%	0	0%	0	0%	0	0%	0	0%
	Dependent	18	6	16	7%	1	4%	0	0%	1	4%	0	0%	0	0%
	Other/No answer	41	13	21	9%	8	32%	5	36%	6	21%	0	0%	1	20%
Japanese	Understand very well	72	23	52	22%	8	32%	3	21%	6	21%	0	0%	2	40%
	Understand	91	29	68	29%	12	48%	0	0%	9	32%	1	17%	0	0%
	Understand a little	119	38	87	38%	3	12%	11	79%	9	32%	4	67%	3	60%
	Do not understand	32	10	24	10%	2	8%	0	0%	4	14%	1	17%	0	0%

(continued)

Table 14.2 (continued)

		Total	%	Aisa	%	North America	%	South America	%	Europe	%	Africa	%	Oceania	%
Occupation	No answer	1	0	1	0%	0	0%	0	0%	0	0%	0	0%	0	0%
	Construction	23	7	19	8%	0	0%	0	0%	2	7%	1	17%	0	0%
	Manufacturing	33	10	24	10%	0	0%	7	50%	1	4%	0	0%	0	0%
	Information and communications	41	13	37	16%	1	4%	1	7%	1	4%	0	0%	1	20%
	Wholesale/Retail	2	1	1	0%	0	0%	0	0%	0	0%	0	0%	1	20%
	Lodging, restaurant or other service business	14	4	11	5%	1	4%	1	7%	0	0%	0	0%	0	0%
	Education, learning support industry	59	19	25	11%	16	64%	2	14%	13	46%	0	0%	2	40%
	Medical, welfare	8	3	7	3%	1	4%	0	0%	0	0%	0	0%	0	0%
	Not working	68	22	58	25%	5	20%	0	0%	4	14%	2	33%	1	20%
	Other/No answer	67	21	51	22%	1	4%	3	21%	7	25%	3	50%	0	0%
Whom do you live with? (Choose multiple answers if necessary)	Alone	126	40	100	43%	4	16%	1	7%	6	21%	4	67%	2	40%
	Parents	8	3	4	2%	0	0%	3	21%	0	0%	0	0%	0	0%
	Husband/Wife	145	46	92	40%	20	80%	11	79%	15	54%	2	33%	3	60%
	Child	85	27	59	25%	8	32%	6	43%	9	32%	0	0%	1	20%
	Sibling	11	3	10	4%	0	0%	1	7%	0	0%	0	0%	0	0%
	Other	36	11	27	12%	1	4%	0	0%	8	29%	0	0%	0	0%

has developed a unique communication style in Japan, which caused specific problems in disaster preparedness. This also indicates that it is possible to find solutions for each group by focusing on their respective problems.

The following common points have been found in several interviews.

- First, most of the interviewees, except for Indonesians, had never experienced a serious disaster so they could not imagine how dangerous it would be.
- Second, all language groups had their own community in SNS. Disaster information was provided in their native language, but it was a mixture of reliable and unreliable information. Some tried to access Japanese or English information provided by the Japanese government or mass media, but most of them found it difficult. Information in SNSs and official information from public sectors are both general and broad. Most of the interviewees couldn't obtain specific, local and timely information, which was necessary to take proper actions.
- Third, Japanese friends and neighbors played an important role in disaster management. For example, a major connection was the homeowner for some interviewees. In particular, those who live alone listed the landlord as "Japanese who they could contact in times of an emergency." Friends are also important. One interviewee said that she raised her awareness of disaster management when many of her Japanese friends warned her to be cautious because a strong typhoon was approaching. On the other hand, some interviewees, who got advice only from their colleagues, did minimum preparation. Interestingly, several couples said that their awareness was raised after having children. They became involved in many local family activities and had opportunities to learn about Japanese disaster management culture.

14.4.1 Chinese Community: Largest Population in Japan

Chinese are the largest group of foreign residents in Japan, 786,000 at the end of June 2019, which is 27% of all non-Japanese residents. The number has steadily increased since China adopted a market-opening reform policy in 1978, and surpassed South and North Korean residents in 2007. This group showed a wide variety of visa statuses. The breakdown shows permanent residents at 38%, students at 17%, workers (engineer/specialist in humanities/international services) at 11%, technical interns at 10%, and others in decreasing order (MOJ 2020a). The face-to-face interviews were conducted at two locations. One was a Chinese restaurant in Tokyo, with three interviewees. Another was a park in Tokyo, where Chinese and Japanese people gather for a friendly chat every Sunday. Here ten people were interviewed. Among the 13 people in total, 6 were students, 4 were workers, and 3 are unknown.

From the interviews, it was found that people rely heavily on Chinese social media such as WeChat and Weibo. They gather and share information about disasters in Japan, which are provided by volunteers who actively translate information from Japanese media into Chinese, forming a huge virtual community. In fact, many interviewees say they prepared for typhoon Hagibis which hit eastern Japan in October

2019, by storing water and reinforcing windows with tape, and these ideas came from SNS.

Therefore, it is recommended that the Japanese government and public organizations open official accounts on Chinese SNS, in order to convey accurate information to every corner of the Chinese community in Japan. Another solution was proposed by a Chinese who promotes Chinese-Japanese exchange through publication and events. According to him, there are many groups related by region, family, or work, making it difficult to recognize all of them. So, it is necessary to create a system to connect these groups and to train leaders in each group.

14.4.2 Brazilians Forming Tight and Large Community of 30 Years

The second group has a different historical background in Japan. The population of Brazilians living in Japan rapidly increased after 1990 when the Japanese Immigration Control Act was amended giving spouses and children of the second generation of Japanese Brazilian the status of "long term residents" and allowing them to work in Japan. The economic slump in Brazil and the labor shortage in Japan accelerated their immigration. Brazilian people formed large communities in Gunma, Shizuoka, Aichi, and other prefectures, working mainly in manufacturing industries. The increase was concentrated in specific areas, so local governments and citizens tried to minimize problems caused by language, cultural gaps, and lack of knowledge about the Japanese social system by providing multilingual services.

The interviews were done in Joso City, Ibaraki Prefecture, one of these areas where Brazilian people live collectively. Eight people were interviewed at the graduation ceremony of a Brazilian school in the city. The school is licensed by the Brazilian government and the children learn in Portuguese. The interviewees were from the 20s through 50s, who lived in Japan for more than 20 years at the most. Many of them weren't willing to speak in Japanese, which is natural for families and friends of the Brazilian school.

It was expected that the Brazilian people would be relatively better informed and their awareness of disaster management would be higher, for two reasons. First, city office and citizen groups are providing information about disaster preparedness in many languages including Portuguese. Second, the area experienced flooding in 2015. One third of the city was suffered flood damage. From the interviews, facts and problems are found as follows.

In time of disasters, for example, when strong typhoon Hagibis hit Japan in October 2019, many followed the city mayor's Facebook account and translated his posts using smartphone translator. They had other information sources, such as television and wireless disaster warning system, but many told that they couldn't understand Japanese. School network was also a major source of information. Families of the students called and mailed the principal asking for advice. The principal issued information and advice via school's Facebook account. Meanwhile, some say that their employers warned them to prepare.

However, there was a high barrier between the Japanese and the Brazilian communities, making it difficult to cooperate for disaster preparation. In a separate interview, a city official in charge of multi-cultural activities said that the city is trying to create trust with the Brazilian people, while admitting that it is still far from sufficient. The city wants foreign residents to become contributors, rather than receivers of supports, because Japanese community is getting weaker, according to the official. This is an important point when thinking of disaster risk management in areas with a large community of foreign residents in general. Such areas depend on foreign manpower because they are suffering labor shortages caused by aging population and outflow of young people to urban areas. It is crucial for those communities to build up inclusive human networks in order to fulfill social needs. Everyone would play an active role there, for example, Japanese elderlies can help foreign residents understand disaster information and young foreign residents can help Japanese elderlies to evacuate.

14.4.3 Vietnamese Disconnected

Following the population of Chinese and Korean population, that of Vietnamese residents is the third largest in Japan at nearly 372,000 at the end of June 2019. It has rapidly increased, to become eight times as large as it was in 2011 when Vietnamese residents were the 8th largest population (MOJ 2020a). The increase is attributed to the growing number of technical intern trainees and students. Technical interns are in a program by the Japanese government which aims "to contribute to developing countries by accepting people from these countries for a certain period of time (maximum 5 years) and transferring skills through OJT." (MOJ 2017) Since they are new to Japanese society, much more needs to be done to understand the problems which they face and proper action should be taken. The interviews took place three times in their housings in Tokyo. The interviewees are two trainees who work at bakeries, two trainees who work at a supermarket, and three students. They share rooms with one another. They were relatively younger, later teenager to early 20s.

In terms of human network, Vietnamese interviewees have only one or two communities in their daily lives, which are school and work. Many of them said that they would rely on the supervising organization in an emergency. Some said that they were so busy working and studying that they couldn't join extra activities such as neighborhood gathering or hobby circles. Their disaster awareness was low. When the strong typhoon approached in October 2019, their information sources were their colleagues, teachers and Facebook groups of Vietnamese living in Japan. They prepared water and food but had no idea to check warnings issued by the weather authority or the local government. They didn't even know where neighborhood shelters were. However, this doesn't necessarily mean that they are not interested in disaster preparedness. Some said they would be willing to join disaster drills and some said they would pay 10,000 yen to buy an emergency bag. Necessary countermeasures are as follows.

– First, local governments, NPOs, companies, and schools should provide as many opportunities as possible for Vietnamese to learn about disaster risks. Roles of supervising organizations of technical trainees and schools of the students are critical because they have the greatest access. Vietnamese trainees and students are a new group in Japan, therefore they have not developed strong social network compared to Chinese and Brazilian residents. It means that they could easily be left behind.
– Second, accurate and timely information should be provided in Vietnamese language in popular media such as Facebook groups. One of those efforts is "NHK WORLD-JAPAN Vietnamese" account on Facebook (NHK 2020a). There should be more of this kind because Vietnamese has a large population and many of them neither understand English nor Japanese.

14.4.4 Indonesians with Religious Differences

Indonesian residents have characteristics in common with Vietnamese residents. For example, their population is growing mainly due to the increase of students and technical trainees. At the end of June 2019, there were 61,051 Indonesian residents in Japan, which had doubled in five years (MOJ 2020a). What's unique about Indonesians is religious differences. 87% of Indonesians are Muslims (Kamenag2020). They are also unique in that their home country has many natural disasters. Group interview was conducted at a university for a number of bachelor and master students.

Their media use in disaster was active. They used multiple sources when the strong typhoon hit Japan in 2019. They checked the English website of the Japan Meteorological Agency, Indonesian community in SNSs like WhatsApp, and personal information from their teachers at the university. However, language barrier and overflow of information made them unsure about what actions to take. The interviewees particularly sited the other challenge, which was religious barrier. Especially during and after the disaster, it is important that halal food is provided at shelters. It is also necessary that they can exercise religious customs such as supplication and dress codes. The population of Muslims is increasing and it is all the more important that Japanese people know the needs of diverse people.

14.5 Role of Media in Enhancing Foreigner's Risk Perception and Preparedness

Here are suggestions based on the survey results in order to improve risk perception and preparedness of foreign residents in Japan.

14.5.1 Provide Information Using Tools Popular Among Foreigners

One of the most important findings from the survey was that each language group had created a large and popular community in SNS in their own language. For example, WeChat and Weibo for the Chinese, Facebook for the Brazilians and the Vietnamese, and WhatsApp for the Indonesians. In order to spread official information to everyone, authorities and mass media must create a different strategy for each language group, by setting up accounts in the major SNSs in the respective communities. At the same time, it is necessary to increase opportunities where foreign residents can learn about disaster risk. There should be more media coverage in diverse forms. Among them are old media such as TV, radio, newspaper, poster, and brochure, as well as new media like SNS, internet, smartphone application, and digital signage.

14.5.2 Reach Many Foreigners by Using "Easy Japanese"

In addition to multilingual information, media should use "easy Japanese" more widely for international audiences. It's communication using simple grammar and vocabulary so that Japanese beginners understand. Easy Japanese has attracted much attention as a useful tool for a multicultural society. Experts and Japanese government are promoting it in the fields of tourism, life support, disaster preparedness, etc. Many local governments are also using easy Japanese in their documents for foreign residents. Among mass media, NHK launched a website with news text in easy Japanese in 2012 (NHK 2020b). NHK WORLD-JAPAN started an audio version of the service in 2019 (NHK 2020c). Easy Japanese has two benefits. One is its ability to reach foreigners of small language groups. For large groups like Chinese, Vietnamese, and Brazilians, providing information through translation might be effective in spite of the cost. But it is impossible to translate into all languages spoken by foreign residents. Easy Japanese is a realistic solution in an effort to access as many foreigners as possible. Another benefit is encouraging communication between Japanese and foreigners, which the survey indicated to be an important factor in raising awareness among foreign residents. Many Japanese want to communicate with foreign people but don't because they are not comfortable in speaking English. But that barrier disappears with easy Japanese. This is critical in an emergency.

14.5.3 Promoting Multicultural Exchange in Daily Life

The case of Japanese conversation class in Kumamoto city is a good example to see the importance of daily communication between foreign and Japanese residents. The Kumamoto International Foundation is operating classes for foreign residents in five different locations for free or up to 100 yen per class. Local Japanese citizens teach them as volunteers. In one of the classes, around ten students and volunteer teachers gather once a week to learn about expressions and basic knowledge of Japanese social system, such as education, medical service, and waste disposal. They also learn unique traditions and expressions of the region. The human relationship of the class members proved to be helpful when the strong earthquakes hit the area in 2016. Many students panicked. But they started to exchange information via LINE, a social media popular in Japan. The communication was first among Chinese speakers in Chinese, and gradually included other language speakers, Japanese teachers, and staff of the foundation. They shared information on whether people were safe, where the shelters were, or about the distribution of food and water. According to a Taiwanese student who played a key role, this action had two merits. One is that they were able to exchange community-based information which was crucial when the disaster occurred. People could get detailed information which they couldn't access on mass media. Another merit was that they could recognize reliable information, which was difficult to do without a Japanese. From the perspective of effective use of social media, the important point is involving Japanese people. Japanese neighbors were essential to understand the local and personal situation. For example, the Taiwanese student brought water bottles to Japanese teacher's house several days after the quake, because she knew where teacher lived and the teacher lived alone. The staff of public organization was important, too. They provided official information and also recognize what kind of problems foreigners were facing. The Japanese conversation class can be an ideal model for many other municipalities in Japan, which face an increase in foreign residents.

14.5.4   Promotion of the Value of Diversity

In principle, media have the responsibility to promote the value of diversity and human rights. For example, presenting foreign residents as contributors to society is important in order to welcome foreigners and to share a positive image of a multicultural society among Japanese. Another approach is to create contents that Japanese and foreigners can learn and work on together. Educational videos about disaster preparedness in several languages are one example.

14.6   Media's Role for "National Minimum" and "Local Optimum"

"National minimum" and "local optimum" are a set of key concept which are used in curriculum management of Japanese public education. "National minimum"means the very basic issues that everyone should be provided at least. In deciding what to include in the "national minimum," careful discussion is necessary in order to avoid sacrificing flexibility and creativity of local educational practices due to excessive control. "Local optimum" is the concept to value the initiative of educators in different places in order to finding the best idea for a specific environment. This framework could be useful when thinking about the media's role in disaster preparedness of foreigners.

"National minimum" is a basic risk perception that every member of society should share. The survey found that a certain proportion of foreign tourists and residents had low or no awareness of disaster risk. They are the group without the "national minimum." Mass media, governments, as well as other public organizations, are responsible for insuring the "national minimum" for all. At the time of disaster, "national minimum" mean that everyone can receive accurate and timely emergency information. To achieve this goal, it is necessary to constantly assess the people's needs and make efficient strategies.

The "local optimum" is similar to the word "localize"which is frequently referred to in the field of disaster management. These words suggest the importance of focusing on the local situation to find out realistic solutions. Therefore, the media must be aware that the goal is to help local people find solutions on their own. In other words, it is necessary to design the media environment as a whole, in an innovative way, using old and new media effectively and to customize information of each target. Participation of foreigners can be one option. The survey showed that both tourists and residents have a diverse set of problems, which means many different strategies are necessary.

In order to spread both "national minimum" and "local optimum," the information needs to be provided frequently, in various styles and through diverse media. In this way, both foreigner's awareness and Japanese awareness of foreigner's needs would rise. This would include disaster preparedness of foreigners as a part of Japanese culture.

References

Honzawa S (2020) Factors affecting foreign residents' disaster prevention awareness. Keio University undergraduate thesis (unpublished)

Hosokawa S (2020) Japan's approach to disaster recognition and behavior of foreign tourists. Keio University undergraduate thesis (unpublished)

Kemenag (2020) Indonesian Ministry of Religious Affairs. http://data.kemenag.go.id/agamadash board/statistik/umat. Accessed March 10 2020

MLIT (2016) New Tourism Strategy to Invigorate the Japanese Economy. (March 30, 2016, English). https://www.mlit.go.jp/common/001172615.pdf. Accessed 15 March 2020

MOFA (2020) Explanation by the Ministry of Foreign Affairs about new system introduced by the amendment of immigration control law. https://www.mofa.go.jp/mofaj/ca/fna/ssw/us/index. html. 15 March 2020

MOJ (2017) New Technical intern Training Program. April 2017, Immigration Bureau, Ministry of Justice Human Resources Development Bureau, Ministry of Health, Labor and Welfare. http:// www.moj.go.jp/content/001223972.pdf. Accessed 10 March 2020

MOJ (2020a) Foreign resident statistics, Ministry of Justice. http://www.moj.go.jp/housei/toukei/toukei_ichiran_touroku.html. Accessed 10 March 2020

MOJ (2020b) Initiatives to Accept New Foreign Nationals and for the Realization of Society of Harmonious Coexistence, Ministry of Justice, Immigration Services Agency of Japan. http://www.moj.go.jp/content/001308076.pdf. Accessed 10 March 2020

NHK (2020a) NHK WORLD-JAPAN Vietnamese. https://www.facebook.com/NHKWORLDVietnamese/. Accessed March 10 2020

NHK (2020b) NHK easy news. https://www3.nhk.or.jp/news/easy/. Accessed March 10 2020

NHK (2020c) Weekly news in simple Japanese. https://www3.nhk.or.jp/nhkworld/en/learnjapanese/audionews/. Accessed March 15 2020

Chapter 15
NHK WORLD-JAPAN's Challenge to Create BOSAI Culture in Japan and Across the World

Midori Kusagaya and Aye Nge Khin

Abstract BOSAI is a Japanese word to express various efforts to mitigate disaster risk. This chapter documents how NHK broadcasters have developed programs and other contents in order to spread BOSAI know-how from the program producers' point of view. NHK WORLD-JAPAN is an international segment of NHK, the Japan Broadcasting Corporation. Its service primarily targets overseas audiences and its content is multilingual. In 2017, NHK started a radio program series of BOSAI, or disaster preparedness. The production team has since sought effective approaches to encourage people to take real action to reduce disaster risk, by expanding its services from broadcasting to online contents, SNS, events, etc. In this chapter, based on the experience of NHK WORLD-JAPAN, the authors focus on the concept of "participatory coverage," inspired by "action research" in the academic world. "Participatory coverage" means that the media and citizens work together to improve society through the process of content production and by utilizing the content. This is especially important in the field of disaster preparedness, where taking action is indispensable to protect lives. The chapter also recognizes a TV program as an example of "participatory coverage," because the collaborators continue learning BOSAI on their own even after the program was over.

Keywords BOSAI · Disaster preparedness · NHK WORLD-JAPAN · Participatory coverage · Action research

15.1 NHK WORLD-JAPAN, History and Current Service

NHK began international broadcasting in 1935, through shortwave radio service, both in Japanese and English (NHK 2015). This served as propaganda during World War II in 24 languages at most, but was ordered by the Allied Powers' General

M. Kusagaya (✉)
NHK Educational Corporation, Tokyo, Japan
e-mail: kusagaya.m-fc@nhk-ed.co.jp; kusagaya.m-fc@nhk.or.jp

A. N. Khin
NHK WORLD Department, Japan Broadcasting Corporation, Tokyo, Japan

© Springer Nature Singapore Pte Ltd. 2021
R. Shaw et al. (eds.), *Media and Disaster Risk Reduction*, Disaster Risk Reduction,
https://doi.org/10.1007/978-981-16-0285-6_15

Headquarters (GHQ) to stop at the end of the war. The service resumed in 1952 as "Radio Japan" based on the principles of freedom and democracy. Radio Japan aired news and programs about Japan in different languages to language-specific areas. Radio Japan was one of the few resources for listeners living abroad to learn about Japan.

While providing international service with short wave radio, NHK added new services to adapt to the changing global media environment. In 1996, NHK's international broadcasting was renamed NHK WORLD. This included both Radio Japan and new TV service in English. It changed its name again to NHK WORLD-JAPAN in 2018. As of 2020, NHK WORLD-JAPAN has radio service in 17 languages, internet service in 18 languages, SNS in several languages, TV in English, in addition to Japanese services for Japanese living overseas.

NHK WORLD-JAPAN covers various topics to meet the needs of diverse audiences. For example, it has programs of current affairs, human portraits, Japanese pop culture, Japanese language lesson, cooking, economics, travel information, science and technologies, etc., both in the Radio and TV service.

In its official promotion brochure in 2019, NHK WORLD-JAPAN explained one of its missions as the following:

> As the world's gateway to Japan and Asia, we reveal the diversity of our culture, traditions and innovations and bring you the latest in business, cutting-edge technologies and creativity from across the region. We treasure our connection with the people who live, work and travel here.

(To avoid confusion, this paper will use the 2020 name "NHK WORLD-JAPAN", in all descriptions including the past when it was called "Radio Japan" or "NHK WORLD".)

15.2 BOSAI Radio Program

Disaster has long been one of the main topics of Japanese media in general. There is wide range of coverages including emergency information, documentaries, educational programs for children, etc. Around the memorial days of serious past disasters, such as the Great Hanshin-Awaji Earthquake in January 1995 and the Great East Japan Earthquake in March 2011, there is much media coverage to pray for victims, remember the need to be prepared and discuss countermeasures for potential disasters. In addition to this, there are always news and programs about disaster preparedness all year round. This is an important part of Japanese media culture.

In parallel, NHK WORLD-JAPAN has covered similar stories as part of its mission to inform overseas listeners about what is currently going on in Japan. In April 2017, a new goal was set to raise awareness in disaster preparedness across the world. In order to provide practical information for overseas listeners, NHK WORLD-JAPAN launched a series of radio programs "BOSAI, Measures for Saving Your Life." The series tells listeners how to be better prepared by providing knowledge and skills that Japan has acquired through experience in the past disasters.

When launching the series, the production team carefully chose the program's presentation style. The message should be easy to understand and enjoyable so that listeners would find disaster issues interesting. Therefore, the programs are carried out in casual conversation style with two people, one of which is the presenter and the other is asking questions. In addition, the presenter gives the "BOSAI quiz" in the latter half of the program. The presenter asks a question with three potential answers, and the right answer is given followed by an expert's comments.

Another point that the BOSAI team needs to be careful about is that program's information should be correct in every place in all locations of the world. For example, Japanese children are taught to immediately hide themselves under desks when earthquake hits. This is because Japanese school buildings are highly resistant. But the decision could be different depending on the place and situation. The scripts were written carefully so that people in any area can learn and think about the best strategy in their own environment.

The BOSAI series has so far covered disasters such as earthquakes, tsunami, floods, volcanos, and lightning. It has also introduced various styles of BOSAI education at schools and communities in Japan. The series has received positive feedbacks from listeners, especially from Asian countries where earthquakes and heavy rain are frequent.

15.3   Launch of BOSAI Website

After one year, the production team began questioning "Is it enough to only provide information via programs?" Radio programs do provide useful information. But the team members were not sure if it actually was encouraging listeners to take actions to protect their lives. Radio programs are generally listened to live. But when finished, the listeners cannot check what they heard. So the BOSAI team decided to make a BOSAI portal website with program archives. This was the starting point of years of trial and error by NHK WORLD-JAPAN to look for effective approaches to create disaster-resilient societies. Throughout the process of developing the content, the BOSAI team has repeatedly questioned "What is the role of public media?" A famous term in the field of disaster risk management "last one mile" means the importance of reaching to each individual at each last corner of society. However, mass media in principle is not good at local and personal communication. Its expertise is mass communication, especially to the people who are already interested in the topics for some extent. So the BOSAI team tried to find the ways to reach "last one mile" by expanding its role from program making to providing various contents to create learning environment for people.

The BOSAI portal website was launched in August 2018 in English (NHK WORLD-JAPAN 2018a). In addition to program archives, the team put some educational materials on the website, to help people to learn by themselves.

One of the web contents is the BOSAI QUIZ, which is a series of question and answer screens with illustrations (NHK WORLD-JAPAN 2018b). It is a visualized version of the BOSAI QUIZ, in the latter half of radio program. People can read the question and three answers on the screen. By touching either of the answers, red circle pops up on the right answer and the answer screen slides in. The screen also has an expert's comments in both audio and text. These contents are designed to enable children with their families at home, students with teachers at schools, people with neighbors at community events to learn about disaster risk reduction. The quiz sheets can be accessed for free. Printout can be shared so that people can enjoy them anywhere without internet access. The BOSAI team hopes that these quizzes motivate people to do further activities, for example, making their evacuation plan, preparing their evacuation bags, or learning the path from their home to a shelter.

Another content of the BOSAI website is "HOW TO CRAFT SAFETY," short video clips (NHK WORLD-JAPAN 2018c). This was originally created by NHK's domestic news section in 2017 and NHK WORLD-JAPAN translated it into English. They are also translated into Chinese, Thai, Vietnamese, and Indonesian. These short videos, 25 in all, provide tips on how to get through emergencies using things at hand. For example, the videos show how to make tableware from newspaper, a bed or a toilet using cardboard boxes, a rain poncho from a garbage bag. The BOSAI team made paper manuals for 10 of the 25 videos and put them on the website so that people can access for free. By using these manuals, the BOSAI team is hoping, people can make the items shown in the video by themselves.

The other content of the website are videos of the TV series titled "BOSAI: An Educational Journey." In the programs, a newscaster of NHK WORLD-JAPAN goes on a journey to learn about disaster preparedness. This series also includes "Message from an Expert," interviews with experts which are specially edited for the website.

15.4   BOSAI Events

By launching the BOSAI radio series and website, it became possible for NHK WORLD-JAPAN to hold events or workshops on disaster preparedness using the online educational contents. For example, the Thai language service team held a promotion event in Bangkok in 2017. Viewing and a demonstration of "HOW TO CRAFT SAFETY" was a main attraction. In 2018, BOSAI team joined a campaign to promote NHK WORLD-JAPAN targeting south Asian viewers and listeners. It conducted BOSAI quiz sessions for children of an Indian school in Tokyo.

The design of these events varies depending on the purpose and situation. In many cases, participants learn by answering quizzes and making materials after watching videos. The BOSAI team found that this is a good way to develop interest in BOSAI. But at the same time, the team thought that these BOSAI contents could be used more effectively and to inspire.

One of the examples is an event for listeners by NHK WORLD-JAPAN's Vietnamese team. It was held in Nagoya in 2018. They chose a video clip which showed how to make rain ponchos from garbage bags. However, they chose not to show the video until the very end of the event. First they ask participants to form groups of three people and discuss ways to utilize garbage bags to protect themselves from rain. Then, the participants gave presentations of their ideas and one of the groups was received an innovation award. Viewing of the video came after all these activities were over.

This is a good example of urging people to think by themselves in an enjoyable way. Thinking is an important process because people actually need to think by themselves in an emergency. Even if they learned how to make poncho from garbage bag from a video that knowledge might be useless if there were no garbage bag. But if people had experienced the process of thinking and finding solutions by using items at hand, they would be able to apply the skills in their own local situation.

Another example of the process where people think and localize that they learned can be seen in activities of Plus Arts, a Japanese Non-Profit Organization which promotes disaster preparedness education. It's Representative Chief Director Hirokazu Nagata is an advisor of the "HOW TO CRAFT SAFETY." One of the video series shows how to make tableware from newspaper. But people in Indonesia and Philippines made the dishes from banana leaves. Another video shows how to make stretcher using a pair of sticks with a blanket or jackets. However, Indonesian people chose to use the saromb, a local traditional skirt for men.

Through these activities, the team noticed the importance of encouraging people to "localize" and "personalize" the general knowledge and skills, in order to spread the BOSAI culture to the world.

Further developments of the contents were made in New York, USA, where the BOSAI team realized that "HOW TO CRAFT SAFETY" had significant potential to inspire people who were not interested in disaster preparedness.

Teachers of New York City's public elementary school came to know "HOW TO CRAFT SAFETY" when they were working with Mr. Nagata as part of Japan Foundation's project. The school conducted drills but they had been focusing on fires and crimes, not natural disasters. But actually the region is prone to floods caused by hurricanes. After Mr. Nagata's workshop for children, teachers at the school began to learn the method of disaster preparedness education. The principal told NHK WORLD-JAPAN in an interview that the idea of using everyday materials for different purposes in emergencies is innovative and that she had realized the potential of disaster preparedness for education (NHK WORLD-JAPAN 2018a, b).

Also in New York, Parsons School of Design, a world's leading design college, held an intensive seminar featuring "design for disaster risk reduction" for the first time in 2017 after being inspired by "HOW TO CRAFT SAFETY." One of the seminar's organizers said in an interview by NHK WORLD-JAPAN that the videos are packed with elements important for future designers. He added that design should respond to the disaster simply and eloquently in ways that are effective, not getting carried away with fanciness, expense, or branding identity. The students came up with many ideas of designs which could be useful in emergencies, such as transforming a shirt and a plastic bag into a container for carrying water, turning lifejackets that refugees used to cross the sea into backpacks, walls which move to block floodwater (NHK WORLD-JAPAN 2018e).

Throughout all the production process of programs, web content, and events, the BOSAI team was conscious about its goal, involving global audience in real activities for disaster preparedness. This chapter calls the team's approach "participatory coverage," to indicate various media activities which commit to the real society through content, as well as, production process. "Participatory coverage" involves people of different sectors and its communication is multilateral. For example, online content such as quizzes and "HOW TO CRAFT SAFETY" are made through collaboration of experts and citizens. The production team also gets feedback to improve the contents, when they are used at local communities and schools. Here, media is participating in real social activities rather than simply providing information.

15.5 Change of Needs and Audience

This part will discuss the history of NHK WORLD-JAPAN focusing on its audience and past coverage of the disasters. It is important for media to recognize the needs of the target audience. However, the audience changes over time, which has had an impact on the BOSAI team's production policy.

Since NHK started international broadcasting in 1935, its communication style was basically from radio station to people overseas. For the audience, the radio service was one of few means to gain information about Japan. However, the media environment has drastically changed and people have access to more information sources. Because international TV broadcasting had become more common in the world and internet service was spreading widely, NHK launched a 24-h all-English TV channel in 2008. As for multilingual radio services, it began providing online news both live and on-demand in the year 2000. Depending on target areas, radio services use a variety of means including Medium Wave, FM, satellite radio, the internet, and smartphone apps. Simultaneously, various media increased the volume of information about Japan in multiple languages. NHK WORLD-JAPAN is now one of many options for people in need of information on Japan.

How did this change affect disaster coverage? When the Magnitude 7.3 earthquake hit the city of Kobe and its surrounding area in January 1995, NHK WORLD-JAPAN had nothing other than shortwave radio service. It intensively covered the disaster, but the target was the listeners overseas, not the people in the quake-hit areas. The situation had already changed when the devastating earthquake and tsunami attacked northwestern Japan in March 2011. NHK WORLD-JAPAN had already launched a live online streaming for both radio and TV. But these services were still new at the time and they were not widely known. It took several more years until NHK WORLD-JAPAN broadcast multi-language disaster information targeting domestic audience of the disaster-hit areas. In October 2019, strong typhoon hit Japan, and NHK's domestic news programs were showing website information of NHK WORLD-JAPAN on the screen and announcers asked viewers to tell foreigners around them about the website.

This new audience was a secondary target for NHK WORLD-JAPAN, but they have become increasingly important. Change in Japan's society has also accelerated the trend. The number of foreign tourists coming to Japan surpassed 30 million a year in 2018. Number of foreign residents has also increased, mainly due to Japan's need to deal with the shortfall of workforce. These people are vulnerable when a disaster hits Japan mainly due to language barrier and lack of knowledge about disaster management system in Japan. In addition, Japan has seen extreme weather conditions which have caused floods, landslides, and heat strokes in late 2010s. Experts say this trend is expected to continue or worsen due to global climate change.

All these changes made the BOSAI team to think about targeting foreigners in Japan. It was not an easy decision, because foreigners in Japan have different needs for disaster preparedness information than those overseas. But after long discussion, the team decided to include them for several reasons. One is because of necessity. The team believes it is the role of public media to provide necessary information to people in need. Another factor was globalization. More and more people move across borders these days compared to the time when Radio Japan started its service. Listeners in their home countries are more likely to come to Japan and vice versa. Also, the media situation is more complex than in the past. Foreign people share the information in and out of Japan, and the virtual communication space has no border. For international media like NHK WORLD-JAPAN, it has become unrealistic to divide audience depending on their physical location.

In this regard, the BOSAI team started a new TV program series in 2020, focusing on basic knowledge necessary for foreigners who are living in Japan. The team is also planning to add new materials on the BOSAI portal website in "simple Japanese" using easy vocabulary and grammatical structures. Experts, governments, and citizens' groups are promoting this "simple Japanese" to encourage communications between Japanese and foreigners. The BOSAI team is hoping that contents in "simple Japanese" would be used by foreign people and Japanese to learn about BOSAI together.

15.6   Raising Awareness Through the Production Process

The next focus is a TV program, which the BOSAI team produced in 2019. The team found its production process to be a good example of "participatory coverage," an approach of contents making in which the media and citizens work together to improve society.

A ten minute program titled "Disaster Preparedness, the First Steps" was broadcast as one of the episodes of TV series "WHAT'S YOUR CONNECTION?" (NHK WORLD-JAPAN 2019) It was aired in the Myanmar language with English subtitles. Currently on the internet, three other versions of Indonesian, Thai, and Vietnamese subtitles are available.

This program answered a question from a Myanmar listener living in Japan, who asked "How can I learn about disaster preparedness in Japan?" The questioner was a member of a community led by a Myanmar Buddhist monastery in Tokyo. She and the chief priest of the monastery appeared in the program to learn about disaster preparedness with other members of the monastery.

In producing this program, the BOSAI team was hoping that these Myanmar people would learn about disaster preparedness by using available resources from their local society, instead of a privilege provided by media people. The team also expected that the viewers, including other language communities who could have similar problems in Japan, could learn how to educate themselves by watching this program.

One of the local resources that the program used was the disaster preparedness center in Tokyo where people can actually experience simulated disasters under the guidance of an instructor. It is run by Tokyo Fire Department and open to citizens including foreign tourists and residents. Myanmar people visited the facility and experienced an earthquake simulation, evacuation under artificial smoke, and how to use a fire extinguisher.

Next, the BOSAI team chose an advisor for the Myanmar community. The team had a human network of experts and some of them were frequently seen in the media. But the team didn't choose a famous personality, because it's not the best solution for ordinary people to follow. Instead, the team used a system already available in Itabashi ward, where the monastery is located. The team applied to the ward for an expert to come to teach interested citizens about disaster preparedness for free. On the day of the shooting, an experienced former official of the Tokyo Fire Department visited the monastery. She checked the whole building, pointed out risky places, and taught how to minimize them. Then she worked with the Myanmar people, for example, fixing furniture, putting film on grass shelves, putting fluorescent stickers on stairs, etc. The chief priest said about his first experience of learning BOSAI, "We haven't seriously thought about disasters until now. I thought today that I should definitely do something about them."

This program proved to be a successful example of "participatory coverage" because it brought a significant change to the Myanmar people even after finishing the program shooting. People at the monastery continue learning BOSAI by themselves, by holding study meetings and town walking for disaster preparedness. In October 2019, typhoon Hagibis, an extremely violent storm tore through Japan leaving widespread damage. Before and during the typhoon, the Myanmar people were supporting one another in how to prepare for the arrival of the typhoon. They shared ideas on SNS, including how to cover windows with storm shutters and how to prevent windows from breaking. They also encouraged each other to store water. It was impressive that the Myanmar people have not only raised their awareness but also spread their knowledge to their community.

The program also served to connect Japanese society with the Myanmar community. The Itabashi ward officials who helped dispatch the instructor said that they were happy to find a foreign community interested to learn about disaster preparedness, because they were always struggling to reach such communities. Also, the instructor showed her willingness to continue to be involved in the Myanmar people's activities. She voluntarily visited the monastery several times even after the program was over. She said that she admired their enthusiasm.

Time has passed since the program was aired, and the Myanmar people's activity continues to develop. They started a bilingual emergency management class for children. Educating children make it possible to educate their families too, because many Myanmar children were born in Japan and speak better Japanese than elder members of their family. The people at the monastery are also planning to launch a website to share disaster management information in both languages for people living around the world.

15.7 "Participatory Coverage" and Challenges of BOSAI

Until now, this chapter has described the process of NHK WORLD-JAPAN's "participatory coverage," an effort to encourage people to take actual actions for BOSAI, or disaster preparedness. For that purpose, the team expanded their contents from programs to online contents and events. The team also tried to help people to engage in disaster preparedness activities through the program making process.

The concept of "participatory coverage" was inspired by "action research." "Research that produces nothing but books will not suffice" is a widely known expression by Kurt Lewin, who coined the term "action research" (Lewin 1948). In the context of the media world, this could indicate that "Media activities that produces nothing but programs will not suffice." Programs are not goals but a means. However, media people's interventions can affect collaborators in both positive and negative ways. Sometimes collaborators become empowered. Sometimes trouble ensues. Sometimes collaborators work hard while being covered, but get tired afterwards. To avoid negative results, media people must ask themselves "Is the goal making attractive programs or improving society through the programs?" Actually, both are important. In fact, the two goals can be compatible. The program that changes the community is a good program. Just same as Lewin's expression "Nothing is so practical a s agood theory" (Lewin 1951).

The BOSAI team uses specifically three methods for "participatory coverage": "collaboration," "utilizing local resources," and "getting feedback." The first method, "collaboration" is necessary to assess the needs of real society and make effective commitments. In making programs and other contents, the BOSAI team involves experts and potential target people including international colleagues. The second method "utilizing local resources" is important to empower local people including collaborators and the audience of programs. As described earlier, the team chose to use local systems in the program to learn disaster preparedness for the Myanmar community in Japan. This enabled Myanmar people to learn through their own initiative. In addition, the program viewers could learn about accessible resources. The third method, "getting feedback," is a condition for successful future "participatory coverage." The team visited and facilitated events where the BOSAI contents were used. These experiences are helpful to develop and improve content.

On the other hand, there is an important point that media people must be careful about when practicing "participatory coverage." They need to keep proper distance between themselves and collaborators. In many cases, especially in the field of disaster preparedness, production teams and collaborators share the same initial goals, but the viewers might not. In order to make persuasive content for diverse people, media people must keep a birds-eye perspective and be critical at all times. This is crucial to maintain a healthy relationship based on trust with the audience. Needless to say, the point of view of the collaborators shouldn't be prioritized in some cases, especially when covering controversial issues or checking antisocial activities.

Now, this chapter closes with two challenges that the BOSAI team is facing: "Grasping a precise image of audience" and "pursuing universal values."

First, grasping a precise image of the audience is necessary in this rapidly changing society in order to set flexible, yet focused strategies. NHK WORLD-JAPAN initially targeted radio listeners outside of Japan, but currently it includes foreign travelers and residents in Japan. The BOSAI team is constantly reviewing the needs of the audience and expanding its service. Currently, the whole world is facing a new challenge under COVID-19 pandemic. It is obvious that the audiences of NHK WORLD-JAPAN are drastically affected and this will change their values and lifestyles. So it is the responsibility of the BOSAI team as well as the media in general to adjust the strategies in order to efficiently contribute to society in the current crisis.

Second, in spite of the fact that the audience is continuously changing, the programs and the contents should pursue universal values. The values here are human rights, international cooperation, respect for diversity, etc. In the 2020s, it is unavoidable for the world to see surprising changes in all fields, including public health, economics, politics, education, climate, etc. In this complex time, priority of values can be confused. Especially in such a situation, it is important that the BOSAI team adhere to universal values, while disseminating practical and useful know-how.

In this regard, "participatory coverage" is expected to become more and more important for the BOSAI team. The team's goal is creating a resilient world by providing opportunities for all people to learn about disaster preparedness and encouraging them to take actual actions. In order to achieve it, it is indispensable to discuss and collaborate with various people such as local citizens, educators, and experts. Through this process, the BOSAI team is hoping, it can find out a new strategy to contribute to the changing world and fulfill its role as a public media.

References

Lewin K (1948) Resolving social conflicts; selected papers on group dynamics. Harper

Lewin K (1951) Field theory in social science: selected theoretical papers. Edited by Dorwin Cartwright. Harper

NHK (Japan Broadcasting Corporation) (2015) A History of International Broadcasting from Japan 80 years of NHK WORLD 1930–2015 CHRONICLE+OUTLINE OF SERVICES. Published and edited: NHK WORLD Department

NHK WORLD-JAPAN (2018a) BOSAI. https://www3.nhk.or.jp/nhkworld/en/radio/bosaiweb. Accessed 10 Oct 2020

NHK WORLD-JAPAN (2018b) BOSAI QUIZ. https://www3.nhk.or.jp/nhkworld/en/radio/bosaiweb/quiz/. Accessed 10 Oct 2020

NHK WORLD-JAPAN (2018c) HOW TO CRAFT SAFETY. https://www3.nhk.or.jp/nhkworld/en/radio/bosaiweb/craft/. Accessed 10 Oct 2020

NHK WORLD-JAPAN (2018d) BOSAI in New York 1: Designing the Future of Disaster Preparedness. https://www3.nhk.or.jp/nhkworld/en/radio/bosaiweb/program/20181225.html. Accessed 10 Oct 2020

NHK WORLD-JAPAN (2018e) BOSAI in New York 2: Planting Seeds of Disaster Prevention Education. https://www3.nhk.or.jp/nhkworld/en/radio/bosaiweb/program/20181226.html. Accessed 10 Oct 2020

NHK WORLD-JAPAN (2019) WHAT'S YOUR CONNECTION? Disaster Preparedness, the First Steps. https://www3.nhk.or.jp/nhkworld/en/ondemand/video/2076019/. Accessed 10 Oct 2020